Custom & Politics
in Urban Africa

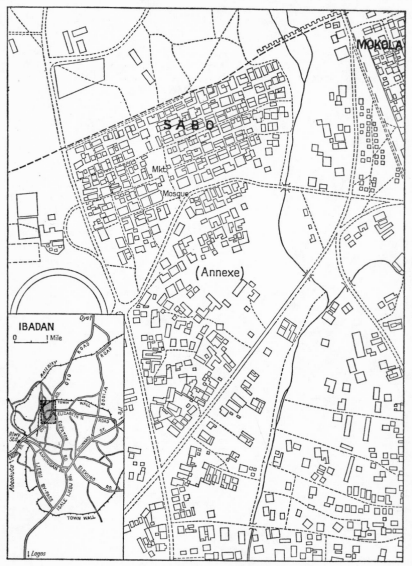

MOKOLA

S A B O

Mkt

Mosque

(Annexe)

IBADAN

0   1 Mile

Oyo

RAILWAY

O
Y
O

R O A D

R
O
A
D

TOWN WALL

ELIZABETH II

B
O
D
I
J
A

R
O
A
D

S
T
.

Abeokuta

RIwy
STN

O
Y
O

EGBETON

ST.

O
G
U
N
M
O
L
A

R
D
.

DUGBE

LIEBU RD.

OGUNPA

ELEKURO   RD.

ISALE IJEBU RD.

IJEBU BY-PASS

TOWN WALL

½ Lagos

Map of Sabo Area, Ibadan

Custom & Politics in Urban Africa

A STUDY OF HAUSA MIGRANTS IN YORUBA TOWNS

by
Abner Cohen

UNIVERSITY OF CALIFORNIA PRESS
Berkeley and Los Angeles

UNIVERSITY OF CALIFORNIA PRESS
BERKELEY AND LOS ANGELES
CALIFORNIA
© ABNER COHEN 1969

SECOND PRINTING
FIRST PAPERBOUND EDITION

LIBRARY OF CONGRESS CATALOG CARD NO. 68–55743
INTERNATIONAL STANDARD BOOK NUMBER 0-520-01571-1 (CLOTHBOUND EDITION)
0-520-01836-2 (PAPERBOUND EDITION)

PRINTED IN THE UNITED STATES

Contents

To
GAYNOR

Preface

This monograph is a study in the role of custom in politics within some contemporary urban settings in Africa. It discusses the processes by which, under certain structural circumstances, an ethnic group manipulates some values, norms, beliefs, symbols, and ceremonials from its traditional culture in order to develop an informal political organization which it uses as a weapon in its struggle for power with other groups, within the contemporary situation. It is based on the detailed analysis of some of the major processes that have been involved in the formation and functioning of a network of socially exclusive and politically autonomous Hausa communities in Yoruba towns, as bases for the establishment of Hausa control over the long distance trade in certain commodities between the savanna and the forest belt of Nigeria.

The monograph combines the analysis of social relationships, history, and individual biography within the same conceptual framework. This is made possible by focusing the discussion on one community, which is thus used as a basis for both analysis and presentation.

The field work on which the study is based was carried out in the Western Region of the Federation of Nigeria, for a period of 15 months, between August 1962 and November 1963. It was financed by the School of Oriental and African Studies (S.O.A.S.), University of London, who later also covered the costs of processing the numerical data through I.B.M. While in the field, I received great assistance from the Nigerian Institute of Social and Economic Research (N.I.S.E.R.), University of Ibadan, who gave me the privilege of appointing me as Associate Research Fellow of the Institute. I am most grateful to both institutions for their generous help.

From among the numerous Hausa who kindly helped me throughout my field study, I want to mention in particular Malam Salisu Atite, Malam Aminu Yahaya, and Malam Dahiru Zungeru, who assisted me not only in the collection of material, in interviews, and in extended visits to different Hausa communities, but also in prolonged discussions about various features of culture and society in the Hausa diaspora in Yorubaland. I also learned a great deal from the endless conversations and discussions which I had with many Hausa malams, particularly with Malam el-Hajji Idrisu na Sarki.

I owe a great debt of gratitude to the Olubadan and to the many officials of the Ibadan City Council and to the various ministries of the Government of the Western Region, and of the Government of the Federation of Nigeria, for their friendliness and kind help which was always combined with a genuine appreciation and encouragement of academic research in their country.

During my field work I was helped in many ways by many colleagues in N.I.S.E.R. and in different departments of the University of Ibadan. Dr. Peter Lloyd, who was at the time Head of the Sociology Section there, was always ready to make available to me his vast first hand knowledge of Yoruba society and culture. I also had frequent and stimulating discussions with many scholars who were in Ibadan at that time, of whom I want to mention: Dr. O. Aboyade, Professor R. Apthorpe, Dr. B. Awe, Professor M. Crowder, Dr. B. Dudley, Professor G. Helleiner, Professor A. Mabogunje, Dr. J. O'Connell, Dr. O. Olakonpo, Dr. K. Post, Professor S. Schatz, Mr. R. Wraith and Mr. C. Wrigley.

I am grateful to many colleagues who have commented on my work. First, Professor C. von Fürer-Haimendorf and my other colleagues in the Department of Anthropology and Sociology at S.O.A.S. who discussed a series of papers which I gave in a special seminar on the subject. Professor Daryll Forde commented on a number of occasions on many parts, as did other members of his Department, at University College London, when I read some papers at their weekly colloquium. Professor F. Bailey read an earlier draft of this book and his colleagues and students commented on my material when I was invited to give a series of lectures at the School of African and Asian Studies, University of Sussex.

In the course of many years, Professor Max Gluckman criticized many of my ideas, gave me valuable advice on my work and contributed greatly to my training in social anthropology in general. Despite a serious illness, he went through an advanced draft and made numerous suggestions.

Professor Ernest Gellner read an earlier draft which he criticized at length. Professor Roland Oliver kindly went through an advanced draft and made useful comment on Chapter IV. Dr. Humphrey Fisher read the whole MS and made detailed constructive suggestions on many points in it. Professor David Arnott not only taught me Hausa but also read my work and commented on it. Professor Ronald Frankenberg and Mrs. Anne Paden commented in detail on Chapter II. Professor George Jenkins generously made available to me some of his notes and criticized some points raised in Chapter IV. I am also grateful to my students in S.O.A.S. and at Cornell who, on various occasions, made some bold and often unexpected remarks about my arguments.

I should like to register my thanks also to Mr. J. R. Bracken for professional advice on the publication of this book and to Miss Catherine Brown for her kind help in office and secretarial matters.

When I went to Nigeria in 1962, I had planned to make a study of a Hausa community in the Northern Region, but for some unexpected reasons it became impossible for me to do so and I had, instead, to study Hausa migrant communities in the South. I am mentioning this in order to point out that my study would not have been possible were it not for the extensive work already done on Hausa culture and society by Professor and Mrs. M. G. Smith, whose material and analytical formulations on the Hausa in Hausaland made it possible for me to study the Hausa in their dispersal.

Finally, it remains a pleasure for me to thank my wife, Gay, who, in the course of my field work, not only looked after our first child and brought into the world our second, but also found time to help me by interviewing secluded Hausa women, looking up references in the library and the archives, and helping me greatly in the collection of census data. In processing the material she also assisted me for many weeks in coding the census data, and later she spent a great deal of time reading and criticizing the script and nagging me into finishing this book. This is why I dedicate the book to her.

Unless otherwise stated, all the information on the history of the communities I studied are from written records. To avoid unnecessary misunderstanding, I hide the identity of some individuals and groups in those communities under pseudonyms.

When the present tense is used in the text, the reference is to conditions existing at the end of 1963.

London, October 1967   A.C.

Introduction

The Problem: Custom in Political Change—Trade and Ethnic Politics in West Africa—The Hausa Trading Network—A Religious Revolution—The Rise of National Politics—Trade and the Process of Ethnic Grouping in Towns—Technical Problems of the Trade—Ethnic Monopolies—Ethnic Distinctiveness Within the New Nationalistic State—The Sociological Problem in a Micro-Historical Perspective.

The Problem: Custom in Political Change

Sociocultural change in the newly independent African states today poses a sociological paradox, for it seems to be producing, at one and the same time, two contradictory phenomena. The one of ethnic groups rapidly losing their cultural distinctiveness, and the other of ethnic groups not only retaining, but also emphasizing and exaggerating their cultural identity and exclusiveness. In the one case an ethnic group adjusts to the new social realities by adopting customs from other groups or by developing new customs which are shared with other groups. In the second case an ethnic group adjusts to the new realities by reorganizing its own traditional customs, or by developing new customs under traditional symbols, often using traditional norms and ideologies to enhance its distinctiveness within the contemporary situation. The process in the first case has been known as 'detribalization', while its opposite has been labelled 'retribalization.[1]

Nowhere are these two processes so dramatically evident as in African towns today, where social interaction is particularly intense and change very rapid. Even a preliminary survey will be sufficient to show that there is no necessary connection between type of process and 'type of town'. Whether a town is of the 'industrial' or of the 'traditional' type,[2] both processes can be found in operation, though one may expect on *a priori* grounds to find more 'detribalization', and less 'retribalization', in the 'industrial' type of town than in the 'traditional' type. In the one process the longer a 'tribesman' stays in town the more 'detribalized' he becomes, while in the second, the longer a 'tribesman' stays the more 'retribalized' he becomes. The two cases should in fact be considered as the two extremes of one continuum, with most ethnic groups falling in-between.

The process of 'detribalization' has been extensively discussed by scholars from different disciplines. It is a process which is well known from the history of Europe during the last two centuries. It is also the process which received much attention from the great sociologists of our time, who described it in evolutionary terms, as a change from a society based on status to a society based on contract, a passage from community to association, from *gemeinschaft* to *geselleschaft*. Some political scientists and sociologists today refer to it as 'modernization', a process by which various types of local, traditional, and status groups are drawn together into a common institutional and organizational framework.[3] New alignments of power are formed which lead to cooperation and to the creation of new patterns of social interaction between members of different ethnic groups. On the other hand, new cleavages cut across ethnic groups so that members from the same ethnic group will oppose one another in the struggle for power. In time, ethnic bonds will weaken and new loyalties which cut across ethnic groupings will predominate.

It is with the second type of process that this study is concerned. Like 'detribalization', 'retribalization' is the socio-cultural manifestation of the formation of new political groupings. It is the result, not of ethnic groupings disengaging themselves from one another, but of increasing interaction between them, within the contexts of new political situations. It is the outcome, not of conservatism, but of a dynamic socio-cultural change which is brought about by new cleavages and new alignments of power. It is a process by which a group from one ethnic category, whose members are involved in a struggle for power and privilege with the members of a group from another ethnic category, within the framework of a *formal* political system, manipulate some customs, values, myths, symbols, and ceremonials from their cultural tradition in order to articulate an *informal* political organization which is used as a weapon in that struggle.

2

Sociologically, this is a process which is as significant in understanding modern African societies as that of political 'detribalization'. Indeed this type of political grouping can be found today as much in a developed society like that of the U.S.A. as in the developing societies of Africa. On a higher level of abstraction, this is but one of the ways in which *interest groups* generally develop in society, with each group forming its myths of distinctiveness, its style of life, and its organization of functions for political action.[4] The more culturally homogeneous the group, the more effectively can it organize for political action. An ethnic political grouping in contemporary society is thus an informal interest group which, from the very beginning of its formation, has the advantage of possessing some of the most essential requirements for the development and expression of its political organization.

The degree to which interest groups can develop in a society depends on the type of state system that prevails in that society. Some states permit a high degree of political 'pluralism', by allowing the formation of a wide variety of formally organized interest groups. Other states are less tolerant in this respect, but do not prevent the formation of *informal* interest groups. Yet other states do not tolerate even such informal interest groups and do their utmost to suppress them.[5] Here, again, ethnic groups are in an advantageous strategic position, for it is difficult and costly for any state to suppress the customs of a group in such respects as marriage and kinship, friendship, ceremonial, and ritual beliefs and practices. And it is these very customs that can readily serve as instruments for the development of an informal political organization. Within the new developing states, a grouping of this type is more stable and more effective in achieving its aims than a formal association in which loyalties derive only from segmental, contractual, interests.

In Africa this kind of political grouping has been labelled as 'tribalism' by laymen as well as by some anthropologists and sociologists. But this term has always been ambiguous and its use as an analytical concept in sociological enquiry has been severely criticized in recent years.[6] The term 'ethnicity', which has been widely used in sociology, particularly in the U.S.A., has been advocated by some writers as a substitute. This, again, is a term lacking in precision but has the advantage

3

over 'tribalism' in that it is more free from value-judgement and can be applied to a much wider variety of groupings. In this study I use 'tribalism' mainly as a native term and use 'ethnicity' as a sociological term. According to my usage, an ethnic group is an informal interest group whose members are distinct from the members of other groups within the same society in that they share a measure of what Smith calls 'compulsory institutions' like kinship and religion,[7] and can communicate among themselves relatively easily. The term 'ethnicity' refers to strife between such ethnic groups, in the course of which people stress their identity and exclusiveness.

I agree with Van Den Berghe that ethnicity should be conceived as a matter of degree.[8] This must depend on the magnitude and combination of the following variables: (1) the compulsory institutions, (2) the ease of communication, and (3) the corporate political interests involved. The strength of these variables should be assessed, not in the absolute, but relative to the rest of the population within the same society.

Theoretically, an ethnic *group* must be distinguished from an ethnic *category*. As Gluckman puts it, 'all culture tends to survive',[9] and when men from one cultural group migrate to town they retain a great deal of their culture even without necessarily forming a corporate political group. They thus constitute an ethnic category. However, an ethnic category often becomes an ethnic group, as a result of increasing interaction and communication between its members.[10] For example, it has been reported in many cases that men in some of the ethnically heterogenous African towns tend to marry women from their own ethnic groups, either from the town, or from the 'tribal' hinterland. They may do this for a variety of psychological, cultural, and domestic reasons. But an unintended structural consequence of this marriage pattern is that, within the new social milieu, these men will become an 'endogamous group', i.e. a group of men who neither give women to members of other ethnic groups, nor take women from them. This alone can lead to intensive social interaction within the group and inhibit such interaction with members from outside the group. In time, the men of this ethnic category may begin to collaborate in efforts designed to keep their womenfolk within the category, particularly if in the new urban situation there are less women than men and there is therefore competition over

4

women. As a result of concerted efforts in this and some other fields, the ethnic category in question will soon develop into an ethnic group.

All ethnic groups can thus be regarded as informal interest groups and can therefore be regarded as political groupings. 'Politics' refers to the processes involved in the distribution and exercise of, and the struggle for, power within a social unit. Power is the control by men over the behaviour of other men and is thus an aspect of all social relationships. In all political systems use is made of a combination of physical coercion, of economic reward and punishment, and of moral and ritual obligations. These factors are combined in various proportions in different political systems. Ethnic groups make extensive use of moral and ritual obligations that bind their members, in order to organize their political functions. The more fundamental the corporate political interests of the group, the more elaborate the political organization of the group. Ethnic groups can thus be heuristically arranged on one continuum, from the least political at the one end, to the most political at the other.

The exploitation of ethnicity in the informal articulation of political interests has been observed almost everywhere in the world. What is of special interest to anthropologists, sociologists, and political scientists is the manner and the processes by which cultural norms, values, myths, and symbols are made to express a number of organizational functions which are essential for political organization by these groups. Every political group must mobilize its resources in order to find solutions to a number of organizational problems: the problem of distinctiveness, of political communication, of decision-making, of authority, of ideology and of discipline. Formal political groups organize these functions legally and bureaucratically. Informal political groups organize these functions through the idiom of custom.

Different ethnic groups organize these functions in different ways, according to their cultural traditions and structural circumstances. Some ethnic groups make extensive use of religious idioms in organizing these functions. Other groups use kinship, or other forms of moral relationships, instead. In the course of time, the same group may shift from one articulating principle to another as a result of changes within the encapsulating political system, or of other developments both within and outside the group. Most ethnic interest groups use a combination of various 'compulsory institutions', usually under an integrating ideology, for this purpose. In all these cases our interest is in how custom is involved in the political process in contemporary situations.

This is a fundamental problem for research in which the detailed analysis of cases which are extended in time can be combined with comparative analysis. In the present study, I concentrate on one such extended case, taking a community of migrant traders in a West African urban setting and discussing continuities and changes in its culture and social organization in response to political changes within the encapsulating political system. Later I place this case within the framework of a comparative scheme.

Trade and Ethnic Politics in West Africa

One of the most significant discoveries in West African studies in recent years has been the magnitude of long-distance trade which is conducted throughout the sub-continent, and which involves the exchange of substantial amounts of money and large quantities of goods, without these being reflected in the official economic figures of the countries concerned.[10] In the course of its operation, the trade brings about intensive social interaction between various ethnic groupings.

By long-distance trade I mean the purchase or sale and the transfer of goods, mostly of perishable nature, across a distance of several hundred miles, principally between the savanna and the forest belt of West Africa. The trade is conducted within the framework of traditional, indigenous arrangements and involves no systematic resort to such modern institutions as banking, insurance, police, civil courts, or the exchange of documents, although very large amounts of money are employed in it, involving extensive credit arrangements, often between total strangers from different tribes.

The trade is organized on centuries-old lines.[11] Long before the Europeans appeared on the scene, the West Africans had operated truly international trade, with developed systems of credit, insurance, brokerage, exchange of business information, transport and arbitration in business disputes. Law and order were normally maintained and strangers honoured their

6

business obligations and deferred to the pressures of moral values and of moral relationships of all sorts. Indeed, the first large-scale European impact on West Africa was more disastrous than propitious. For, the trans-Atlantic slave trade, the magnitude of which dwarfed the local slave trade, inevitably brought disruption to the flow of long-distance trade. Furthermore, it introduced many demoralizing processes into an ongoing system of exchange which at some periods had linked the various parts of West Africa into one economic unit and had connected it with the countries and civilizations of the Mediterranean.[12]

The fact that this indigenous system of trade continues to operate today is not an indication of ignorance or primitiveness on the part of people conducting it. The West African long-distance trader is fully aware of the existence of the railway, the bank, the post office, the solicitor, the police and the court, and he is not less rational in his economic activity than the European business man. Indeed, it is specifically because he is rational in the conduct of his business that he continues in the old traditional ways.

The trade has developed against the background of a number of geographical, cultural, and social conditions. Ecological conditions vary widely in West Africa, with a sharp division into savanna and forest belts running parallel to the coast from east to west across the sub-continent. This tends to stimulate exchange and economic interdependence.

These ecological divisions frequently overlap with tribal divisions. In Nigeria alone, which, as Forde points out,[13] represents a cross-section of the various physical conditions of West Africa, there are over 200 different ethnic groups. This means that trade between different ecological areas involves inter-relations between individuals and groups from different ethnic groups.

The trade involves difficult technical problems which, in the pre-industrial conditions prevailing in these areas, have been most successfully overcome when men from the same ethnic group controlled all, or most, of the stages of the trade in specific commodities. But this control can usually be achieved only in the course of continual competition or strife with men from another ethnic group. In the process, the different ethnic groupings are forced to organize themselves for political

7

action, within the political sphere in which they happen to operate.

Thus at nearly every stage in the chain of the trade, economic institutions are closely inter-connected with political institutions. And both types of institution are embedded in a web of social relationships between the people involved. So that at every step the study of the organization of the trade poses problems of inter-connections between economic, political, and other social factors.

These are problems of direct interest to economists, political scientists, geographers, historians, sociologists and anthropologists. One way of approaching them is through conducting extensive surveys which cover wide geographical areas, numerous communities, different kinds of commodities, transport arrangements, credit facilities and other practices. Extensive surveys of this kind will certainly be of great value to administrators, investors, and economic planners. But, apart from the fact that such surveys are difficult to conduct in the present circumstances, they will inevitably give restricted accounts of these highly complex phenomena. This is because the institutions which are involved in the organization of the trade, interlock, not in a standard fashion throughout the chain of the trade, but in a variety of ways depending on varied circumstances in each local community or network of such communities.

An alternative technique in the analysis of these problems can be the intensive monographic study of the social organization of a tribal community which is specialized in this trade. Through the use of special, intensive techniques, analysis within such a limited field of social relations can be made of processes and of sociological relations of much wider applicability.

The Hausa Trading Network

One of the best-known ethnic groups who are active in long-distance trade throughout West Africa is the Hausa.

The Hausa trader is ubiquitous in the towns of the forest belt of West Africa, hundreds of miles away from his original homeland in the savanna country, in parts of what is known as the Northern Region of the Federation of Nigeria and the Niger Republic. Aloof and distinct in his white robes, proud of his customs, Islamic beliefs and practices, and of his 'Arabic learning', he is often regarded by the host peoples among whom he lives or moves as an exploiter, a monopolist, rogue and trouble maker. When his business fortunes are at an ebb, he may pose as an Islamic teacher, diviner, barber, butcher, commission agent, porter or beggar. His high degree of mobility, skill and shrewdness in business are widely acknowledged and have earned him the reputation of having a special 'genius' for trade. On a closer analysis, much of this 'genius' turns out to be associated, not with a basic personality trait,[14] but with a highly developed economico-political organization which has been evolved over a long period of time.

This economic organization is at the basis of a far-flung diaspora, which consists of a network of localized Hausa communities, where each community usually occupies a special quarter within the foreign town, and is headed by a Hausa chief, the *Sarkin Hausawa*, who is recognized as such by the local authorities. The community is formally established on the basis of Hausa cultural distinctiveness under the Hausa motto: 'Our customs are different'. These customs, which are far from being a replica of northern Hausa culture, provide a stable institutional set-up which facilitates mobility of people and makes the establishment of further outposts of Hausa trade possible. Hausa trade and Hausa customs have gone hand in hand, each supporting the other, in the dynamic process of the continual ramifying of the Hausa network.

Within this network, there are clusters of neighbouring communities between which social interaction and economic co-operation are particularly intense. One such cluster is that formed by the Hausa communities in the main Yoruba towns of the Western Region of Nigeria. At its centre is the Hausa community in the city of Ibadan where the main fieldwork of this study was carried out. This community occupies a special quarter, locally known as 'Sabo', an abbreviation of *Sabon Gari*,[15] on land which was allotted for the purpose by the Ibadan Native Authority. As Ibadan is the capital of the Western Region and is an important junction on the roads and railway line between Hausaland, southern Nigeria, and Ghana, Sabo has become the centre of this cluster. In 1953 the communities of this cluster formed what they called a 'Federation' and elected the Chief of Sabo as their Chairman.

9

A Religious Revolution

When I began my field study in 1962 I was immediately struck by the intensity of Sabo's religious activity. In a Middle-Eastern Arab Moslem village which was particularly known for its orthodoxy in the area, and which I had studied a few years earlier, the performance of ritual was almost confined to the elderly, who spent a total of 30 to 40 minutes daily on prayers.[16] These prayers were mostly performed individually and it was only on Friday and on feast days, that a larger proportion of the men gathered in the one and only village mosque to perform a collective prayer.

In contrast, all Hausa men in Sabo, excluding only a handful of men who practise the 'pagan' *bori* cult, observe the five daily prayers. Only the morning prayer is performed individually, while the other four are performed collectively, in groups, twenty or more strong, under the leadership of a malam.

In addition to the five daily prayers, the Hausa of Sabo also perform the elaborate rituals enjoined by the Tijaniyya Order, to which the overwhelming majority of the men belong. A major part of these rituals consists of loud choral recitation of certain phrases and passages, each of which is repeated a prescribed number of times. The counting is done with the help of a long rosary which is a constant companion of every Hausa man. Some of the phrases and passages are repeated hundreds of times in the normal daily ritual. In the Friday two-hour *dhikr* ritual, the name 'Allah' is recited over a thousand times. On the whole, an average Hausa man spends on the perform-ance of ritual about an hour and a half every week day and three and a half hours on Friday.

Another feature of Sabo religion is the relatively large numbers of malams engaged in its activities. In the Middle Eastern Arab village which I studied there were only two, part-time, religious functionaries, in a population of 2,300; i.e. less than one in 1000.[17] In Sabo, on the other hand, there are 119 full-time malams in a population of about 4200; i.e. about 30 in 1000.[18] Very few of these malams combine some trade with religious work. The overwhelming majority devote their entire time to attending to the ritual requirements of the population, to teaching, and to increasing their own Islamic learning. Also, in the Arab village, the two religious function-aries played no significant role in the political organization of the community, whereas the malams of Sabo perform crucial political roles.

Furthermore, Sabo religion embraces a wider range of social life than was the case in the Arab village. Apart from the collective ritualism of the prayers and the ritualization of the life cycle, there are various mystical practices from which men hope to attain wealth, success in love, and health, or to prevent the evil machinations of rivals, or even to cause harm to enemies. In Sabo belief there seem to be no limits to the mystical powers of the malams and there are countless stories current among the inhabitants to prove their exploits in effecting dramatic changes in individual fortunes and in interpersonal relationships.

⌐For the Hausa man, the good life is a combination of success in trade and the progressive attainment of Islamic learning. Both wealth and Islamic learning are forms of power and success, and each gives support to the other. All Hausa education in Sabo is Islamic, or as the people call it 'Arabic'.[19] In 1963 only seven Hausa children from Sabo were getting 'secular' education in a near-by Catholic School. All the rest of the children attended Arabic schools run by the malams and the malams' assistants within the Quarter. For many, learning does not stop at maturity. Adult Arabic classes, given by some of the leading malams, have an average daily attendance of about one hundred men, and are held during the morning and the afternoon. In these classes the men read, one after the other, from theological texts in Arabic, which the malam then translates and explains in Hausa. Through success in trade, men attain leisure which they devote to learning and one of the most coveted prizes which wealth brings to a man is to perform the pilgrimage to Mecca.

But sociologically the most significant point about Sabo religious activity is that its intensity is only a recent development. Up to the late 1940's only a few men in the Quarter belonged to any Islamic mystical order at all, the majority being ordinary Moslems with little collective ritual. The massive affiliation of the majority to the Tijaniyya order occurred dramatically in the course of one or two years after an important shaikh of that order had visited Sabo and appointed local ritual masters[20] who eventually initiated the men into the Order and gave them the ritual instructions of the Order. This led to far-reaching changes in the Quarter's religious organization. In 1952 Sabo formally became an autonomous ritual community when the Hausa decided to hold the Friday midday prayer[21] in a central mosque in the Quarter instead of holding it in the Ibadan Central Mosque which was predominantly Yoruba, as they had done for the past 40 years. The married women of Sabo became fully secluded and there is ample evidence from documents as well as from informants that the number of malams rose steadily only during the past decade. Again, at the beginning of the 1950's only 6 Sabo men had been to Mecca to perform the pilgrimage and to attain the title *Al Hajji* but by the end of the decade the number rose to 45. During the two years 1959 and 1960 alone, 28 men performed the pilgrimage.

The Rise of National Politics

These dramatic changes in religious beliefs, practices and organization, were in many respects, interconnected with equally dramatic changes in the nature and organization of political authority within Sabo as well as in the political relations between the Hausa and Yoruba within the Ibadan polity. Today, the Hausa refer to the period in which those political changes had occurred as 'the time when politics came',[22] a phrase which recurs in almost every conversation on the economy and the politics of the Quarter.

The 1950's brought the rise of Nigerian Federal politics, following the development of a Nigerian nationalist movement and a series of constitutional reforms after the Second World War. Federal politics brought about political parties which were in principle national and not tribal, and the subsequent elections as well as the reorganization of the administration, effected a shift of power, which was gradual but steady, from the traditional 'tribal' chiefs who had controlled the Native Authorities, to a new, nationalistic, Western-oriented elite. The word 'tribalism' became associated with imperialism, reaction and the antithesis of progress.

Three major political parties had evolved, and within a short time they established branches in Sabo and went into full activity to win support among its people. According to the 1952 census, there were in the Western Region about 41,000 Hausa but even then it was known that the actual figure was far higher, as many Hausa did not register themselves either because they were temporary migrants or because they were afraid of taxation. The two southern parties, the National Council of Nigerian Citizens (N.C.N.C.) and the Action Group (A.G.), hoped that through their activities in Sabo, they would influence not only the other Hausa communities in the Western Region, but also the massive population of the North. These parties condemned tribalism and in Ibadan declared on many occasions, that Sabo men should be treated no longer as native strangers but as equal citizens.

These developments brought an increasingly bureaucratized administration to the Ibadan City Council which no longer officially recognized Sabo as a Hausa Quarter. The territorial principle of Hausa exclusiveness had thus come to an end, and in 1952 the Ibadan District Officer wrote that the Ibadan Local Authorities would no longer support 'tribal areas'. This meant therefore that they would not give any more land to extend the Hausa Quarter and that any individual Hausa who wanted land should make his own arrangements with private Ibadan landowners.

By this time the City of Ibadan had grown substantially and its built-up area had crept northwards, outflanking Sabo. Sabo had thus been transformed from a well-circumscribed village to a quarter within a large city—the largest in tropical Africa.[23] In the meantime Sabo had become more congested than ever before and some Hausa migrants had to seek space in the peripheral areas of Mokola and Ekotedo.[24]

An additional process which threatened to undermine the Hausa identity of the Quarter was the very rapid growth of Yoruba Islam. When the Quarter was founded half a century ago, the number of Yoruba Moslems in Ibadan was insignificant. In fact the Hausa themselves had played a crucial role in spreading Islam in the city: Yoruba Moslems had looked up to the Hausa as superior, more enlightened Moslems and many of them had gone to the Quarter for ritual help and religious guidance. Yoruba Islam, however, developed very rapidly and today Ibadan is predominantly Islamic. Yoruba Islam became efficiently organized and Islamic learning among the population made great advances. The Hausa of Sabo were thus rapidly 'swallowed' by the masses of Yoruba Moslems and they were no longer distinct as a religious group.

The weakening position of the traditional chiefs of the city under the Olubadan began to undermine the effectiveness and legitimacy of the authority of Sabo's chief, which in the past had been derived from the formal support of the Olubadan and, indirectly, of the District Officer. The ability of the Hausa chief to serve as mediator between his people and the city's authorities dwindled, as a great deal of that function was passed on to the secretaries of the Sabo branches of the three major political parties. The records of the period are full of petitions presented by these secretaries to the authorities, in protest against all sorts of alleged injustices and acts of discrimination, including the alleged oppression by the police of the Quarter's 250 prostitutes.

These political developments constituted a direct threat to the identity—indeed to the very existence—of Sabo as an autonomous, well-organized, Hausa community. The Hausa of the Quarter became apprehensive and, as the years rolled on, they became more and more anxious that for one reason or another the Yoruba authorities might 'scrap' the Quarter or remove it from its present site.

Trade and the Process of Ethnic Grouping in Towns

Hausa anxiety in this respect arises from fear of losing their source of livelihood, rather than from the fear of suffering the ultimate loss of Hausa cultural identity. This is because Hausa identity and Hausa ethnic exclusiveness in Ibadan are the expressions not so much of a particularly strong 'tribalistic' sentiment as of vested economic interests.

Rouch seems to argue that Hausa migrants are particularly predisposed towards forming exclusive 'tribal' communities in the foreign towns to which they migrate.[25] In his study of migrations to Ghana, he makes the observation that different groups of migrants organize themselves differently in the foreign towns to which they migrate. The forms of their organization fall into a continuum between two extremes. At the one end are migrants who form only segmental, ephemeral 'tribal' associations. At the other end are migrants who, like the Hausa, form autonomous, multi-purposive, 'tribal' communities. Rouch does not analyse this difference in detail but he tends to explain it in terms of differences in tribal traditional culture.[26]

There is no doubt that Hausa customs and institutions have contributed in important ways to the formation of a closely knit Hausa community in Ibadan and in other Yoruba towns. The Hausa themselves explain their ethnic exclusiveness within these foreign towns, in cultural terms, repeatedly offering the simple, cliché-like motto: 'Our customs are different'. But the culture and system of social relationships in these communities are far from being reproductions of the culture and the social system in Hausaland in the North. What is more important for this discussion is that not all Hausa migrants into Yorubaland find it necessary to live within these autonomous Hausa communities. There are tens of thousands of Hausa who migrate annually to southern Nigeria to seek seasonal employment, who live in small, scattered, loosely knit gangs of workers without forming or joining organized communities. Hausa cultural tradition therefore is not the crucial factor in the formation of these communities in Yoruba towns. In the course of his study, Rouch intercepted Hausa annual migrants at points of entry into Ghana and collected information from them. But in order to study their groupings and their relationships with the host communities in which they worked, he did not follow the same people whom he had questioned, but went to the settled Hausa communities in the Zongos. These Hausa settlers however are a different occupational category altogether.

The study of Sabo and of a few other Hausa communities in other Yoruba towns has shown that their development and their structure are closely interconnected with the development and organizational requirements of long-distance trade, between the savanna and the forest, in which most of their members are directly or indirectly engaged.

These two geographical zones of Nigeria are in many respects economically interdependent. The North sends to the South millet, groundnut oil, dried meat, dried fish, cassava flour, butter, milk and cattle. The South sends to the North kola nuts, sugar, salt, scrap iron and a variety of imported manufactured goods.[27]

But in Sabo economic organization two articles of trade between North and South are particularly dominant: cattle and kola. Because of the tse-tse fly,[28] no cattle survive in the forest zone[29] and the inhabitants depend, for their beef supplies, on the cattle brought down from the savanna. The savanna peoples, on the other hand, depend on the forest zone for all their supplies of the kola nut which is an important item of consumption among them.

Of the 1984 mature males of the Quarter, 452 (22.8%) work directly in these two trades.[30] This figure represents only those who are permanently engaged in these trades. At peak seasons, particularly in the case of the kola, more men are employed. Some of these additional recruits are drawn from those settlers who are engaged in marginal occupations. Others are drawn from the transient population.

Traders in these two commodities, together with traders in some other commodities[31] provide business and employment for nearly all the porters, transporters, men of the different services, labourers and others.[32]

Most of the traders in category No. 9, Table I, call themselves 'petty traders'. They are mostly young and they walk around peddling pencils, torchlights, sun glasses and the like. For many of these this is a training phase for more permanent trades.

Thus about three-quarters of the men in Sabo are engaged in jobs connected with long-distance trade. In terms of wealth and of income, the proportion is higher. Historically, the Quarter was founded by men connected with the cattle trade. Later, these men were joined by men connected with the kola trade. The men who control these two trades maintain the Quarter and dominate it both politically and economically.

The trade in each commodity has its own history, its own social organization, and its own pattern of politics. In order to simplify the sociological issues which are the subject of this monograph and to reduce the number of variables, I shall focus only on the social organization of kola and cattle.

The trade in these two commodities is conducted within the framework of traditional, indigenous, institutions.

Thus, in the Ibadan cattle market, locally known as 'Zango', nearly 75,000 head of cattle are sold every year. These herds are collected principally from the semi-nomadic Fulani by Hausa dealers from the North and are then brought southward to be sold with the help of Ibadan Hausa commission agents to Yoruba butchers who are total strangers to the Hausa dealers. All sales are on credit and there is always an outstanding total amount of about £100,000 current debt. No documents are signed and no resort is had to the services of banks or to the official civil courts: the whole organization is entirely indigenous.[33]

On the other hand millions of pounds worth of kola is collected annually by Hausa brokers from various producing centres in the Western Region of Nigeria and is sent through a chain of intermediaries to the consuming centres in the North. This trade, again, involves credit arrangements in many of its stages and the whole business is still organized on traditional indigenous lines.[34]

Technical Problems of the Trade

Under the pre-industrial conditions prevailing in West African countries, long-distance trade is attended by a number of technical problems.

The first of these problems is that of securing the continuous and rapid exchange of information between traders in the various centres about conditions of supply and demand.

The demand for cattle in the forest belt in Yorubaland fluctuates from one week to another. Most of the consumers are town dwellers whose livelihood depends on the marketing of cocoa (75% of town dwellers are farmers). This means that the demand is affected not only by the cocoa seasons but also by the fluctuations in cocoa prices in world markets. Within the consuming areas demand also fluctuates from one area to another, following local circumstances. Furthermore, as the cattle markets throughout Yorubaland form an inter-connected network, the sometimes wild fluctuations in the demand for cattle at the Lagos market for export to the neighbouring countries, and particularly to Ghana, create unpredictable conditions. Also, as most of the cattle are sold to local butchers on credit, financial or political crisis will affect the volume of credit given and hence will greatly affect demand. Thus during the second half of 1963, there was a squeeze on credit in the Ibadan cattle market as a result of the political and financial disturbances in the Western Region.

The conditions of supply also vary. The Fulani are the main source of cattle and their willingness to sell is affected by various ecological and social factors. The trade involves a long chain of sellers, dealers, drovers, commission agents and other intermediaries of all sorts and the availability of manpower is also a factor. Thus during the rainy season when most of the men in the North are engaged on the land there is an acute shortage of men for some of the stages of the trade and this often leads to a restricted supply. Since a large proportion of the cattle are now brought by train, changes in the conditions of railway service affect supply. This is particularly so as the number of wagons available for the transport of livestock is limited. Sometimes a herd has to wait for several days around the railway station area in the North in the hope of having the necessary wagons. Often the owner of the herd will decide that under the circumstances it would be best for him to march his herd on the hoof, which means a delay of about 40 days. During September 1963, when I was working in the area, there was a complete stoppage of railway service when the lines were disrupted by floods and the supply of cattle in southern markets was therefore highly restricted.

It must be remembered that cattle are a highly perishable commodity in the South. Once a herd reaches the forest area the animals become infected with the disease (*trypano somiasis*) and unless they are slaughtered within one or two weeks they are likely to die. This means that one cannot keep a herd in the consuming area in the hope of an improvement in the sellers' market, and as there is competition in the business and the margin of profit is narrow, miscalculations or mis-information can bring ruin. Very large amounts of money are involved and traders therefore have to exchange current information.

Similar variations in the conditions of supply and demand affect the kola trade. To begin with, there are different types of kola. The nuts vary in size and in shade and, generally, the larger the size and the lighter the shade, the higher the price. They differ also in flavour. In the major producing regions, such as the Western Region of Nigeria, different areas produce their own peculiar type and flavour of nut. Also, different areas have different kola seasons. Thus, in the Shagamu area, the season is October to January while in the Ibadan area, which is only about 50 miles further north, the season is January to March. Continuity of supplies for the off-season period is secured by storing the nut under special conditions. The kola is a very delicate nut and perishes easily so that the stored supplies have to be examined continuously and tended in special ways. The storing has to be arranged in the producing areas of the South because the dry climate of the North is hostile to the nut. According to men in the business, stored kola greatly improves in flavour; and, because of the scarcity of fresh supplies, of the expense of storage, of the cost of expert care, and of the risks of speculation, off-season stored kola fetches nearly twice the price of fresh kola.

In the North, too, conditions vary. Different consuming areas favour different types of kola. Also, some areas can be supplied by rail and road, others only by road. Retail prices fluctuate all the time in relation to changes in the forces of supply and demand.

It is thus essential that traders should have day-to-day knowledge about the changing conditions of supply and demand. Almost every day decisions have to be taken by the trader about what to buy, in which areas to buy, and which of these areas offer supplies at the lowest price. He has also to know which consuming area will offer the widest margin of profit. Often as a herd of cattle is on its way to the markets in the South the owner will precede it to the various markets en route to Lagos to find out which of the markets offer the best price. Similarly, while kola is being transported to the North in the lorry, the trader may decide, on the latest information given to him, to change course and to proceed to markets offering better prices than those he initially aimed at.

The second technical problem in the trade is that of speed. The trader must have immediate facilities for despatch, transport and sale. Like cattle the kola too is perishable, and has to be packed in the supply area in a special way which will give it protection for the duration of the journey. Speed is also important for the additional reason that dealers cannot afford to keep their capital tied up for a long time in goods. Credit, it is true, is involved at every stage, but its volume is not unlimited and although no centralized planning agency is involved, it tends under ordinary circumstances, to stand in a certain proportion to the capital circulating in the trade.

The third technical problem is that of the organization of credit and trust, without which trade will not flow. Butchers in Ibadan sell to retail consumers on credit. They buy their cattle on credit. The cattle-dealer entrusts all of his money to the care of the local commission agent. Herds of cattle worth thousands of pounds are entrusted to the drovers. Similarly large consignments of kola are entrusted to lorry drivers. At every stage in the chain of the trade total strangers have to trust each other. Thus, kola dealers from the North send thousands of pounds to the local agents, while business landlords entrust all their fortune into the hands of their clients.

Ethnic Monopolies

Under the pre-industrial conditions of Nigeria the difficulties in dealing with these technical problems are numerous. Literacy is low and no regular exchange of correspondence takes place. The problem of communication of business information is made difficult and complicated by the differences in language and cultural traditions between northern and southern centres —or more specifically between Hausa and Yoruba. Often the long chain of the trade involves in one way or another people from different ethnic groups. Credit, too, is beset by various difficulties. Because of the lack of a high degree of effective centralization, contractual relations cannot be easily maintained or enforced by official central institutions, while modern methods of insuring goods in the various stages of transit between suppliers and retailers are not developed, since security of property is not yet very high.

My material suggests that under these pre-industrial conditions, the technical problems can be efficiently, and hence economically, overcome when men from one tribe control all or most of the stages of the trade in specific commodities.[35] Such a tribal control, or monopoly, can usually be achieved only in the course of continual and bitter rivalry with competitors from other tribes. In the process, the monopolizing tribal community is forced to organize for political action in order to deal effectively with increasing external pressure, to coordinate the cooperation of its members in the common cause, and to mobilize the support of communities from the same tribe in neighbouring towns.

The question of which tribe controls the trade in which commodity within a certain area depends on a number of factors—economic, political, cultural, and historical. The monopolizing tribe may be the main producer or the main consumer of the commodity, but it may be neither of these.

The Hausa produce neither cattle nor kola and yet they control the trade in both. Up to the early 1940's they also controlled the butchering industry in Ibadan and in other towns, but they lost this as a result of subsequent developments.

In the course of evolving ways of meeting the technical difficulties, the Hausa have managed to develop an extensive, intricate business organization which covers most of the stages of the trade in cattle and kola. A closely knit network of Hausa centres for the sale of cattle, and for the purchase, storing, packing and transporting of the kola to the North, sprang up in the course of the first half of the present century all over Yorubaland. Hausa communities already established for the sale of cattle and some other commodities served as bases from which other men operated the kola trade. These communities consequently expanded and their organization became more complex. In areas where no such Hausa communities had been in existence new Hausa communities were founded. From all these communities there branched out smaller Hausa communities and Hausa trading stations spread among the Yoruba.

The process, as manifested in the histories of the few communities which I have studied, seems to have been similar everywhere. A number of Hausa commission agents would lodge temporarily with Yoruba house-owners, and then, as their number increased, and as they were joined by men from related occupations, they constituted a social problem within the polity of the settlement. The Yoruba population would complain that the Hausa were harbouring burglars, pickpockets and other categories of 'undesirables' who endangered law and order in the community. To meet this danger, and also to meet the simultaneous clamour of the Hausa to live on their own— 'because our customs are different'—the local chiefs would decide to allot to the Hausa a special Quarter within the settlement and would recognize one of the Hausa men of influence (always one of the important 'business landlords') as chief. He would then be held responsible to them for the conduct of his people, inform the authorities about the undesirables in his community, and help in the collection of taxes. More men would then join the community, such as tailors, barbers, malams, petty traders and beggars.

At the same time women would come, or are brought, and

consolidate the community in other respects. Prostitutes arrived in the early stages, and many of them were eventually married and slipped into the respectability of family life. Men who were already married brought their wives to settle with them. The women bore children and also fostered other children. They soon also established a trade, usually the preparation of cooked food for the large number of bachelors and strangers in the community. In the process, the community organized itself in ways which made it possible to accommodate and serve a large number of Hausa men who came for business. With its development and consolidation and with the development of the business, the community became the basis from which further ramifications of the Hausa network was possible, and Hausa business penetrated deeper into the forest area.

Thus, for the people of Sabo, as indeed for the people in all these communities, Hausa culture is not just a way of life, but identification with it is in many ways a political ideology, emphasizing identity as well as exclusiveness. This identification is upheld not only by recent migrants but also by old timers. It is important for the Hausa business landlords and for their assistants to emphasize over and over again that they are Hausa, because in the circumstances Hausa northern dealers will entrust their goods and money only into the hands of Hausa 'brothers abroad', who live within a highly stable and organized Hausa community. Also, it is essential for this community to organize politically in order to maintain Hausa monopoly in trade, by preventing foreigners from infiltrating into the organization and by preventing Hausa 'self-seekers' from disrupting it. This political organization is achieved under the banner: 'Our customs are different; we are Hausa'.

Ethnic Distinctiveness Within the New Nationalistic State

Thus, the threat to the autonomy of Sabo in the early 1950's was in fact a threat to Hausa control over the long-distance trade in certain commodities.[36] The threat was twofold. Firstly, the basis of Hausa distinctiveness, i.e. of their unity and exclusiveness, was no longer officially recognized. Indeed this basis was regarded as a creation of the colonial power and was thus deemed incompatible with national unity, independence and equality of citizenship. Secondly, the structure and legitimacy of authority within the Quarter were undermined. This meant that individual members of the Quarter were no longer formally bound to submit to the authority of the local chief for the purpose of maintaining the autonomy of Sabo.

The fact that the members of the community share common interests does not mean that they will always automatically act in conformity with the general interests of the Quarter. This is because there is always potential conflict between the interest of the individual and the group to which he belongs, in respect of rights and obligations. Men in general are always happy enough to claim their rights in the group but often they feel constrained when they are called upon to fulfil their obligations to the group. To use the terms of Fortes and Evans-Pritchard: In its pragmatic and utilitarian aspects, the autonomy of the group is a source of immediate private interest and satisfaction to the individual.[37] But as a common interest, it is non-utilitarian and non-pragmatic, a matter of moral value and ideological significance. People are usually so preoccupied with their private interests that they do not always see the common interests on which they depend. This problem is further complicated by the fact that the maintenance of the autonomy of the group often requires the organization of functions such as communication, coordination, and decision-making, which cannot be left to the private consideration of the individual.

Thus, the threat to the authority of the chief in the Quarter was in fact a threat to the very continuity and distinctiveness of the community.

It was in reaction to this threat that Sabo adopted the Tijaniyya, which articulated the varied interests of the Quarter's people within their communal interests by means of a strong religious belief leading to effective centralized organization.

This does not mean that religion had no political significance during the period of Indirect Rule.[38] The political organization of a local group may be regarded as that aspect of the total social relations of the group which contributes to the maintenance of the group as an autonomous polity. Many principles of social organization are thus involved, but different principles are differently emphasized in different systems. When the contribution of one principle diminishes within a system, other principles are exploited to take its place. The power on which authority is based is always composite, as it is derived from different kinds of social relationships. In simple, pre-industrial, societies one principle, like that of unilineal descent, may ideologically articulate the whole political system so that the whole universe of social relationships tends to be conceived in terms of the values, myths, rules and practices governed by that principle. But all this does not mean that that principle is the sole or main basis of the structure. It only means that the principle serves as an idiom around which different social forces—loyalties, sentiments, norms, ideologies, myths, etc.—can be mobilized, though every principle tends to exploit more of certain kinds of social forces than of other kinds.

An 'experimental situation' for the analysis of this complicated nature of political organization into its different constituent elements and of the ways in which these elements interact to produce an on-going political system, is present when a relatively small community goes through the process of dramatic change from one stage to another and its social organization becomes dominated by a new articulating principle. Such a situation has been occasioned in many small ethnic groups in British West Africa by the collapse of Indirect Rule, when many autonomous groups have suddenly become local communities within new national states. Under the protection of the colonial power these groups had developed corporate economic and political interests of their own, and their political autonomy, under Indirect Rule, had become a vital vested interest shared by most of their members. But with independence, their autonomy, and hence their common interests, were undermined. Indeed this situation seems to be common in other parts of post-war Africa as well.[39]

The reaction of these groups to the new threat varied with circumstances. Some of them succeeded in reorganizing their autonomy on new political lines which were in conformity with the new political realities. But others, like Sabo, who could not do so effectively, articulated their political autonomy in terms of other principles of social organization like religion and thus gave rise to the phenomenon labelled as 'tribalism'. This is essentially a phenomenon of the distribution of, and the struggle for, economic and political power. Under certain circumstances in the contemporary situation in African societies, ethnic loyalties and ethnic customs are used to articulate, in an informal way, a political organization which cannot be formally institutionalized.

The Sociological Problem in a Micro-Historical Perspective

The first heuristic requirement for the analysis of the nature of this interconnectedness between religious, political, and economic processes in the Hausa diaspora, is to draw clear boundaries for the area of social relations within the context of which these variables can be considered. This is essential in the study of every community today, but it is more particularly so in the case of a community of migrants, like Sabo, whose members maintain vital and live links with individuals and groups outside of the Quarter, in three main directions— Hausaland in the North, Yoruba Ibadan, and the network of Hausa communities in other Yoruba towns. In such a situation the investigator is always in danger of being drawn farther afield in tracing chains of relationships and studying 'feed back' processes.[40]

To avoid this difficulty in the study, relations which lead outside the Quarter will be traced to 'only one link', as Bailey puts it.[41] Thus, if a landlord in Sabo has business relations with a dealer in Hausaland, no account will be taken of the social network of that dealer, other than his relation with the landlord.[42]

The second heuristic requirement is to draw clearly the boundaries of time within which the processes are to be considered. This is because Sabo has been continuously changing since its creation. Within the flow of this change, two major kinds of process are found.[43] The first, which has been called 'cyclical', refers to repetitive developmental changes in the life of an individual or of a group. Thus, even if it is assumed that Sabo social structure is stable, it will still be found that people pass from one role to another in their life careers. People are born, get married, procreate children, develop in business, and then die and are replaced by others in those roles. Similarly, migrants in Sabo pass through a series of roles until they occupy the roles of settlers, and thus replace those settlers who have died or left the Quarter.

But Sabo social structure has been changing since it was founded early this century, so that cyclical change has been going on together with structural, or 'historical', change. The

Quarter has been changing demographically, economically, politically, and religiously.

Therefore, to isolate economic, political and religious processes and to analyse their interdependence, it is necessary to study their concomitant variations in the course of events in historical time. These events are thus used experimentally and not so that they may serve as parts of a narrative history of the community, though I have tried in the final presentation of the monograph to arrange the events in such a way as to give a running narrative.

It will perhaps be better if this procedure is described as 'Micro-history', to distinguish it from 'Macro-history', which tends to deal with general, large-scale, structural changes, and from 'case studies' which deal with isolated social events that are analysed statically, without the analysis of interconnections between them. Micro-history in this sense deals with local, small-scale events. It deals with macro-events which involve the grand organizations of power within a large-scale society only as these events are manifested in the local, small-scale face-to-face community. On this level, it is easier to have control over different variables and to examine sociological hypotheses.[44]

Micro-history has certain advantages. Firstly, it deals with only a few and specific variables that are relevant to a particular sociological problem. Secondly, it selects for intensive analysis, events which reveal more clearly than others the operation of those specific variables. Thirdly, it spans relatively short periods of time, the duration of which is determined by the extent to which significant continuities in cultural and social formations exist in the community studied. Fourthly, it has close reference to a contemporary situation 'on the ground' which is the starting point of observation and of analysis.[45] In the course of the study the analysis of the past helps in the analysis of the present, and the analysis of the present helps in the analysis of the past.[46] The aim throughout is to isolate variables and to analyse their interaction, not to explain the present in terms of precedents.

This is not the kind of history that is usually given as introductory 'background' in monographs, but is an integral part of the central analysis of the study. Indeed, its logical position in the final presentation is not the beginning, but the middle or the end of the monograph, after some of the main variables, which are relevant to the problem of the enquiry, have been sufficiently identified and isolated, within the context of the society in which the study is carried out.

Micro-history in this sense is now becoming part of the routine procedure of social anthropological analysis and I mention it here only to draw the attention of readers who are not anthropologists to this aspect of the present study. Turner has referred to this orientation as the study of 'social drama' and Gluckman as the study of 'extended cases'.[47]

Within these boundaries in space and time for this study, I present in the first two chapters an analysis of the processes of mobility and stability of population in the Hausa diaspora. The first chapter focuses on the processes of settlement within Sabo, as the migrant moves progessively from one role to another and thereby becomes increasingly more assimilated within the Quarter and, hence, increasingly more 'tribalized' within the city context. The second discusses the operation of two conflicting principles governing the recruitment and settlement of Hausa women within the Quarter and points out its political, economic and religious aspects. In the third chapter I discuss the social organization of the trade and thus deal with the different roles played by the thirty landlords of the Quarter, in economic, domestic, moral and political fields. The fourth, and longest chapter, analyses the interdependence between economic, political and, later, religious variables, in the course of discussing extended events which often involve the same persons and groups, spanning the period 1906 to 1950 when the system of Indirect Rule in Nigeria virtually collapsed and Sabo distinctiveness was thereby no longer formally recognized. In the fifth and sixth chapters, some processes of the religious revolution mentioned earlier, are discussed in relation to political processes, both within the Quarter and between the Quarter and other political groupings outside it.

In the Conclusion the results of the monographic analysis are brought to bear upon the phenomena of political ethnicity in general. Comparative situations from different African towns and from towns in other parts of the world are drawn upon. Political ethnicity is considered as a sociocultural strategy for informal political grouping under special structural circumstances. Basic political functions, which in formal political groupings are organized legally and bureaucratically, are organized by these ethnic groups indirectly through the manipulation of symbolic formations which are derived from their traditional culture. A comparative scheme by which different types of symbols are used in the organization of different organizational functions is discussed. This is then related to the wider problem of the study of political change. Social anthropology is seen as a branch of political science which is concerned with the study of the dynamic involvement of the symbolism of custom in the changing relations of power between individuals and groups in contemporary society.

CHAPTER ONE

The Migratory Process: Settlers
and Strangers

---

*The Quarter and the People—Processes of Settlement—Rights
in Housing—Occupational Stability—Residence of Wife
and Children—Primary Relations within the Quarter—
Relations with the Chief—Old Timers and Transients
—Social Security in Institutionalized Begging—On Becoming
a Diaspora-Hausa*

Hausa control of long-distance trade in kola and cattle in
Nigeria has required the formation of a network of highly
stable Hausa communities in the towns and villages of Yorubaland. In the face of fierce and continuous competition by
Yoruba traders, much of the success of the Hausa depended on
the rapidity with which they could establish and develop these
communities. This has involved various kinds of mobility of
population through which continual demographic adjustments
in the age, sex, and occupational structures of the communities
have been made. Different Hausa traditional customs and
institutions were closely interconnected with these demographic
processes.

When a Hausa man from the North comes to live in Sabo he
does not automatically become a citizen of the Quarter.
Settlement in the Quarter is a complex process which involves
passage through a series of roles, ranging from that of the
stranger to that of the permanent settler. As the migrant
becomes more settled, by being drawn into active participation
in the social life of the Quarter—economically, politically,
morally, and ritually—he becomes increasingly more *retribalized*. His Hausa identity becomes the expression of his
involvement in a web of live social relationships which arise
from current, mutual interests within a new social setting.

The Quarter and the People

When the present Quarter was established in 1916, about 400 Hausa were settled in it.[1] But this number steadily increased and by the early 1930's the Quarter had become highly congested and some new migrants had to settle in a peripheral area on land which they acquired from Yoruba owners. In subsequent years a few hundred Hausa eventually also sought accommodation in the centre of the town in houses owned by Yoruba.

Today there are 3,400 Hausa living within the original settlement and 762 living in the adjoining peripheral areas.[2] For all social purposes, and for adequate sociological analysis, this second group of settlers constitute an integral part of the Quarter and will be treated as such throughout the monograph.

The Hausa living in the nearby Mokola area,[3] together with Nupe and some other migrants, and the Hausa living in the centre of Ibadan, among Yoruba settlers, fall into a different category. They do not own houses but live as tenants in houses belonging to Yoruba landlords. They do not form part of the Sabo community, nor do the people of Sabo regard them as forming a part. They are mostly temporary settlers, who usually stay in Ibadan for a few months and then leave. They will therefore be treated as a separate category in this discussion.

Within the original Quarter, there is, in addition to the Hausa, a group of 382 settlers who fall into a special ethnic category. They are bilingual, speaking both Hausa and Yoruba, though they speak Yoruba among themselves. In interaction with the Yoruba they claim to be Yoruba, but within the Quarter they claim to be Hausa in origin. They claim to have been settled in Yorubaland for so long that they cannot remember their homes of origin. But according to the Hausa of the Quarter a true Hausa must be able to name his place of origin in Hausaland,[4] even though he was born in Ibadan. Thus, when in conversations these settlers say they are originally Hausa, the Hausa often retort: 'But what about your home settlement?' which, in Hausa is *'kaka gida!'*. The group is, accordingly, known within the Quarter as 'Kaka Gida'. It is believed that at least some of the families within this group are descendants of former slaves from the North who had been owned by Yoruba masters. When they were eventually

30

emancipated they could not find a place within the Yoruba compounds which belonged to freeborn Yoruba lineages, and so when a Hausa settlement was established they joined it. During the first two or three decades after the establishment of the Quarter they played an important part socially in the Quarter. They had their own chief who was turbaned by the Hausa Chief of the Quarter to whom he paid allegiance. But, as Ibadan grew bigger, as Yoruba from everywhere in Yorubaland came to settle in the city, and as the significance of lineage affiliation began to dwindle, most of the Kaka Gida began to work with Yoruba. With the intensification of party politics after the Second World War, the Kaka Gida began to identify themselves more with the Yoruba than with the Hausa. Today, the Quarter is for most of them mainly a place of residence. They and the Hausa have intermarried little.

Processes of Settlement

Of the 2,614 Hausa who were born in the North, 2,334 (89.3%) came to Ibadan between 1943 and 1963, while only 280 (10.7%) had migrated before 1943.[5] These figures reflect only the incoming migrants who were still living in the Quarter at the time when the census was taken. They do not show how many of the migrants who had lived in Sabo during the past 47 years had eventually died or returned to their homeland in the North or moved to join other Hausa communities in southern Nigeria or in other countries in West Africa. It was difficult to overcome these limitations in the general census by carrying out an extensive genealogical census, as many of these former settlers did not leave relatives behind. In 1963 I attempted to trace the fate and whereabouts of the 394 Hausa men and women who had founded the Quarter in 1916 and whose names and occupations had been listed at the time by a British official. I found that of these Hausa, 20 were still living in Sabo, 239 had died in Sabo, and 43 had left Sabo. No information could be obtained about the remaining 92.[6]

However, although it is not possible to obtain accurate and exhaustive figures in these respects, much can be learnt about the processes involved from the intensive study of events from records and biographies. In any case, it is established beyond any doubt that the total number of Hausa settling in Ibadan has been steadily increasing almost all the time, except during the Second World War period when the rate of increase became very small.[7] All this means that the number of migrants who have settled in the city is greater than those who have left it. The total number of those Hausa in Sabo who were born in Ibadan or who have been living in Ibadan for 9 years or more is 2,909, which is nearly 70% of the total Hausa population.[8]

The settlers themselves are not only aware of this fact but are even inclined to deny that there is any reverse migration. When informants are reminded of some specific well-known cases of men who have left the Quarter, they try to argue that those men had not been settlers but only 'strangers' living in the Quarter for a short period of time.

The Hausa of Sabo clearly distinguish between a Hausa settler[9] and a Hausa stranger.[10] Length of residence in the Quarter is by no means the most important criterion for this categorization. For example, men who have been sent by northern dealers to act as their permanent agents in Sabo are regarded as strangers even though some of them have lived in the Quarter for many years and have had their families with them. On the other hand, others who have been in the Quarter for a shorter period, but who act and regard themselves as permanent settlers, are not categorized as strangers.

To put it briefly, there are within Sabo social organization, distinct sets of roles for Hausa settlers and for Hausa strangers. Between the two there are graded in-between sets of roles, which mark the different degrees of commitment to settlement in the Quarter. This means that the process of social assimilation, or settlement, within the Quarter can be viewed as a movement on a continuum between the status of the stranger and that of the settler. This continuum of sets of roles consists of highly overlapping scales of roles, with each scale presenting a different criterion for settlement within the society in the Quarter. Men become more settled, not as a result of a slow process of 'acculturation' or 'socialization', but of a dramatic movement from one role to another on the same scale and from one set of roles to another.

Important among these scales, or criteria, of settlement are (1) rights in housing and space accommodation within the Quarter; (2) type of occupation; (3) the residence of wife, or wives, and children; (4) primary relationships within the Quarter and (5) relationships with the Chief of the Quarter.

Rights in Housing

Housing is crucial to settlement in the Quarter in many respects. Without some kind of permanent housing arrangement a man cannot become a citizen of the Quarter and cannot actively participate in the economic, political, and other social life of the community. He will need increasingly more housing space to accommodate his expanding family and often housing is also essential for the conduct of his business.

Since the early 1930's the Quarter has become increasingly congested. More people have settled in it without proportional expansion of the allotted area. Housing has become the scarcest, and hence the most expensive, commodity in Sabo.

When the Quarter was first founded the land was distributed in plots of equal size among the original settlers, but since then many changes in the distribution and ownership of the houses and of the plots have taken place. The land on which the houses have been built is public land but individuals have rights in the use of the plots of land which they hold. This right is inherited and it can be sold. A man can remain the 'owner' of land even though another man can own the building on which it stands. A tenant in such a house may spend money on substantial repairs, or on adding rooms to the house, and will thus have the right to a part of the value of the building. When a man dies, his rights are inherited by his kin, some of whom may not be resident in the Quarter. Sometimes a man dies leaving no heir in Sabo and after a time—in some cases after many years—someone may come from the North and claim to be an heir. In the meantime, according to custom, when a house owner dies without leaving an heir the house will be inherited by the Chief of the Quarter, presumably for use in the interest of the whole community. Therefore, because of the mobility of people, of a high rate of mortality, and of frequent bankruptcies which nearly always result in selling rights in housing, a most complicated situation has evolved, with continual claims and counter claims being made.

This situation is further complicated by the fact that a client who is accommodated in a house owned by his patron acquires in the course of time, a 'moral' right in the house. This moral right will in due course be considered by the public to be 'legal' so that even if the man loses his job, for one reason or another, in the business house of the landlord, he may still continue to have the right to the house. I have come across a number of cases of this kind, with the Chief of the Quarter, and his advisors, supporting this right, when he arbitrated in disputes.

Thus, to become a citizen of Sabo, a man has to acquire rights in housing and, other things being equal, the more such rights he acquires the more settled he becomes in the Quarter.

A man can certainly acquire housing rights outside the Quarter, by becoming a tenant in a house owned by a Yoruba landlord, and indeed he can do this at lesser expense than within the Quarter. But because by doing this he puts himself out of the control of the Chief, and hence of the community, he will not be regarded as a citizen of the Quarter and he will have no creditworthiness within it.

Occupational Stability

As in most migrant communities, the degree of settlement in the Quarter is closely inter-related with the kind of occupational role a man occupies. There is a great deal of occupational differentiation and specialization in Sabo. Within most occupational categories there is a hierarchy of roles, from that of the business landlord at the top to that of his lowest client at the bottom.

Occupational roles in Sabo can be arranged on a graded scale representing progressively higher degrees of commitment to permanent settlement in the Quarter. This scale is based on a number of criteria which overlap considerably.

The first criterion is the amount of investment in housing in the Quarter which the role calls for. A tailor needs a shop, as well as a residence. A small-scale landlord needs at least one house for the accommodation of stranger dealers who conduct their business through him. A large-scale landlord needs houses for his wives, his stranger dealers, his employees and their families, and so on. The more housing the occupational role necessitates, the more committed is the man in the role, to living within the Quarter.

Secondly, of great importance is the amount of money invested in giving credit or loans to assistants, agents, and customers, as well as the amount of money 'invested' in the form of presents to various categories of men, and of alms given to malams and to beggars. Here again, the greater the amount invested in the course of fulfilling the requirements of an occupational role, the more is the occupant of the role committed to settlement in the Quarter.

The third criterion is the stability and regularity of the role over time. Some roles are seasonal while others are constant, and some roles are temporary or intermittent while others are more continuous. Some roles, like those involved in the cattle trade, have existed and remained continuous since the beginning of Hausa migration into Ibadan, while others, like those involved in lorry transport, are of fairly recent origin.

Fourth, there is the amount of income which the role yields. The level of income is generally speaking higher in southern than in northern Nigeria and the higher the remuneration from an occupational role in the Quarter the more committed the man is to settlement in Sabo.

The fifth criterion is the amount of experience and training in local conditions which the role necessitates. Some roles require a great deal of connections with people in Sabo, in Ibadan, in the North, and in the other Hausa communities in the South. This experience is an investment and is often not transferable, so that a man acquiring valuable experience of working in the South will not be able to make great use of that experience in the North.

Residence of Wife and Children

A man shows a high degree of commitment to living in the Quarter if his wife, or wives, and his children live with him in the Quarter.

This criterion, however, is not by itself as significant as it is in many other migratory situations in Africa. Hausa marriage, both in the North and in Sabo is highly unstable.[11] In Sabo it is easy for a man to find a wife and it is also easy for a woman to find a husband. I recorded numerous cases of men who left their wives in the North and married a second wife in the South. In both the North and in Sabo, housewives conduct a trade in their own right and nearly always have some capital, as well as an income, of their own. Children are no handicap to mobility of either parent. There is on the one hand avoidance

35

between children and parents, and, on the other, a widespread practice of fostering of children. In accordance with Islamic law, when a couple are divorced children must remain with the father. But cases studied in Sabo show that nearly half the divorced men left their children with the divorced mother.

It is nevertheless the case that a married man who has his wife, or wives, and children with him in the Quarter is more committed to settlement than if he had his family staying in the North. His degree of settlement will be highest if his wife was born in Ibadan and if her parents live in the Quarter. This is because Hausa wives are attached to their parents, particularly their mothers. A Sabo housewife will always press her husband to let her go to visit her kin in the North for many weeks. In many cases which I recorded the wife had extended her visit and even stayed indefinitely, sometimes insisting that the husband should move back to the North. Sometimes the wife contracted a lover and finally divorced the husband. In a number of instances which occurred during my field work period or shortly before, a young husband would go to the North to bring back his wife and would decide or be prevailed upon to stay there indefinitely.

Primary Relations Within the Quarter

A Sabo settler is also a man whose moral universe is largely confined to the Quarter. His friends are Hausa, not Yoruba. His strongest moral obligations are toward people in the Quarter, not in the North or in the rest of the town. If he develops relationships of friendship with Yoruba men he will be looked upon with suspicion by people in the Quarter.

By moral universe I am referring here to the network of primary relations that a man develops in the course of informal interaction with other men. This network exerts a great deal of moral pressure on him and affects his behaviour. Relations of this kind develop between members of one's kind, and between various categories of friends. Friendship arises in interaction in the course of conducting business, religious worship, or leisure seeking.

These relations are described as 'moral' because, unlike contractual relations, they are ends in themselves and have an intrinsic autonomy in their own right. They are governed by

36

what Kant called 'categorical imperatives'. Partners in the relationship regard one another as an end in himself and not as means to realize an end. Participation in the relationship involves the total personalities of the partners and not segments of those personalities. In contrast, contractual relations are governed by 'hypothetical imperatives' in which men partake with only a segment, not the total, of their personality and in which they use one another as means to an end, not an end in himself.

The total primary relations of a man comprise his moral universe and to a large extent it is this universe which mediates between him and his social world.

The significance of these moral relations in the economic and political organization of the Hausa of Sabo will be discussed in detail later in the monograph. What I want to emphasize here is that a man will be regarded as settler in the Quarter only if he will be fully involved in such moral relations with members of the community.

Relations with the Chief

A settled man identifies himself with the Quarter politically and pays allegiance to its Chief. When he marries, the Chief witnesses, validates, and records the marriage, and when his children are born he goes through the naming ceremony at the Chief's office. When he becomes involved in a dispute in business or in matters of inheritance he asks the Chief to arbitrate. He gives the Chief specified fees as well as presents for all these services. When he passes by the Chief's office he kneels down as a greeting and token of respect. When the Chief requires him to act in a certain way which is deemed necessary for the general interest of the Quarter he will obey unquestionably.

The Chief is an indispensable reference for the honesty and the creditworthiness of a man in Sabo. Strangers coming for the first time from the North to do business with the help of men in the Quarter, nearly always seek the advice of the Chief. The right testimony given by the Chief is sufficient for the strangers to entrust a man with their business. In many contexts the Chief's help and testimony, in dealings with the local authorities, are of great importance. Similarly, the Chief will mediate on the man's behalf with chiefs in other Hausa communities in the North or in the South, and in marital and inheritance problems.

In the course of continual interaction between a settler and the Chief, some personal, informal, dyadic relationships which develop are often expressed in terms of father–son or brother–brother, depending on the respective ages of the two men. And as the settler's children grow up they call the Chief by the term 'father'.

Old Timers and Transients

On the basis of these highly overlapping criteria of settlement in the Quarter, the Hausa of Sabo, at any one time, can be classified for sociological purposes into three major demographic categories.

The first can be called 'the Settlers'. It consists of a permanent core of old timers, or Hausa men born in Ibadan, who have their families with them, regard themselves as permanent settlers and are usually house-owners, or have some kind of permanent housing arrangement. They are often engaged in occupations which necessitate long experience in local affairs and wide connection in the host city, and in other centres of the Hausa diaspora in Yorubaland.

The second category, 'the Migrants', consists of relatively recent migrants who are mostly males, many of whom are either unmarried or have their wives back in their native land in the North. They usually lack both the experience and the capital to engage in business on their own, though many of them work as itinerant traders with a very small capital. They are mostly accommodated in rented single rooms, with two or more men sharing the same room. Many of them are uncertain whether they will settle permanently in Ibadan, or return to the North, or migrate to other parts of the Hausa diaspora.

A third category, 'the Strangers', consists of people who come to stay in the Quarter temporarily, some for a few months, some for a few weeks, and many for a few days. Among them are northern dealers who come to Sabo to have goods sold or bought for them in the city. Others are visitors who come to stay with their kin or friends for some specified or unspecified time. There is also a continuous stream of Hausa transients who are on their way to other Hausa centres, further south in Nigeria or in Ghana or in other countries in West Africa. Sabo travel-agents, who run the two lorry parks in the Quarter, and provide various services to men in transit, also specialize in getting Travel Certificates for those who travel out of Nigeria. For a number of reasons it is much easier for these transients to get travel certificates in Ibadan than in their own settlements of origin in the North.

The strangers are accommodated in the scores of 'houses for strangers' that are run by settlers, where they are also provided with food. Other strangers stay in the houses of relatives, or friends, if these are available.

The number of these strangers fluctuates from season to season, but there is hardly a day when they do not total a few hundreds. Although the individuals change all the time, the category as a whole is a permanent part of the social structure of the Quarter. Strangers are the customers who are served by settlers and are in fact the source of livelihood for the settlers.

It is clear that at any point in time, these three categories are not mutually exclusive and that in some cases they overlap or shade into one another, so that a man who is in one category by virtue of one criterion is in another by virtue of another criterion. A young man who is from a family of settlers may fall into the category of Migrants because he is not married, has no fixed residence of his own, and is engaged in an occupation which does not tie him permanently to the Quarter. Similarly, a man may be regarded as a stranger because he has been in the Quarter for a relatively short time, but may have his wife and children with him, after having been invited by a relative or friend settler to take up a permanent job and also a permanent residence in the Quarter.

Although the categories are permanent features of social organization in the Quarter there is a continuous process of mobility of personnel from the category of strangers to that of migrants and then to that of settlers.

From the general massive flow of Hausa from the North to the South, some men and women find their way to Sabo where for a shorter or longer period they stay as strangers. For one reason or another, some of these strangers prolong their stay in the Quarter and eventually pass into the category of migrants, thereby replacing those migrants who have moved up to the category of settlers, or who have left the Quarter altogether through emigration or death. A stranger who came to visit relatives in the Quarter may be offered a job as well as accommodation by these relatives and may thus be induced to stay on. Many settlers told me that they had initially come to the South to look for a 'brother', who had left the North and never come back. They drifted southward visiting Hausa communities on the way and finally found the missing relative in Sabo and joined him. Some labourers who come during the dry season and work as porters in the railway station or as carriers in kola yards may stay on indefinitely if there is continued demand for their services. Itinerant petty traders, beggars, malams, barbers, herbalists and other categories of mobile Hausa who pass through the Quarter as strangers may find it profitable to stay on. Also, pupils who are sent to study for some time with Sabo malams often stay on with their master to help him tutoring junior pupils and thus become migrants. Agents of northern dealers who are sent to Sabo to conduct their business sometimes decide to settle in the Quarter and to sever their relation with their patrons in order to start in business on their own. The crucial factors at this stage for strangers to become migrants are housing and occupation, both of which are often provided by the same landlord.

Similarly many migrants eventually become permanent settlers to replace those settlers who have died, migrated back to the North, or drifted to other Hausa communities in the South. As most of the migrants are single men, the most crucial factor in the movement to the Settlers' category is marriage, particularly if the wife was born in Ibadan. Marriage in Sabo always entails the acquisition of relatively permanent housing arrangements, as no man can marry without giving his wife at least one separate room of her own. Marriage is also crucial in that the man becomes more creditworthy and hence he has a chance to pass on to a more responsible, more profitable, and more stable occupational role. Soon his wife will set up some trade from within her seclusion inside the house and will in many ways indirectly connect him with more people. More contacts will be made when children are born. As his wife becomes settled in her trade she will foster one or more children from her or his relatives. In short, marriage will push up the position of a man on all scales of settlement.

These cyclical processes operate all the time even if the demographic and social structure of the Quarter remain static.

But in reality this structure has been continually changing. The ratios between the sexes, the various age groups, and the occupational divisions, have been changing all the time. The number of settlers has been steadily increasing because more men enter this category than men die, or return back to the North out of it. This can be seen from the age distribution of the population which, unlike that of many other migrant communities in African towns, shows a relatively high proportion of old people.[12] All this means that unlike other migrant communities, men reaching old age or becoming physically handicapped do not have to seek security in their community of origin. This is because in Sabo, as in other Hausa migrant communities in Southern Nigeria, there are fairly adequate institutions for social security.

Social Security in Institutionalized Begging

A large proportion of the massive stream of annual Hausa migrants from the North to the South eventually return to their homes. The general pattern in the North is that men work on their land during the wet season and migrate for work or trade during the dry season. A few of these seasonal migrants come to Sabo for some seasonal work, particularly when the kola season is at its peak in the South.

However, the majority of those migrants who stay permanently in Sabo are not engaged in this type of mixed economy. Many of them have no land of their own in the North. The few who do have, find that they are economically better off in the South. Many Hausa in Sabo rationalize their permanent settlement in Ibadan on the ground that in the North land is poor, that employment is not available, that the climate is harsh; and some informants would add that the regime of the emirs and chiefs is oppressive and exploitative. In any case there are many Hausa migrants who, for a number of reasons, prefer to stay in Sabo if they can.

For those migrants who settle in the Quarter there is obviously no strong 'pull' back towards the North. In other parts of Africa migrants to places of work are often under pressure to return back to their native settlement. The pressure comes from two sources: kinship obligations and the lack of social security in the centres of migration.[13]

Most of the Hausa in Sabo have no strong kinship obligations to return to the North. The Hausa generally are bilateral and the range of economically, politically, or morally significant kinship relationships among them is very narrow. Many men in Sabo do not remember the names of their grandparents on either side. And because of the high rate of divorce, of the wide practice of child fostering, and of estrangement between parents and children, primary relations within the family itself are not very strong.

All this means that the moral pressure on a man to return to the North to fulfil obligations to kin is not a very strong one. It also means, on the other hand, that a man does not rely for social security, in time of need, on a group of kinsmen in the North. In other parts of Africa migrants keep in touch with their kin in the tribal hinterland, send them gifts and remittances and pay regular visits to them for the very purpose of providing security for themselves in the hour of need. Most migrants eventually return to their native settlements when they are ill unemployed or too old to work, because no effective institutions of social security in the centres of migration are available.

In Sabo, the situation is different because there are institutionalized ways in the Quarter for providing for the bereaved, the physically handicapped, and the old.

To begin with, if a man is wealthy and his business is continued by his sons or by his leading clients then there is no problem. Also, a client who has reached old age and ceased to work for his patron will remain in the accommodation given to him by the patron. Moreover, his patron is under moral obligation to help him with food and clothing. In addition, the Chief of the Quarter controls scores of houses, on behalf of the community, where he is under obligation to accommodate needy settlers and in some cases even to provide food for them.

But by far the most important institutionalized arrangement for social security in the Quarter is that of begging. Among the Hausa of Sabo, as among the Hausa elsewhere in West Africa, begging is a highly organized industry which plays a crucial role in the migratory process and in the organization of the Hausa diaspora.

Begging among the Hausa, as among some other Moslem peoples, rests on the principle of alms-giving, which is one of the five pillars of orthodox Islam, and which requires that a believer should pay a small part of his annual income to the needy.[14] In Sabo, most, if not all, of the business landlords regularly give alms, though it is difficult to say how meticulous they are about the exact percentage of these alms in their total annual earning. Alms-giving in the Quarter is a well established public institution.

What is sociologically significant in this context is the question as to who qualifies for receiving these alms and how public assistance is generally organized.

Among the Hausa there are a number of traditional occupations which border on begging. In Sabo musicians and praise singers are regarded as beggars, though they form a special category on their own. They are usually described as 'official beggars' (*maroka*) and are organized under a chief of their own, known as *Sankira*, who is appointed and 'turbanned' in this position by the Chief of the Quarter. The Chief of the Musicians is also the Public Announcer (*maishela*) of the Quarter. Informants in Sabo insist on describing the musicians as beggars on the ground that these attend to play and sing in weddings, naming, and other ceremonies, without being invited. In contrast there is in Sabo a professional drummer who is never described as a beggar because he only drums, without singing praise songs, and he attends ceremonies only when invited. Sociologically, praise singers cannot be regarded as 'beggars', but many beggars use praise singing as a technique for getting alms.

Another profession bordering on begging is that of the malam, or the religious functionary. There are different types of malams. Some men sit near their own residence and recite the Koran throughout the day, either loudly or faintly; and people pay them alms in money or food. Others act as rhetorical 'advisors', who on Fridays and feast days stand or sit beside groups of men, and utter exhortations to piety and to good social conduct. When they finish they are paid a small sum of money. Many men who pay alms in the Quarter seemed to me to hold the view that it was not only more meritorious, but also a better investment, to give these alms to malams rather than to ordinary beggars. Even the most eminent of the malams in Sabo live principally from the alms—often described as gifts —given to them by their patron landlords. Malams are believed to bestow some of the blessing (or *baraka*) which they possess on those believers who give them alms and there are countless

43

stories, current in the Quarter, of men who gave alms to malams and were enriched or helped out of great difficulties by the mystical help of one or another of the malams to whom they gave alms or presents, or whom they sheltered and fed. As one goes down the scale of the hierarchy of malams it becomes in some cases difficult to determine whether a man is a malam or a beggar. This is particularly so because many of the ordinary, publicly-styled beggars recite passages from the Koran while begging.

Again, some men who describe themselves as 'petty traders' act as beggars either intermittently or in the course of peddling a few simple articles. Some of them work throughout the week as petty traders and beg only on Fridays.

There are some other occupational categories which merge, in their lower periphery, into begging. Indeed many Hausa migrants who travel hundreds of miles from their native settlements engage in begging for part of the way to enable them to pay, with the proceeds, for their transport for the remaining part of the journey. Almost the same pattern is reported in a large scale study of destitution in the Gold Coast (now Ghana). A report, based on this study, points out that many Hausa beggars who were begging in Gold Coast towns in 1954 had walked from Sokoto to Kano, then travelled free on the train to Lagos, begging in towns on the way, and begged in Lagos until they had money to pay their fare to Accra.[15] It emerges from the accounts of some informants in Sabo that in the course of their trek from their native settlements in the North to places of work in the South, some migrants alternate between begging, working on farms, petty trading, posing as malams or selling charms and amulets. Begging is thus a traditional trade, the skills of which are learned by many men for use in the hour of need.

In all these cases, begging is informal and is not organized. But full time, formal, begging in Sabo is a highly organized institution. Beggars, who are called *al majirai* as distinct from *maroka*, are clearly categorized, and each category forms a separate association with its own structure and rules. Each category is organized under a chief who holds a special title and who is officially turbaned by the Chief of the Quarter in a special public ceremony. Thus, the blind beggars have a Chief of the Blind, *Sarkin Makafi*, the lame beggars have a

Chief of the Lame, *Sarkin Guragu*, and the leper beggars have a Chief of the Lepers, *Sarkin Kutare*.

Within each category membership is well defined and organization fairly strict. Members pay tribute, in money or in service, to their respective chief. The Chief of the Blind runs a house for the accommodation of blind beggars. Each beggar is provided with a guide and is assigned a place, or places, for begging. Earnings from begging during weekdays belong to the beggars themselves, but earnings on Fridays are paid to the Chief of the Blind.

When a man in Sabo becomes disabled or old, he usually goes to the Chief of the Quarter and asks his help. The Chief of the Quarter then recommends him to the chief of that category of beggars into which he fits best. The beggars' chief will then enrol the new member and discuss rules and areas for begging with him. During my period of field work, a commission agent in the cattle market became blind and was unable to continue in his job. The Chief of the Quarter suggested that the man should become a beggar and should enrol with the Chief of the Blind. The man agreed and the Chief of the Quarter duly talked to the Chief of the Blind. The man was admitted into the organization. He was provided with a guide and assigned places for begging. He continued to be accommodated in the house given to him by his former business landlord.

But Sabo does not pay the whole of its social security bill. It is only the very old and infirm beggars who are assigned by their respective chiefs to beg within the Quarter. The rest of the beggars are dispersed daily in the city to beg in specified places. The Hausa have an almost complete monopoly over the begging industry in Ibadan. Most of the beggars use Sabo as a base from which they 'raid' the Yoruba city for donations.

Thus a great proportion of the alms given by the Hausa of Sabo is paid to the malams and to the very old beggars who beg within the Quarter. For the rest of the beggars, Sabo only provides free accommodation, shelter, a place for respite, for washing and for changing clothes, and makes the Yoruba hosts pay the rest of the bill.

Most of the Hausa beggars in Ibadan are clean, well dressed and well fed, and they often are very cheerful. Earnings from begging vary according to skill and according to the day of the week and the season. But on the whole they are not inferior to earnings from the other ordinary trades. Many of the beggars travel daily from the Quarter to their special place of 'work' in the town, in a taxi.[16]

The best strategic places for begging in Ibadan are markets, business streets, lorry parks and the neighbourhoods of places of worship. On Fridays the entire beggar force of the Quarter concentrates in the Central Mosque area in the middle of the town. On Sundays, the beggars disperse to sit near Christian churches to beg while chanting passages from the Koran.

Some of the beggars beg in teams. One group of blind beggars beg on Friday in an organized team, having one guide and one blind malam who is skilled in reciting the Koran.

During the 'begging high season', when the Yoruba of the town have much money from the sale of their cocoa produce, the permanent begging force of Sabo is augmented by migrant beggars who lodge with one or another of the chiefs of the beggars in Sabo, and beg under the chief's auspices paying the chief part of the proceeds. For the economy of Sabo as a whole, this is an additional income which consolidates the Quarter's institutions of social security.

Here again, Sabo is not unique in this elaborate organization of its beggars. Similar arrangements exist in other Hausa communities in other towns in southern Nigeria and in Ghana. In a survey of beggars in Lagos in the mid-1940's it was found that 139 out of a total of 153 of the beggars were Hausa. Of these, 132 were permanently resident in Lagos. In the Gold Coast survey of 1954, 353 out of a total of 596 of the beggars in the survey were Hausa.[17] The Report quotes the Hausa Chief of the Zongo in Accra as saying that he accommodated in his own houses many beggars for whom he provided also two meals a day.

Less systematic information, scattered in the literature on West Africa indicates that begging is a universal institution throughout the Hausa diaspora in West Africa. Sabo's beggars form part of a special beggars' network which extends to all Yoruba towns, and farther beyond, through which information is communicated as to changes in the 'carrying capacities' of different localities for begging. While there is a hard core of permanently settled beggars in each Hausa centre, there is also a mobile force which circulates from one centre to another according to local possibilities.

All this suggests that there is in Sabo a great measure of stable arrangements for social security providing for the physically handicapped and the unemployed. Indeed the evidence shows that these institutions are adequate to serve not only the permanent population of Sabo, the migrants and the settlers, but also the Hausa strangers from the North.

Thus, it is possible for migrants to settle in Sabo without the need to go back to their native settlements. This should explain the steady growth of Sabo and of the other centres of Hausa migration in the towns of the forest belt, throughout almost the whole of West Africa during the present century.

On Becoming a Diaspora-Hausa

It has been suggested that ethnic exclusiveness in African towns is due to the fact that migrants are only temporary town-dwellers and that therefore they tend to retain their tribal identity because their residence in the host town is too short to allow of much cultural assimilation and also because they are constantly aware of the 'pull' of their native communities, partly for considerations of economic security and partly for kinship obligation. But it has been seen above that there is in Sabo a highly settled population who do not intend or need to return to the North. And yet, it is specifically this population and not the strangers or the migrants, who uphold, emphasize and keep alive Hausa exclusiveness in Ibadan, even though many of these settlers have been in the Quarter for two or three generations.

Hausa culture in Sabo is not an extension of Northern Hausa culture. In fact there is no uniform, homogeneous, Hausa culture. There are some significant cultural variations between the various concentrations of Hausa communities in Northern Nigeria.[18] The Hausa generally maintain a diversified economy which is far removed from the subsistence level and which involves a great deal of occupational differentiation. Some Hausa live in indigenous, long-established, towns while others live in rural areas. And across differences in type of settlement there is a great deal of class differentiation. It is for this reason that some writers describe the Hausa as a 'nation' and not as a 'tribe'.

47

These differences in region and type of settlement, are reflected in a survey of the origin of the Hausa of Sabo on the basis of my census.

Of the 4,184 Hausa living in the Quarter, 1,570 were born in Ibadan, but these are mainly young people. Of the remaining 2,614, about 55% were born in Kano province, 10% in Sokoto province, 10% in Katsina province, 17.7% in other places in the North, and 0.6% in other Hausa centres in the South.[19] Cutting across this difference in place of origin is the difference in the type of settlement of origin. Nearly three quarters of the migrants came originally from rural areas and a quarter from the towns.

But within the context of Sabo society, place of origin is of only limited importance in inter-personal relations. Some men are known in the Quarter by their first name and by the name of the town or village from which they came. This is especially the case with those who settled in the Quarter in its early stages, when the number of settlers was relatively small. There are also some differences in accent between settlers hailing from different parts of Hausaland, and there is some stereotyping current in the Quarter in terms of place of origin. Also, a new migrant in the Quarter expects more help from men from his own settlement of origin than from others. And, relatively speaking, there is probably more trust between people coming from the same place, and dealers from the North try, when possible, to do business with landlords from their own settlements of origin. Similarly, business landlords tend to recruit clients from their home settlements when possible.

On the whole, however, place of origin is of little significance within Sabo social organization. There is no correlation between place of birth and social status or such criteria as political affiliation, occupation, average length of residence in the Quarter, proportion between the sexes or between age categories, or the choice of partners in marriage. The Hausa of Sabo themselves stress that, being a minority of 'strangers' who are under constant economic and political pressure exerted on them by the host society, they cannot afford to emphasize differences within their own camp.

Sabo social organization and the Sabo brand of Hausa culture are new phenomena which can be explained in terms of the economic and political circumstances in which the Hausa diaspora in Yoruba towns has developed and not in terms of Hausa patterns in the North. Hausa culture in Sabo is in many ways a new culture and a Hausa newcomer from the North has to learn it and to adjust to it. He will not become 'one of us' simply because he comes from Hausaland and he speaks Hausa. He will achieve this status only through the process of progressively acquiring the role of a Sabo settler.

Indeed it is possible for some non-Hausa to acquire such roles and thereby to become, in effect, Sabo Hausa. Not all the Hausa of the Quarter are 'authentic' Hausa. The term 'Hausa' is generic and refers to those people who speak Hausa as their first language. In Sabo a man can qualify as Hausa if he satisfies the following conditions: (1) speaks Hausa as a first language, (2) can name a place of origin in one of the seven original Hausa states, (3) is a Moslem, and (4) has no tribal mark on his face which indicates affiliation to another tribe.

From the census data which I collected in the Quarter it can be seen that there are many cases of men and women who satisfy these conditions and yet who are not full Hausa by birth. Some of them had only one of their parents as Hausa. In other cases both parents were non-Hausa. In Northern Nigeria many non-Hausa ethnic groups are interspersed between Hausa settlements within the same province. The long-standing political dominance of the Hausa-Fulani states has led to the adoption of both the Hausa language and of Islam by some of those ethnic groups. For some of these groups or for their individual members, identification with the Hausa has meant an upward social mobility. In Sabo an insurmountable obstacle to a man's acceptance as a Hausa is a permanent facial tribal mark which indicates clearly affiliation to a foreign ethnic group. However, as a result of the spread and progressive consolidation of Islam, many Moslems in Northern Nigeria have stopped the practice of marking the faces of their children. This has facilitated the assimilation of non-Hausa within Hausa communities. Furthermore, as the Hausa are essentially bilateral, a man does not need an elaborate genealogical evidence to prove that he is Hausa. As the Hausa traditional polities are centralized, and not segmentary it has been possible to incorporate within them different ethnic stocks. The acceptance of Islam by some of these groups has meant the acceptance of a universalistic, as against tribal, law, governing the organization of the family. This must have led to intermarriage. As a result of these conditions non-Hausa individuals and groups have become 'Hausa-ized'.

The Hausa of Sabo are aware of many of these processes whereby non-Hausa become Hausa, and many cases of individuals who are in various stages of becoming Hausa are known in the Quarter. The fact is that for both the Hausa and the Hausa-in-the-making, being a Diaspora-Hausa must be achieved and is not simply an acquired status.

As the migrant becomes more and more settled so he becomes more and more of a Diaspora-Hausa. He becomes socially assimilated within Sabo and he identifies himself with the Quarter. In the process he also becomes progressively more culturally exclusive, emphasizing among Hausa northerners as well as among Yoruba, that he is culturally distinct. A migrant may work in a town and mix with Yoruba. He may have Yoruba friends, pray with Yoruba and eat with Yoruba. But a Sabo settler cannot do so without losing much of his 'ethnic' identity. He must be truly Hausa even though he may interact in business with the Yoruba.

This ethnic distinctiveness is, again, not an extension of an indigenous Hausa trait from the North. Indeed as indicated earlier the Hausa are by no means fanatic about their tribal identity. They tolerate outsiders, and provided these are Muslims, they admit them into their settlements and eventually give them the same ethnic status.

Sabo's Hausaism and Diaspora-Hausaism generally, is manifested in the occupation of certain roles within Sabo structure. It is a living system of roles which has developed under certain economic and political circumstances in Nigeria.

CHAPTER TWO

The Migratory Process: Prostitutes
and Housewives

---

*Mystical Dangers of Yoruba Wives—Prostitutes and Satan
—Housewives In Seclusion—Prostitution and the Mobility
of Women—Trade from Behind the Purdah—Accumulation
of Capital and Conspicuous Expenditure—The Mobility of
Women in the Perspective of Sabo's History*

In the course of a few decades Sabo's female population has
been getting increased through the operation of two conflicting
sets of customs which govern the position of women. The first
set is associated with the free and mobile prostitute, while the
second is associated with the secluded and settled housewife.
And through frequent divorce, many women oscillate between
prostitution and wifehood a number of times in their marriage
career.

One of the most fundamental demographic processes in the
building up of the Hausa network of communities has been the
recruitment of women. A sizeable and stable stock of women is
always necessary to ensure stability of settlement. Women
provide sexual services and companionship for the men, maintain households, bear children, and run special trades.

It is for this reason that sociologists have often measured the
stability of migrant communities in African towns by the
proportion of the women to the men in them. The more even
this proportion is, the more settled the community tends to be.
Those tribal migrant groups who suffer imbalance between the
sexes, usually resulting from shortage of women, are highly
unstable and their men maintain a restless existence in the
centres of migration until, after a short period, they go back
to their tribal settlements. As described in the last chapter, the
bachelor migrants in Sabo become finally settled only when

ve their wives living with them in the

the many migrant groups which he studied
basis of this criterion and ranks the Hausa
most settled, with nearly 400 women to every 1,000
the Accra community.[1] He implies that this is achieved
a custom among Hausa migrants of taking their women and
children with them as they move. He points out that during
the 19th century, Hausa men migrants took their women and
children with them and were thus 'ready to settle anywhere
and develop their community without any contact with the
natives other than those demanded by trade'.[2]

But the study of Hausa migration in recent decades gives a
very different picture. In a survey of the annual labour migration from Sokoto province in 1954, Prothero reports that the
men migrated alone, without their women.[3] And my own study
of how Hausa migrate in Yorubaland gives the same result.
Male migrants to Sabo have always come alone. Those of them
who were married, left their wives and children behind them,
at least for some time. Nevertheless, Sabo is a highly stable
community with a relatively high proportion of females to
males.[4] Of the 1,570 Hausa who were born in Sabo, 891 are
females and 679 are males.[5] Among the rest of the population
who were born elsewhere the number of women is nearly half of
the number of men. But this should not be taken to indicate
that within this category there is a shortage of women of
marriageable age. Indeed there is much evidence to show that at
no time in its development has the community experienced
a shortage of women in relation to the demand for them. The
analysis of the demographic history of the Quarter indicates
that whenever there has been a need for women in Sabo there
has been an appropriate supply to fill that need. The principal
reason why there is such a high proportion of bachelors in the
Quarter is the shortage of accommodation in Sabo. During
field work I knew many bachelors who wanted to marry and
get settled in the Quarter but could not find the appropriate
accommodation. I also knew a number of men who had one or
two wives with them, and who wanted to marry an additional
wife but could not do so for the same reason. In all those cases
the men had the necessary money to make the marriage payment as well as a steady income to maintain the wife, and in

certain cases the men also had specific eligible wome
to marry them.

Mystical Dangers of Yoruba Wives

The Hausa of Sabo have relied for the supply of women almost exclusively on Hausa women born in Sabo or in Hausa-land in the North. Hausa men in the Quarter do not take Yoruba women as wives. Of the 950 housewives in the Quarter, only four who come from the half-Yoruba/half-Hausa group known as Kaka Gida, which I mentioned earlier in the mono-graph can to some extent be described as Yoruba.

There are strong beliefs current in the Quarter about mystical dangers which can afflict the Hausa man who marries a Yoruba woman. Informants support these beliefs by reference to specific cases. In two recent cases, marriages with Yoruba women against the advice of the divining malams, had ended in disaster. In one case the man died within two months after the wedding and in the other the man became seriously ill and eventually divorced his Yoruba wife.

These beliefs can be related to some political dangers which are likely to result from Sabo men marrying Yoruba women. In the long run, such intermarriage can be highly subversive of Sabo ethnic exclusiveness and political autonomy and this would be fatal to Hausa economic interests. As the Hausa of Sabo are not strongly patrilineal, Yoruba women are not likely to be 'absorbed' within Hausa kinship groupings. Indeed the opposite can be true. Yoruba women can pull their husbands towards increasing involvement in Yoruba society. This is particularly the case because Yoruba wives will have their own kin living nearby in Ibadan or within a relatively short distance from the city. Furthermore, Yoruba married women, unlike Hausa married women, are not secluded. They are traders in their own right and they compete freely with men in the economic as well as the political arenas. Children born from such a mixed marriage are likely to be torn between their father and mother between Hausa society and Yoruba society and their political alignment will be ambivalent.

On the individual level, a Hausa man who is married to a Yoruba woman will not be trusted by northern Hausa dealers to conduct their business in Ibadan. In 1963 a cattle landlord, with whom I was very closely acquainted, fell in love with a

used to see in the neighbourhood of the
ecame very keen on marrying her but did
using accommodation, particularly as he
ives and also had his deceased father's wives
male relatives living in his three houses. The
ly changed when one of his wives died in
fter a few weeks he decided that the time was
narry the Yoruba girl. However, his two leading
busines...   s, whom he regarded as 'fathers' because of their
senior age and long-standing service under his deceased father,
strongly opposed the proposed marriage. Reluctantly he gave
in to their will. In conversations which I had with them later,
they were emphatic that the marriage would have ruined the
business of the landlord and, in addition, would have imperilled
his health or even his life.

Again, in a dispute within the Hausa Quarter in the neighbouring Yoruba city of Oyo, the Chief of the Quarter, together
with some of the leading landlords, demanded the dismissal of
the Hausa Chief of the Cattle Market, on the ground that he
had become Yoruba 'by naturalization' when he had married
a Yoruba woman.

Because of the continuous struggle between Hausa and
Yoruba over control in trade, a Hausa settler in Sabo is in
political opposition to the Yoruba. Marriage to a Yoruba
woman can therefore inhibit a man from fulfilling the requirements of his role as a citizen of Sabo.

The Hausa of Sabo are thus opposed to marrying Yoruba
women. Social interaction between Hausa and Yoruba is in any
case, minimized and opportunities for Hausa men to become
involved with Yoruba women are thus greatly reduced.

Hausa men in Sabo therefore neither brought women with
them nor took women from the Yoruba. However, by exploiting
a number of Hausa traditional institutions they succeeded in
accumulating a large stock of women, who are today the
basis of stability and settlement in the Quarter.

Prostitutes and Satan

There are in Sabo today (1963) 1,753 females in a total
population of 4,184.[6] These figures do not cover the strangers,
whose number runs to many hundreds and who include several
categories of women. Of the 1,753 females, 483 are children,

54

under 15 years of age. The remaining females fall into two main categories: 950 housewives and 250 prostitutes. A residual category numbering 70 women consists of old widows and of women who have just been divorced. The main division of the women into housewives and prostitutes is in keeping with local usage and ideology and represents one of the most important organizational features of Sabo society.

All the prostitutes are former housewives who have either divorced their husbands, been divorced by them, or run away from them. As Smith asserts of the Hausa in Northern Nigeria, every adult woman is or has been married.[7] Womanhood is a social status and a female acquires it only on marriage. Marriage is thus the rite of passage from childhood to woman-hood. If, after divorce a woman remains single, she will be called *karuwa*, or prostitute. The passage from wifehood to prostitution after divorce is not automatic. A divorced woman who does not immediately practise prostitution and who remains at home, with her parents or other relatives is called *bazawara*, which means literally a formerly married woman who is currently not married. But if the *bazawara* does not marry within a short time and if she begins to go out of the house in daylight she becomes known as prostitute.

In Sabo society, prostitution does not carry the same stigma which it does in Western or in some other societies. The Hausa *karuwa* is idealized in the culture as a woman of strong character, intelligent, and highly entertaining. In many Arab communi-ties, when a woman becomes a prostitute, her brothers and father's brothers' sons are put to shame by the community until they kill her and, as the Arabs put it, 'wash away the shame with her blood'.[8] Among the Hausa, on the other hand, no great shame is inflicted on the parents or other relatives of the prostitute, though it is nearly always the case that women leave their natal settlements when they become prostitutes.

Of the 250 prostitutes of Sabo, only 2 were born in Sabo, while all the others were born in the North. In comparison, 407 of the 950 housewives of the Quarter, were born in Sabo. Even after the puritanic tendencies brought to Sabo religion during the past fifteen years by the Tijaniyya order, to which the overwhelming majority of the men adhere, it is not shame-ful for a man to visit a prostitute. It is true to say though that if a business man frequently visits prostitutes, he is likely to

55

lose some financial trustworthiness in his trade, as people will be afraid that he may squander on the prostitutes money entrusted to him in the course of business.

In Sabo, the prostitutes are coveted and admired by men and are always sought after in marriage. Male informants in the Quarter say that the prostitutes make ideal housewives in many respects. They are entertaining companions, they excel in the arts of lovemaking and, when they are in love with a man, they are most devoted and sincere to him. Informants emphasize, however, that to marry a prostitute a man must have a strong character himself, as, because of her love of freedom and of independence she needs to be tamed and kept under constant control. Male informants also believe that prostitutes are endowed with special mystical characteristics which make them immune from illness and, somehow, even from death. Informants who have been settled in the Quarter all their lives state that while in their lifetime scores of women in the Quarter have died every year, they do not recollect even one prostitute having died. They also state that while housewives often fall ill, no prostitute seems to suffer from any illness. Thus men combine their admiration and idealization of the prostitute with some apprehension of the unknown mystical forces believed to be associated with her.

Nevertheless, men marry prostitutes all the time and in 1963 I recorded 12 such marriages which had been contracted during the previous two years. In one of these cases, the man was a malam, a religious functionary. Prostitutes are very selective in the choice of both lovers and future husbands and there is always a great deal of demand for them. Informants are agreed that if all the prostitutes of the Quarter decide to get married immediately they will all find husbands on the same day without much difficulty. Such a dramatic turn of events did actually take place once in 1931 when the Ibadan Native Authority chiefs ordered that the prostitutes of Sabo had either to marry immediately or leave the town. The records indicate that the prostitutes did in fact get married, at least temporarily, and that the Chief of the Quarter had collected a sum of 2/6 from every one of the prostitutes in order to organize a collective wedding celebration for them.[9]

Many of the housewives are therefore former prostitutes. Divorce among the Hausa is easy and very frequent. It is far more frequently sought by wives than by husbands. In Islam, generally, it is easy for men to divorce their wives, but exceedingly difficult for wives to divorce their husbands. In Sabo, however, a woman can either ask her husband to divorce her by pronouncing the divorce formula and signing a letter for her confirming it, or, if he refuses, she can ask people to put pressure on him to do so. If she fails in such efforts, she can go to the Chief of the Quarter and put a case before him and his counsellors. Judging from the cases which I recorded, the Chief will nearly always grant a wife a divorce and his judgement is only important in determining whether the wife is obliged to return the marriage payment or not. If the worst comes to the worst, the wife can, as a last resort, just run away from her husband and pose as a prostitute. The Chief justifies the ease with which he grants divorce to wives, on the ground that if he did not, the wives would become prostitutes somewhere else. A wife whose marriage is annulled by the Chief, gets from him a written document to that effect so that when she wants to remarry in another place she will produce it in evidence. In a random sample of 164 married women in Sabo, 46 had divorced once, 37 twice, 9 three times or more, and 91 had not divorced. According to Smith, the average Hausa woman in the North probably divorces two or three times before the menopause.[10] Many of the divorced women become prostitutes for a shorter or longer period before they eventually re-marry.

Of the 164 women in the random sample, 22 were known to have solicited as prostitutes in the past. When the figures are broken down by the birthplace of the women, it turns out that of the 38 Sabo-born women in the sample, 4, or nearly 10%, had solicited before, while of the 104 North-born women in the sample, 18, or 17% had been prostitutes before. If we assume that the sample is representative of the 950 housewives of the Quarter, then we can see that 132, or nearly 14%, were formerly prostitutes. I believe that, for a number of reasons these proportions are underestimates, and that a larger number of the housewives were, in the past, prostitutes.

The important point to be emphasized here is that prostitutes frequently marry and slip into the anonymity of wifehood, and wives frequently divorce and emerge into the freedom and independence of prostitution. In men's thinking these two roles represent two aspects of womanhood. Some women move from one status to another a number of times in their career. Thus every woman is a potential prostitute.

In Sabo belief, as in that of Hausa society in the North, prostitution is closely associated with the bori cult which, according to the prevailing attitude in the Quarter, is the work of Satan. The bori is an old, indigenous, pre-Islamic Hausa cult which involves the belief in spirits known as *isokoki*, which under certain conditions can possess men and harm them. The Hausa malams have been continuously and consistently fighting against it, but, as Greenberg points out,[11] instead of dismissing the spirits as mere myths, the malams have admitted their existence, and hence their mystical power, by identifying them as the wicked among the many categories of *jinns* whose existence and characteristics are discussed in the Koran. In this way the popular belief in these spirits has been indirectly accommodated within Islamic belief and today one of the most important missions of the malams in Sabo and among the Hausa generally is to carry on the relentless battle against the spirits and those who perform their cult.

This association between prostitution and the bori cult in Sabo, however, is largely a matter of belief and is not supported by empirical evidence. Only 10 of the 250 prostitutes of Sabo are known to be active initiates in the cult. On the other hand, a number of respectable housewives are known to be secret participants in the cult. Moreover, the impression one gets from men informants is that most of the housewives support the cult financially when in the case of their own illness or in the case of the illness of their children they apply to the local initiates to hold special ritual sessions on their behalf to seek a cure for their afflictions. Thus, in effect every woman is a potential bori initiate and hence a disciple of Satan. This belief is mixed, in men's minds, with the Islamic attitude towards ritual purity and pollution. A man who performs the ritual ablution in preparation for prayer will have to perform the ablution once again if he even in the meantime talks with his wife, let alone comes into physical contact with her. Similarly, when a man is about to have sexual intercourse with his wife he utters the formula: 'I seek refuge in Allah from the wickedness of Satan', and he has to have a bath after intercourse in order to purify himself. Thus in Sabo it is indirectly regarded as the religious duty of every man to be on his guard against the potential mystical dangers and machinations of women and to keep women constantly under tight control.

Housewives in Seclusion

In Sabo, all the housewives, with the exception of the very old among them, are strictly secluded from public life and from contact with men. Islam has always been associated with the seclusion of women, but the nature of this association has not always been clear. The Koran, which is the principal source of Islamic belief and practice is not at all conclusive over this point. Some passages in it refer to a revelation by the Prophet Muhammad that he should order his wives and daughters and those of the believers not to leave their hair and face uncovered when they go out of doors.[12] In Islamic societies, the interpretation of this injunction was left to the religious leaders of the community where guiding religious principles were flexible enough to enable them to push the interpretation to one side or to the other, in order to accommodate local conditions and local customs. Thus, some Moslem communities seclude their women and others do not.

But not all the Islamic communities who observe the seclusion of women do so on religious grounds. In some Arab Moslem villages which I studied a few years ago[13] I observed a movement of veiling of women for purposes of prestige and upward social mobility. Men from those villages abandoned farming and took up well-paid jobs in neighbouring industrial towns. At the same time the villages obtained a central supply of piped water and, in many cases, also of electricity, into the houses. In this way many women in the villages became emancipated from farm work and from the necessity of collecting water for domestic purposes. And because the women of the formerly landed and wealthy families were veiled, this custom became one of the symbols of upward social mobility and many men began to veil their wives. Yet none of these men claimed that he was doing so on religious grounds. When a man veiled his wife he was said by the villagers 'to have made her into a civilized woman'.[14] Indeed in one of the larger villages upward social mobility was expressed in two incompatible ways, one of veiling and the other of unveiling. The former peasants who had become labourers, veiled their wives to emulate the former wealthy families. Some of the latter, however, began to unveil their hitherto veiled women, mainly in order to re-emphasize their superior social status by having their women adopt Western appearance. A distinction developed in that village between what the villagers described as 'peasant non-veiling'[15] and 'civilized un-veiling'.[16] Thus in one and the same Moslem community veiling and unveiling served as symbols of higher social status. Smith points out that in some Hausa communities in Northern Nigeria too, men seclude their wives in order to gain higher social prestige.[17]

Another point to be noted about veiling in Islamic communities is that it is often an individual, not communual, concern. In the Arab villages mentioned above, as well as in some parts of Northern Nigeria, some men seclude their wives and some do not.

Finally, in both the Arab villages and in Hausaland in the North the women involved are not only willing but also proud to be secluded.[18] Amongst other things, seclusion has made them women of leisure and has given them a high prestige among women.

The seclusion of the married women in Sabo differs markedly on nearly all these points from the Arab and Hausaland cases.

In the first place, it is upheld on strictly religious grounds and men are so deeply concerned about it that they justified the Quarter's secession from Yoruba Islam in Ibadan on the ground that important Yoruba Moslems allowed their wives to go out to trade in the marketplace during the day.

Secondly, seclusion is a public, and not only an individual, concern. Men are under constant communal pressure to isolate their wives from public life. In July 1963, while I was still in the field, a public meeting was held in the central school building of the Quarter and was attended by the Chief, nearly all the business landlords, the leading malams, and a number of men from the permanent core of the population. The meeting decided unanimously to accept the instructions of the malams that the seclusion of the married women of the Quarter should be tightened further by prohibiting the women from attending weddings, even at night, where they were likely to encounter men. Thus the seclusion of the married women became almost total for at least those who are under fifty. Seclusion is so well established that when a housewife is seen in public in the street people immediately conclude that she has been divorced. The housewives are secluded not only from secular but also from religious public life. It has been often asserted that Islam is essentially a man's religion and women have little or no part to play in it. In Sabo this is doubly so, because the Tijaniyya order, since its dramatic penetration into the Quarter in the early 1950's has localized, intensified and collectivized ritual in Sabo, and has excluded Sabo women from joining it, though I understand that in Northern Nigeria women are allowed to join the order.

Thirdly, the seclusion of housewives in Sabo is in many respects uneconomic. Only ten per cent of the houses in the Quarter have piped water supply. The rest of the houses are supplied by water from two local public taps where people have to queue for a long time for their turn. Husbands are obliged therefore to ensure the supply of water to the secluded wives, and this is usually done by employing young Yoruba girls from Ilorin for the purpose. Because of the shortage of water for domestic purposes all washing of clothes is done in a stream well out of the Quarter and because the housewives cannot go out, all washing is given to specialized washermen, of whom there are 50 in Sabo. Another factor unfavourable to female seclusion in Sabo is the congested conditions of housing. Usually many families live within a single compound, each housewife occupying one room, but the houses are surrounded day and night by hundreds of single men, strangers or recent migrants, many of whom sleep in verandahs, yards or even the sides of the roads.

Prostitution and the Mobility of Women

The mystical beliefs which Sabo men hold about women are related to a basic conflict between two organizational principles concerning the role of women in Sabo society. The first principle is manifested by the free, mobile, prostitute and the second by the secluded, settled housewife. The free mobility of women is necessary for continuous demographic adjustments within Sabo and within the whole network of Hausa communities in the area. But the settlement of women, once they are in the diaspora centre, is equally necessary.

When Hausa men began to migrate and to settle in Ibadan they were soon followed by increasing numbers of prostitutes. In the 1916 list of the names of Hausa settlers in the Quarter, there were 122 women, in a total population of 394. Of these women, 114 were described as 'petty traders'.[19] In the Nigerian censuses of 1962 and of 1963 the prostitutes of the Quarter registered themselves as 'petty traders' while the married women were registered as 'housewives' even when they were in fact engaged in trade. Informants who were in the Quarter in 1916 confirm that the majority of those women were prostitutes. Until today in Yorubaland, Hausa prostitutes continually move with the mobile men within the network of Hausa communities. During the period October–January, when the kola season begins in Shagamu, 50 miles south of Ibadan, and when hundreds of men connected with the kola trade move from Ibadan to Shagamu, between a third to a half of Sabo's prostitutes move with them. In the same way, when the season in the Ibadan district starts in January, both men and prostitutes return to Sabo.

As it is a general tendency for a woman who becomes a prostitute to leave her home town or village, at least for some time, and to drift to other settlements, prostitution has become for the ramifying network of Hausa communities in Yorubaland and perhaps also in other parts of West Africa, an institution which frees women from the ties of their natal homes and renders them mobile within the network. The significance of this institution is not that it has supplied migrant men with sexual pleasures in foreign lands, but that it has been perhaps the most important channel for mobilizing potential housewives for the pioneering communities.

Until today, when the proportion of the prostitutes to other females of marriageable age in Sabo is perhaps at its lowest (mainly because of the steadily growing proportion of Ibadan-born marriageable girls),[20] men would often prefer to marry a prostitute rather than a woman from Hausaland. When a man gets married in Sabo, people always ask whether the bride is, as they put it, 'long' or 'short', by which they want to know whether the man married her in the North and brought her to Sabo or whether she was born in Sabo. A housewife recruited in the North creates numerous problems for her husband because she wants to travel to the North frequently to visit her kin. Men complain that when such a wife asks permission to spend a few weeks with her kin she ends up by spending a few months. In many cases she does not come back and the marriage comes to an end. When a woman goes for a visit to the North she, in effect, gets out of the control of her husband and is likely to be seduced by men in the North. Apart from these risks which the husband takes, every visit to the North costs a large amount of money, both in fares and in presents. The fares alone often come to about £6. Today the ideal woman in marriage in Sabo is a girl born in Sabo, and next is the prostitute. A prostitute costs less money to marry and her links with her kin are usually weak or broken.

In Sabo, prostitution is formally institutionalized. The prostitutes are organized under a 'Chieftainess of the Prostitutes', known as *magagiya*, who is officially installed in this position by the Chief of the Quarter. The *magagiya* attends to many of the problems and disputes involving prostitutes and she represents these in front of the Chief. She has two uniformed prostitutes who act as her official messengers.

The prostitutes have always been a significant factor in the politics of the Quarter. This has been particularly so since party politics came to the Quarter as from the beginning of the 1950's. The prostitutes soon organized in separate female branches of the two major south Nigerian parties, the N.C.N.C. (N.E.P.U.) and the Action Group. As the housewives are secluded from public life, they have not voted in the federal, regional, or municipal elections which have taken place and they did not take any part in party political activities. In contrast, the prostitutes registered their names in the voters' lists in those elections and have been very active politically.

From the records of the history of the Quarter, the Yoruba authorities in Ibadan seem to have taken a hostile attitude towards the Hausa prostitutes, even though these have not operated among Yoruba men. In records dating from the early 1930's there are references to many periods in which native authority police harassed these prostitutes and sometimes arrested many of them. There were also many petitions from Sabo people protesting against police action in this respect, and, as from the early 1950's, similar petitions were also presented by the local branches of the major political parties.[21]

The Chief of the Quarter has often had trouble with the local Yoruba authorities over the prostitutes and it seems to me that, in order to avoid such trouble, the prostitutes have been accommodated in houses which have been sold to Yoruba men living in the town, who come to the Quarter only once a month to collect rent. In this way Hausa landlords and the Hausa Chief can avoid direct responsibility for harbouring the prostitutes.

Today there are 11 such houses in Sabo and nearly all the prostitutes are concentrated in them. But unlike prostitution in other societies, there is no racketeering in the organization of prostitution in Sabo. Each prostitute retains all her earnings for herself and is in almost every respect her own master.

Trade from Behind the Purdah

But while it has been important for the development and functioning of the Hausa network of communities in Yorubaland to have a population of women, in the persons of the prostitutes, regularly circulating in the various communities, following the men, it has been equally important for the functioning of the same network of communities that women should be completely settled in order to perform the many domestic, economic and biological roles without which a community will not continue to exist.

The housewives bear children, run the households and ensure domestic stability for men who are often on the move. Apart from this, however, housewives play an important role in the economy of the Quarter. This is the business which they run, from their seclusion, as traders in their own right. It is one of the most significant paradoxes in the position of women in Sabo society that they can engage in business and amass wealth for themselves when they are in the bondage of seclusion and wifehood, but cannot do so when they are free as prostitutes.

Apart from the few very young and very old, all the housewives are engaged in business from behind their seclusion. About a third of them dominate the business of retailing the local sale of such popular items as kola, oranges, and plantain, while the remaining two-thirds dominate the cooking industry of the Quarter.

The Hausa menu is highly varied, with scores of different kinds of dishes, snacks and beverages. Women specialize in preparing particular kinds of food and become widely known in the Quarter as being highly skilled in their specialities.

This cooking and the sale of cooked food caters first and foremost for the thousands of bachelors of the Quarter and for the stream of strangers coming through the two lorry parks of the Quarter. But the women also cook food for one another's households. This may sound strange, but as the menu is varied and the cooking is done on wood fires, there are many economies which can be realized by specialization and by production on a large scale. Most of the households in the Quarter cook only the evening meal themselves and rely for breakfast and lunch on the cooked snacks and dishes which they buy from the other households. Even when a meal is cooked within the household it is supplemented by some cakes, cooked vegetables and drinks, which are brought from other households. As a result of these economies of scale and of specialization many women are emancipated from having to cook for their own household and enabled to produce for the market. This is particularly feasible for them as the food bought for their own household is paid for by the husband, while the money which they earn from their trade belongs to themselves.

The housewives do all the purchasing of their merchandise and raw materials and, then, all the selling, from behind the purdah, without going out of the house. It is here that children, mainly girls between 7 and 14, perform their most important contribution to Sabo economy. Without child labour a housewife is completely cut-off from business and from the outside world.

A housewife can mobilize child, female, labour in three main ways. By bearing and raising up her own children, by fostering children from her brothers, sisters, sons or daughters, and, failing these, by hiring Yoruba girls from Ilorin, of whom there are nearly 200 in Sabo. In her lifetime, a housewife may make use of all these three sources. Generally, if she has no children, or if her children are too small to be of any help, she resorts to fostering.

Child fostering among the Hausa is very widely practised and has been one of the most important institutions of Hausa migration, in the building up of the network of Hausa communities, because of its role in the rapid demographic adjustments required by the economy of these communities.

The Hausa refer to this institution by the word *yaye*, and clearly distinguish it from adoption, for which they use the term *tallafi*. The term *tallafi* is used only in the case of a child whose parents are dead and who is therefore adopted by a relative. Fostered children remain the legal children of their legal, not their fostering, parents, visit their legal parents regularly and can marry the children of their foster parents. In a random sample of 120 fostered persons in the Quarter, 74 were female and 46 were males. Of the fostering parents, 75% were women and 25% were men.[22] The corresponding figures for the Zaria communities given by Smith[23] show a higher proportion of males among the fostered children, and a far higher proportion of men over women among the fostering adults.

It is not necessary here to go into details about the institution of fostering in Sabo, but it is sufficient to emphasize in brief only two relevant aspects of it. Firstly, the institution helps housewives to have a more or less regular service of child labour. Many women foster a child, or children, twice in their business career; early in their married life when by custom they can foster their brothers' or sisters' children and, much later, as their fostered and their own children mature and leave, when they can foster their grandchildren.

The second aspect is that a prostitute cannot foster children. In fact almost all the prostitutes who have children of their own see to it that those children are fostered by some kin, if they are not already in the custody of their legal father, as the Shari'a (Moslem law) stipulates. A prostitute thus can give children to be fostered but she is not given children for fostering. For some obvious reasons, rearing children and prostitution do not go together. The prostitutes are often on the move and sometimes two or more prostitutes have to share the same room and it is therefore very difficult for them to keep children.

For these and some other reasons a prostitute cannot engage in business in the Quarter. This means that they have no income other than that which they get from soliciting. The prostitutes lead an exciting, free, and independent life but they are not well-off, and the majority possess only a number of glossy gaudy dresses, and very little, simple furniture. Only a few of them have, in addition, a little jewellery.[24] It is evident therefore that their situation is vastly different from that of the housewives.

Accumulation of Capital and Conspicuous Expenditure

Immediately on her marriage, a woman acquires an initial capital in the form of her marriage payment, to which she is entitled by the Shari'a and with which she can start business. But a more important source of capital-formation is the small amounts of money which she 'cuts' for herself from the household money, which her husband hands over to her daily. Men complain bitterly of this 'stealing' but they seem incapable of doing anything about it, as, according to custom, it is the wife's right to be in charge of household money. In polygynous households, co-wives develop an agreement among themselves as to the amount of the 'cut' which each should take for herself when her turn to manage the household comes.

A third source of capital which the housewife can accumulate is that created by the productivity of the labour of her own daughters or of her fostered girls who work for her. These girls are usually adolescents and for many of them selling in the streets of the Quarter is a means by which they eventually 'fall in love' with a man and marry him. They do not get any immediate reward for their services from their mothers, but when they marry they are given by these mothers a substantial dowry consisting principally of brightly-coloured, enamelled, Czechoslovakian-made bowls, in the purchase and amassing of which the housewives sink most of their profits from trade. And here we come to a significant point about the position of women in Sabo society.

The prostitute is free to participate in public life but cannot acquire much wealth. The housewife, in comparison, can accumulate a great deal of wealth. Unlike the prostitute, she pays no rent. She and her children are fed and clothed by her husband, and, being settled and leading a respectable stable life, she is worthy of credit and she has a steady clientele. She also enjoys a steady source of capital from the 'cut' which she takes from the household money and from the productivity of her children. Thus her possibilities for acquiring wealth are great, but because of her seclusion, she cannot invest this wealth in expanding her business by entering into competiton with men.

A few women own houses bequeathed to them by their deceased parents or husbands and a number of them are said to possess large sums of money in cash allegedly hidden in some secret place. Some of them also have a great deal of jewellery. But the particular craze among nearly all the housewives in recent years has been to sink all their profits in acquiring ever increasing numbers of Czechoslovak-made, brightly-coloured, enamelled bowls. Within the world of Sabo housewives, these bowls have become the most important status symbol and women are ranked in status in proportion to the number of bowls they possess. Some housewives in the Quarter have managed to accumulate hundreds of them, which they meticulously arrange in ceiling-high columns in their small dark, rooms. A business landlord invited my wife once to visit his two wives, but these asked him to fix the time of the proposed visit at a date which would give them nearly two weeks' grace, during which they could wash and rearrange their treasured bowls. Space is scarce in Sabo and husbands are greatly annoyed by the mountains of bowls. A current, sardonic, complaint among the married men of the Quarter is that, because of the bowls, a man cannot nowadays find space in his wife's room for even his morning prayers.

A housewife thus continues to accumulate bowls and when her own daughters or her fostered daughters get married she gives them part of her treasure, usually in proportion to the length of time the daughter has served her. In 1963 a woman with 500 bowls gave a dowry of 50 bowls to a foster daughter. A housewife will attract and retain more marriageable girls from her kin, the more bowls she accumulates. The older a woman is, the more settled as a housewife she becomes, and the more girls she attracts to her service. And, for the developing Sabo community, the more housewives become settled, the more girls they will recruit for the community.

The Mobility of Women in the Perspective of Sabo's History

One aspect of these arrangements is that Sabo men are saved from the kind of tragic fate of some Nupe men. Among the Nupe, according to Nadel, married women are traders who travel widely in the course of their trade, who use contraceptives to avoid pregnancy, who engage in adulterous liaisons with other men, who frequently work on the side as part-time prostitutes, and who often lend money to their poor husbands who are thus enslaved to the wives for life. The only reaction which Nupe men seem to offer to this fate is to escape into the fantasy of witchcraft beliefs, in which women figure as evil witches and men as benevolent wizards.[25] Sabo husbands have also escaped the lot of many Yoruba men whose trading, unsecluded wives frequently sue for divorce in order to marry new lovers whom they have contacted in the course of their business, and who usually pay the expenses of the divorce proceedings.

In Sabo, in comparison, the wealth which the housewives might have used in economic competition with men is, because of enforced seclusion, mostly directed to harmless, conspicuous expenditure. Moreover, this wealth serves to stabilize marriage, as women can steadily increase it, by continuing in marriage. For the community as a whole, this wealth also helps, not only in keeping Sabo's stock of women, but also in increasing it, by attracting to the women the daughters of their relatives in the North. Divorce among Sabo women, though frequent as compared with some societies, seems to be less frequent than in Hausaland in the North, judging from the difference between my figures and those of Smith.[26] The figures from Sabo also show that Sabo-born housewives divorce less frequently than Northern-born housewives in the Quarter, although these trends should not be stressed too far because many other factors such as average age and residence after divorce can be important.

In Sabo, the seclusion of wives is an institutionalized ritual act, separating the mobile prostitute from the settled housewife, both of whom are necessary for the development, functioning and continuity of the network of communities. The marriage ceremony is not the only mark of the passage from prostitution to wifehood in Sabo. On the eve of her marriage, a prostitute goes to a malam, pays him money and asks him to offer a special prayer on her behalf, presumably to absolve her from her former unholy association with Satan.

In Sabo, and in the other Hausa communities in Yorubaland, such issues as prostitution, divorce, wifehood, seclusion, and mobility of women, are communal, and not only individual, concerns. Divorce is always dangerous to the community in that it may lead to the reduction of the stock of housewives, and hence weaken the community demographically and economically, because in the on-going migratory process, a divorced woman may become a prostitute and leave the Quarter. On the other hand, if she was born in the North, she may go back to her natal home, or she may marry one of the thousands of unsettled bachelors who crowd the Quarter and eventually drift with him to another place. Every divorce carries with it also the potential loss, not only of the woman involved, but also of her daughters or foster daughters who will almost invariably follow her if she leaves. In a community where many men are often on the move in accordance with the requirements of trade, married women provide social stability and continuity.

The sociological significance of the processes which have been discussed can be assessed only when they are considered in the perspective of historical time. The analysis of the census material shows, firstly, that the stock of females in the Quarter has been steadily increasing in relation to that of the males. Secondly, the number of Sabo-born females has been steadily increasing. Thirdly, more Sabo-born females remain in the Quarter than Sabo-born males.[27]

Today, Sabo-born housewives constitute nearly half of the total number of housewives in the Quarter.

The material also indicates that the proportion of housewives to prostitutes has been steadily increasing. Before World War II, the prostitutes were more numerous relative to the housewives than they are today. Informants often speak of the pre-War period as the period of moral corruption when almost every man, from the business landlord to the smallest client, frequently visited the prostitutes and drank beer and palm wine with them. Today, the informants claim, those men are married and have grown-up children and grandchildren and have therefore become virtuous.

Thus while the stock of the housewives in general, and that of the Sabo-born housewives in particular, have been increasing, the proportion of the prostitutes has, relatively speaking, been decreasing. But the prostitutes continue to be a source of housewives for Sabo.

Hausa men in Sabo thus uphold two organizational principles governing the position of women in their society. The first is the ideal of the prostitute as a woman freed from the ties of her natal community who is thus rendered mobile and capable of following male migrants to their new settlements. The second is that of the settled housewife who maintains the household, bears children, and renders important services within the economy of Sabo.

But these are incompatible principles which are in perpetual conflict with one another. This is a conflict which is, in the present stage of the demographic development of the Quarter, irresolvable.

CHAPTER THREE

Landlords of the Trade

The Politics of Housing—Hotel Keepers—Commission Agents—Inhibited Dealers—Risk-Taking Entrepreneurs—Investment in Primary Relationships—The Landlords in Politics—The Nodal Position of the Landlords

Sabo social organization is based on the position and manifold economic and political activities of nearly 30 business landlords, known to all, Hausa and non-Hausa alike, by the Hausa term *maigida*.[1] By the criteria of settlement in the Quarter which were discussed earlier, these are the most settled men in Sabo. Indeed in their various roles they run, support, and maintain a framework of institutions which ensure stability of structure despite the mobility of various elements of the population.

Their high degree of settlement is made necessary by the crucial economic roles which they play in the organization of long-distance trade and by which they provide mechanisms whereby the technical problems of this trade are overcome. These economic roles give them power over large numbers of men and enable them to act politically both within and outside of Sabo polity.

In the course of playing these economic and political roles they link Sabo with Hausaland in the North, with the network of Hausa communities in Yorubaland, and with different Yoruba individuals and groups within the city of Ibadan or within the Western Region of Nigeria generally.

The Politics of Housing

Between them, the landlords control over half of the housing of the Quarter. Housing is the most important capital asset of a business landlord. Apart from the house in which he and his immediate family live, he needs housing for the accommodation of his clients—brokers, assistant-brokers, clerks, servants, errand boys[2]—and of their families. Further housing is needed for storage and as a place of work for the secluded wives. The kola landlord also needs space for kola packing. As his business expands he will require more housing for the accommodation of more clients and their families. At the same time his problems will increase and his need for the services of malams in the mystical world will become greater and he will therefore need more housing to accommodate more malams.

With the expansion of his business he will need increasing financial and social credit and the amount of housing he controls will become the most important asset by which his credit-worthiness is measured. No house or right in housing can be sold in Sabo without the knowledge, mediation, and hence approval of the Chief of the Quarter. The Chief acts as arbitrator in cases of disputes over business matters and he can force a business man to sell more, or in some cases all, of his housing rights in order to settle his debts. This means that no man can pull out of the Quarter easily in order to escape from his financial obligations. To a very large extent, his housing rights are a pledge in the hands of the community, as represented by the Chief. As a man sells some or all of his rights in housing, he proportionally loses part or all of his creditworthiness. As there is little conspicuous consumption in the Quarter and as men are not used to entrusting their money to banks, housing has also become the most important form of saving.

Command over housing is thus command of economic power, and because of the increasing scarcity of housing fierce competition between the business landlords has developed. Most of the important political disputes within the Quarter have been the result of an underlying struggle for control over housing.

Hotel Keepers

A landlord must also have at least one house for the accommodation of northern dealers who come to the Quarter to conduct business through his house.

Of the twelve cattle landlords in Sabo in 1963, one had six houses for strangers, a second had four, two others had two houses each and the remaining eight had one each. The nine kola landlords ran between them, fourteen houses for strangers. The transport landlords ran ten. In all, the thirty landlords of the Quarter ran a total of 51 houses for strangers, which is equivalent to about a tenth of the housing space of the whole Quarter.

A house for strangers contains an average of fifteen small rooms. The rooms are furnished with beds and mattresses. When the house is not crowded with dealers each dealer is given a room on his own, but when business is high only important dealers are accommodated in separate rooms while the rest share rooms, sometimes up to five men in one room. If a landlord has at any time more dealers than he can accommodate in his houses for strangers, he will accommodate them in the houses of his relatives or friends, or in the houses of strangers which are run by the transporters. He will never, however, accommodate them in the houses for strangers which are run by other landlords within the same trade.

The dealer-strangers are given by their host three meals a day. Some of the meals are cooked by the landlord's wives and some are bought from enterprising women cooks. The food is served in trays which are carried by 'boys' from the landlord's house to the rooms of the dealers. Each dealer eats his meal separately in his room.

A landlord who has more than one house for strangers, usually accommodates strangers in accordance with their province of origin. He may thus have one house for dealers from Kano, another for dealers from Sokoto, and so on. On the whole dealers tend to associate themselves, whenever possible, with landlords from their own province of origin.

A landlord regularly entertains his dealers, for a few minutes at least, every evening by paying them courtesy calls and having conversations with them.

A big landlord who has many houses for strangers and whose wives cannot cope with cooking for all his dealers usually 'allots' some of the houses to his most senior clients. These have the food cooked by their own wives. In return they get a higher commission from the transactions.

In both the cattle and the kola trades the landlord does not charge the dealers anything for accommodation or for food, no matter how long they stay. The travel agents, who operate in the two lorry parks of the Quarter, receive a special 'gift', in money, from the strangers who are accommodated in their houses. The landlords' expenses are usually covered by part of the commission which they receive from conducting the business of the dealers. For, when a dealer lodges in the house of a landlord, it automatically means that he is entrusting his business to that landlord. When a dealer is for some reason dissatisfied with the services of a business landlord he 'changes house', which literally means moving to a house of strangers belonging to another landlord and having his business conducted by the new landlord.

Commission Agents

The principal business function of the landlord is that of mediation between dealers from the North and from the South, against the receipt of a special commission, widely known by the Hausa term, *lada*.[3] For the purpose of fulfilling this function of mediation, the landlord has a number of clients who work for him as commission agents, while he himself devotes much of his time to directing the general affairs of the agency, though he remains responsible to the dealers for the business conduct of his own clients.

When a cattle dealer arrives at the Quarter and lodges with his landlord, the latter entrusts the sale of his herd to one of his commission agents. The dealer then accompanies the agent in the cattle market and remains with him until the cattle are sold. No dealer can sell his cattle directly to the butchers. Sale is nearly always on credit which is extended over two to four weeks. The money is collected by the clerk of the landlord and is kept by the landlord at his home until the dealer asks for it, just before returning to the North. The landlord receives no direct reward whatsoever from the dealer, but his expenses are covered by the commission which he collects from the buyer, in cash, on the sale of the cattle. In 1963 the landlord received only 7 shillings as commission on the sale of each head of cattle to cover all his expenses.[4]

In the kola trade the landlord acts as a buyer for northern kola dealers. A few of these dealers come down to Ibadan themselves, bring their money with them and lodge with the landlord. They will then go in the company of a commission buyer, who is a client of that landlord, to the sources of supply, buy the quantity they need, return back to the Quarter with the goods, supervise the packing and then despatch the bundles, or actually accompany them on the journey to the North. These are relatively small-scale dealers, amongst whom are some who may send a permanent representative, who is usually a relative, to lodge with the landlord and conduct the dealer's business with the help of the landlord.

The majority of the dealers, however, trust the local landlord to act as their agent, sending him orders and money, and leaving the conduct of the business at the supplying end to his honesty and discretion. The dealer will just send an amount of money with a simple request to 'buy good kola' of a certain type. There is no question of specifying the exact quantity of the consignment or the price at which it should be bought. Conditions change from day to day and it is not possible to exchange correspondence and quote exact prices. The whole job is left entirely in the hands of the landlord and it is he who decides on the spot what to buy with the money, where to buy it, and at what price.

The commissioned buyer gets his commission from the seller of the kola and not from the landlord. He is thus paid nothing by the landlord.

The kola landlord also runs a packing service. The kola is packed in a special way, in basket-like bundles, about four feet in height and two feet in diameter. The main packing material is rope, which is imported from the North, and special fresh green leaves from the forest. The packing is done by skilled workers. Usually three men work as a team on each package. One of them is the chief packer, the second his assistant, and the third is a 'measurer' who ascertains the exact quantity of kola in the package, by bringing nut which has been taken from a large heap in a special standardized basket, to the packer. A bundle will usually take about 20 minutes to pack. The chief packer gets two shillings for each bundle and out of this he pays sixpence (in 1963) to his assistant. The measurer is paid separately by the landlord. Usually there are, in each packing yard, several teams of packers. In addition to packers and measurers, the yard is also served by several carriers whose sole job is to carry the nut from the lorries to the yard and to carry bundles from the yard to the lorries.

The transport of the goods to the North is arranged by the landlord who maintains for this purpose, connections with transport commission agents, who are Hausa living within the Quarter. If the consignment is to be sent by rail, it is taken by lorry to the railway station where it is immediately entrusted to a porters' supervisor, who is the head of a number of porters. In the Ibadan railway station, there are between 200 and 300 (the actual number depending on the season) Hausa porters, who are organized within four business houses under four landlords in the Quarter. Under each landlord work a number of supervisors whose task is to receive the goods from the lorries and to make all the paper arrangements with the railway authorities and, finally, to supervise the loading on the wagons by the porters.

If the consignment is to be sent by lorry, then the arrangements are made in one of the two lorry parks of the Quarter. Business in these lorry parks is dominated by two transport landlords who have under them several commission agents, each of whom is aided by a number of 'boys'. One of these two landlords bears the title 'Chief of the Transporters', after nomination by the men in the business and after official installation by the Chief of the Quarter. The transporters of the Quarter are commission agents who negotiate business for lorry owners and lorry drivers who regularly call at the Quarter's two lorry parks. The transport landlords also run houses for the accommodation of lorry drivers and lorry owners as well as for passengers in transit.

In recent years more kola has been sent by lorry than by train. The railway authorities are trying to lure back the traffic by offering cheaper freight charges and by providing lorry services between kola yards and stations. But the advantages of the lorries are still numerous. Lorry service is more personal than that of the railway which is highly bureaucratized. In the case of the lorry, the trader entrusts his goods into the hands of a responsible transport landlord who is permanently settled within the Quarter, and who is reputedly a trustworthy person who undertakes to compensate the owner of the despatched goods for any loss incurred in transit. The transport landlord and his agents, in their turn, are personally acquainted with the lorry owners and drivers. Lorry transport is also faster than rail transport and is more convenient in that the goods are taken straight from the yard in the South to the dealer's place in the North. Those northern kola dealers who travel themselves south to supervise the purchase of a consignment usually travel back to the North in the lorry carrying their kola. Some of these dealers even manage to sell all or some of their consignment on the way, towards the end of the journey. Sometimes, the consignment is redirected at the last moment to another destination, still in the North, where sale conditions are known to have become more favourable.

In the case of the kola, the landlord's commission is not fixed. He is in fact at liberty to fix his own commission. But in order to retain the dealer's confidence he cuts that commission down to a minimum. The landlord's commission is nearly always in the form of a lump sum, deducted from the amount sent to him, and not in the form of a percentage.

Inhibited Dealers[5]

Sometimes landlords also engage in trade on their own account. This is the case in both the cattle and the kola trades.

Two out of the 12 cattle landlords have clients in the North who act as their own agents, buying cattle from the local markets and sending them regularly by train to Ibadan. These clients are Sabo settlers who reside in the North on temporary basis, as 'strangers'. Other cattle landlords deal in cattle on their own account only sporadically and in an opportunistic manner. A landlord who happens to know at any one time that prices in Lagos are particularly high, while prices in Ibadan are low, may be tempted to purchase a herd which he will take by lorry to the Lagos market. In some other Hausa centres in Yoruba towns some Hausa cattle landlords have also ventured into the butchering industry, buying cattle, slaughtering them locally and selling the meat to local retailers.

But this tendency of cattle landlords to act as dealers in their own right is thwarted by a number of factors. Those landlords who have agents in the North to send them cattle have continually suffered losses through misjudgement, mismanagement and, sometimes, default on the part of their client-agents. Various stages of the trade have in recent years become specialized and a landlord who wants to operate successfully as a dealer must have a special network of different categories of intermediaries in the North. He must also himself frequently visit the North to supervise his agents. But by extending his interests and his social network in this way he will prejudice his interests and his standing as a commission agent. Dealers from the North will be reluctant to entrust the sale of their cattle in Ibadan to such a landlord for fear that he will attend more to his own private interests to the detriment of their interests. He will be suspected of manipulating the market so that he can buy at a cheap price and thus harm the interest of dealers. Dealers will also suspect that the landlord is using their own money, which is kept for some time with the landlord, to conduct transactions on his own and thus run the risk of losing their money in cases of his own loss. To be a cattle dealer is a specialization in its own right, requiring a great deal of experience and a special network of social relations with both Hausa and Yoruba, in both the North and the South. A landlord who is only an occasional, amateur dealer is likely to fall into the many traps of the business and to suffer the loss of his money. The cattle may die or may be stolen on the way and he may be sold unhealthy cattle. Prices may also fluctuate very wildly so that he may eventually have to sell at a much lower price than he anticipated.

In 1963 I followed closely one cattle landlord, who had not regularly traded in cattle on his own account, in the various stages of a speculative enterprise, from the moment he felt that the market offered a great opportunity for a profitable deal until he sold his herd. It began when he heard that prices in Lagos had suddenly gone up while those in the Ibadan market remained normal. He was very tempted to buy. He had money of his own and he deliberated over the prospects with his leading clients. There were many pros and cons to the venture. When he finally became inclined to act, he went to his malam and asked him to divine the chances of his enterprise. The malam was acquainted with the whole picture and was well informed about the cattle trade, especially, as his own son and his sister's son were in the trade. The answer from the mystical sources was favourable. The landlord then acted quickly. He bought a herd of 30 head, loaded the beasts on lorries and went himself with them, direct to the Lagos cattle market, where he eventually sold the cattle for cash, accepting a lower price than that for credit. It took him three days to sell. There was all the time the danger that some of the animals might become sick and die. There was also the danger of theft, and the price he received was much lower than he had first anticipated. He came back to Sabo and went through the account and found that he did not make any profit. The transaction had cost him a whole week of work, worry and tension. He did not mourn his failure to make a profit and attributed that to the will of God which should be accepted unquestioningly. Indeed he was grateful that he did not lose money and he even gave some alms for that. During that week he had neglected his work as a commission agent. He did not supervise his clients in conducting the business of his dealers. His dealers did not like his absence. They wanted him on the spot because it was only through him that they could entrust his own clients with their business. In addition he was not there to greet them in his houses as was customary.

Under some other circumstances this or another landlord might be more fortunate, whereas he might just as easily be unlucky. But it is clear that being a dealer does not accord with being a commission agent and that there are various sources of pressure which inhibit a landlord from developing too much interest in being a dealer.

The same conclusion can be drawn from the accounts of the attempts of some cattle landlords in other Hausa centres in Yorubaland to act as butchers. Here again the role of the landlord as 'buyer', in the very cattle market in which he operates as commission agent, antagonizes the northern dealers who entrust him with the sale of their herds, for fear that he may artificially lower prices or that he may be trading with their own money which is kept with him. On the other hand, it also antagonizes the local butchers, who are the usual buyers, and hence debtors, in the market. The butchers have always resented and sometimes opposed violently the competition of the stranger landlords in their own town. In 1963 the attempt by some Hausa cattle landlords in Abeokuta (a Yoruba town about 50 miles south west of Ibadan) to slaughter cattle on their own account, led to a drastic concerted action on the part of the Yoruba butchers. These officially stopped paying their debts to the landlords and completely paralysed the market for about five weeks. In the end the dispute was successfully arbitrated by the Chief of Sabo in Ibadan who ruled that the Hausa landlords had no 'right' to enter the butchering industry and to try to deprive members of the host community of their source of livelihood.

In the kola trade, conditions are different but the lesson is the same. Often a kola landlord finds it necessary for his business as a commission agent, to act also as a dealer in his own right.

When he receives money from a northern dealer to buy a consignment, he sends to the dealer, along with the dealer's order, a consignment, of his own, which he buys with his own money, and entrusts its sale in the North to the dealer. He does so mainly to gain the confidence of the northern dealer by showing him reciprocal trust. Some kola landlords, however, operate as dealers on a larger scale. And, as in the cattle trade, in this case, too, a kola landlord cannot concentrate on his own dealings without adversely affecting his interests as a kola landlord. Northern dealers may in the long run suspect that he is using their own money in advancing his own interests as dealer. They will also resent the appearance of the landlord as a seller competing with them in the North, in the very markets in which they operate. Here, too, the landlord has to have special connections with people in the North, and the wider the network of such connections is spread, the more risky the business becomes. And like the cattle trade, the kola trade is highly competitive and requires a great deal of experience. It is, therefore, given to an intensive degree of specialization and sooner or later a man will have to decide whether he should become principally a landlord or a dealer.

Being a landlord, in both cattle and kola, requires all the cunning, the experience, the organizing ability, and the judgement that a man can muster. This is particularly so because the landlord is also an insurer and risk-taker.

Risk-taking Entrepreneurs

The landlord is entrusted by the northern dealers with large sums of money or goods for which he becomes solely responsible. But, in order to carry on the manifold activities of his business, he is forced at various stages, to entrust money and goods to buyers, clients, and other dealers and landlords. He is thus continuously burdened by great financial risks and a great deal depends on his experience, sound judgement, and character.

In the cattle trade, where nearly all sale in the cattle market (*Zango*)[6] is on credit, the landlord is the guarantor that the money will eventually be paid. Should the buyer default, the landlord will pay the full amount to the dealer from his own money. This obligation means that he must be very well acquainted with the buyers, and it is only through long experience in the business that he comes to acquire the necessary knowledge. He has to know not only where a buyer slaughters the cattle, or where he has his shop or market stall, but also where he lives, who are his relatives and associates, what is the size of his business, and how honest and trustworthy he has proved himself to be in his dealings in the past. In this way, every butcher in the market is informally graded by the landlords and their brokers on a scale of creditworthiness from no-credit up to about £1,000 of credit, for a period of up to four weeks. No sane landlord will give a butcher credit in excess of the latter's 'quota'. Misjudgement in this respect can ruin the business house of the landlord. This actually happened, early in 1963,[7] to one of the landlords, when a number of butchers who had bought cattle through him defaulted, and he eventually failed to pay the money himself to the dealers. These dealers stopped lodging with him and put their case before the Chief of the Quarter, in his capacity as the Chief of the Cattle Market. In accordance with the Chief's ruling, the landlord had to sell his only house of strangers to meet his obligations. He subsequently became a kind of free-lance commission agent[8] operating for one landlord or another, when those landlords happened to have more business than their regular client-agents could cope with.

Thus cattle landlords need to have not only a precise assessment of the buyer's social background and of his business conduct in the past, but they must also be continuously vigilant about his day-to-day purchases in the market. For, while a dealer is attached to one landlord at a time, the butcher is free to buy through any landlord, and he usually makes his purchases through many. It is conceivable therefore that he may succeed in buying, within a short period of time, from several unsuspecting landlords in excess of the limits of his creditworthiness. The only way in which the landlords can meet this potential danger is by the continuous exchange of business information. And, as there are no formally institutionalized channels for the exchange of such information, various mechanisms and informal relationships are used for this purpose.[9]

But, although the cattle landlords are forced to co-operate in order to protect their collective interests, against the Yoruba butchers-buyers, it is in the nature of their business also to compete and it happens sometimes that a landlord may suppress information from the other landlords. I witnessed in 1963 a case of a butcher who failed to pay, on time, a debt of a few hundred pounds to a landlord, but promised to do so as soon as his business improved. The landlord withheld this information from his colleagues, since otherwise the other landlords would have refrained from selling cattle to the butcher, who would thus have been without business and would have failed to settle his original debt. An unsuspecting landlord eventually sold cattle to the butcher involved, who duly settled his debt to the first landlord but defaulted in payment to the second. When the first landlord was later blamed for his unethical conduct, he replied that no one had specifically asked him to give the information which he had withheld.

In the kola trade, the risks are also numerous. Very often the kola landlord assumes responsibility for money or goods from the moment he receives an order from a northern dealer to the time when the kola is packed and loaded for despatch. In the process, money is entrusted to commission-buyers, clerks, servants, or other categories of clients working for the landlord. Scores of men handle the purchased kola, particularly when it is packed, and the danger of theft is always present. Moreover, if the kola is not well looked after it can deteriorate and the landlord will be held responsible. The kola landlord also risks hundreds of pounds' worth of kola which he sends, as a dealer in his own right, to northern dealers who will act as his sales' agents and who will eventually send the proceeds back to him. In the course of loading and transporting, packages of kola are sometimes lost and, although the porters' landlords, or the transporters' landlords, should assume responsibility for such losses, the kola landlord will have to meet part of the loss. This is because when cases of loss are arbitrated by the Chief of the Quarter, the Chief tends to spread the loss as widely as he can.

Another risk which landlords have to shoulder in the course of carrying on their business is that of keeping cash belonging to the stranger-dealers who conduct business with them. Strangers do not want to carry cash while they are staying in Ibadan and so they leave large amounts of money with their landlord. For a variety of reasons the landlords cannot deposit the money in banks. The stranger-dealers do not usually have a precise time-table and their departure from Ibadan is unpredictable, depending on the arrangements they make for their journey with lorry owners or drivers. The departure can take place at any time, during the night or the day, on weekdays or at week-ends, and as soon as it is fixed the dealer will go to his landlord and ask for his cash back. Landlords explain that the stranger will be greatly suspicious, or, at best, greatly inconvenienced if he is told that he should wait until the money is brought back from the bank which may be closed at the time. The result is that every landlord has to keep the cash in his own house, usually in a wooden chest, which is protected by Koranic charms as well as by a special guard from among his clients.

Risk-taking is thus one of the most fundamental roles which every landlord has to play. It is built into his position and he cannot avoid it without seriously prejudicing his other business roles.

In fulfilling the requirements of his different roles, the landlord can perhaps best be seen as an entrepreneur who employs different factors of production: land, labour, capital, and experience. Different trades require different proportions in the combination of these factors, and within the same trade, different landlords combine the factors in different proportions. Expansion of the volume of business can be achieved by increasing the proportion of some or all the factors, subject to the law of diminishing returns. The more the business is expanded, the more the profit, but also the greater the risks of loss.

As a business landlord expands the scale of his enterprise he is forced to employ more men to work in his 'house'. As he does this, he takes greater and greater risks. This is because, as the study of the life careers of landlords indicates, the greatest financial danger to the landlord comes from his clients. Clients sometimes exploit the trust which their landlord places in them and embezzle money or default, and during the period of my field work alone a number of such cases occurred. In one of these cases a clerk embezzled about a thousand pounds from his landlord.

It is for this reason that the creditworthiness of a business landlord is determined not only by his own assets, experience, and personal integrity, but also by the trustworthiness and reputation of members of his business house. The formal business relation between the landlord and his client is a contractual relationship whereby the client undertakes to perform certain economic roles for a specified amount of remuneration. But contractual relations can effectively operate only when they are backed by a fair, efficient and effective judicial system which is upheld by a centralized authority and is ultimately supported by organized physical force. Such a system, however, is not well developed in a pre-industrial society. For a number of reasons, the Hausa of Sabo find the formal civil courts rather ineffective. In the conduct of trade, no documents are exchanged and no detailed accounts are kept nor is any use made of insurance or banking. Some money and goods are certainly lost in the process. Cases of theft, embezzlement, default, and loss through negligence or misjudgement are many. But generally, the losses constitute only a small proportion of the total volume of the trade. The analysis of cases indicates as mentioned earlier, that through arbitration by the Chief of the Quarter, the incidence of the losses is spread as widely as possible. Thus, the system continues to function as an on-going concern. The question is, what mechanisms keep it going?

In all economic systems which involve credit there are social mechanisms, both formal and informal,[10] for the organization and maintenance of credit relations. These mechanisms are different in form, in the type of pressure they can mobilize on potential defaulters, in the motives they appeal to, and in the interests, sentiments, symbols, myths, norms, values and ideologies which they exploit. There are economic mechanisms, political mechanisms, ritual mechanisms and moral mechanisms. All these operate in all credit systems. However, credit systems vary in the degree to which the different mechanisms are exploited and in the manner in which they are combined.

In the industrially advanced and highly differentiated societies, great emphasis is placed on formal and political (legal) mechanisms. Extensive use is made of formal, standardized arrangements by which the solvency of debtors is closely assessed, securities against possible default are provided and the conditions of the contractual agreements are upheld by legislated rules and sanctions which are administered by centralized rules and highly bureaucratized courts and police.

These formal economic and legal arrangements are supplemented by the informal organization of a variety of ritual and moral mechanisms.

Even an elementary acquaintance with the history and the

contemporary operation of the credit system in a country like Britain will be sufficient to show how close-knit networks of credit relationships exist between members of certain religious groupings,[11] and since Weber and Tawney the interconnections between aspects of the credit system and of religious belief and organization have been increasingly recognized. The oath on the sacred book, which is administered in courts in legal proceedings indicates, at least symbolically, the significance of ritual mechanisms in the organization of trust.[12]

Similarly, it has now become clear to sociologists that primary relations which are developed in the course of informal social interaction in school, club, intermarriage and the like, greatly affect the organization and operation of credit systems at many points.[13]

Thus, in western industrial society, ritual and moral mechanisms, which are officially exterior to the formal bureaucratic organization of the credit system, are in fact integral parts, without which the system will not operate. The creditworthiness of a man is measured not only in terms of his solvency, judgement, and enterprise, but also of the network of primary relationships in which he is involved and hence in terms of the amount of moral pressure which operates on him. Similar emphasis is placed on the network of primary relationships of a candidate for such a position as a cashier in a bank, or indeed any position which requires trust and confidence in its performance.

Nevertheless, the greater emphasis in the organization of credit in western industrial society is on formal political and economic mechanisms. Through legislation continuous effort has always been made to express as much of the ritual and primary relationships in terms of contractual (legal) relations. But of course there are limits to this tendency because primary and ritual relationships are phenomena *sui generis* and can never be completely reduced to contractual relationships.

In a pre-industrial society, like Nigeria, on the other hand, greater emphasis is placed on moral and ritual mechanisms. This is because of the relatively little developed means of communication, centralization and bureaucratization of economic and political functions. At those points in the credit system where economic and political mechanisms are not effective, moral mechanisms are strongly mobilized. Primary relationships which are not ordinarily exploited are exploited, others are consolidated, and new ones generated.

Investment in Primary Relationships

This is why a business landlord in Sabo invests a great deal of his wealth, time, and sentiments in developing dyadic primary relationships between himself and his clients.

As businessmen do in many other societies, Sabo landlords often try to exploit kinship relationships by recruiting business clients from among their own sons, relatives, and affines. A few of the landlords have one or more of their sons assisting them. But, generally speaking, the father–son relationship in this community is very often fraught with tensions of various sorts. The Hausa are polygynous and most of the landlords have two or more (up to four) wives. And as divorce is frequent children may either stay with the father, in accordance with the injunctions of Islamic law, or they may go with their mother, though the tendency is that sons stay with the father, and daughters go with the mother. Further complexity is brought about into the father-son relationship through the observance of father-son avoidance, especially with the first born son.

It is mainly for this reason, that not many of the landlords employ their sons as clients. The father–son relationship in business is strongest when the landlord has an only son. In that case the son knows that he will eventually inherit not only the wealth but also the whole business concern of his father. When his father dies, the structure of the business house will remain intact and the son will step into most of the roles of his deceased father as landlord. Until that time his relations with the clients of his father are those of 'brother–brother', particularly if they are not much older than he is. After the death of his father he will continue as 'brother', but will develop other dyadic relationships with them to mark his passage into the headmanship of the business house. Business will then go on as usual.

But the situation is different when a landlord has more than one son. Here there is always tension between the sons over inheritance and over opportunities in the business house when the father is still alive. In all the cases of this type which I recorded, the death of the father led to the collapse of the whole house. The property had to be divided between the sons and this often led to the liquidation of the house for strangers. The clients of the house were disbanded. Formerly the clients were held within the house through the dyadic relationships between them and the landlord. But when the landlord has died, the relationships between the house and the different categories of individuals and groups outside it—in the Quarter, in other Hausa centres in the South and in Hausaland in the North— are also disrupted.

As a result of all these changes, the creditworthiness and reputation of the house will drastically diminish and the business will dwindle and come to a standstill. One of the sons may continue in business with his share of the inherited estate but things will never be the same as before.

It is for these reasons that landlords do not always employ their sons as assistants.

A second, and in many ways better source of recruitment of business clients is that of fostering. In a survey mentioned earlier, 25% of the fostering parents were men. Men tend to foster male rather than female children, usually their brother's sons. Nearly 20% of all fostered male children in the survey were of this type.[14]

There is hardly a landlord in Sabo without a number of fostered sons. There are various reason why men foster children. In some cases as a man in Sabo becomes successful in business, his brothers and sisters in the North will try to send one of their children to his care so that the child will grow up in a well-to-do house and will learn a lucrative trade. In other cases the Sabo landlord is under obligation to 'relieve' his brother or sister of the first born son. At the same time, the more successful the landlord is in business the more inclined he is to foster male children.

Fostered sons call their foster father by the term 'father' and very frequently a strong moral bond develops between the two. A foster son inherits from his original, not foster, parents and is thus in many respects a better business client than a legal son. His relationship with his foster father is governed by a great deal of sentiment and is not vitiated by money matters. As the foster son continues in the service of his foster father's business house, the moral bond between himself and his foster father becomes stronger and develops in stages into greater complexity as the son marries and begets children.

Sons and foster sons, however, will make up only a small

proportion of the large number of clients which a landlord needs in his work. The majority of the clients are therefore men who are not related to the landlord by ties of kinship. Formally, their relationship with the landlord is contractual. But in fact this relationship will not be effective unless it is backed by informal moral relationships which develop between landlord and client in time. These are personal relationships and are governed by categorical, not hypothetical, imperatives.

These moral relations develop in different stages. Assuming, as is generally the case, that the client is junior in age when he begins his service with the landlord, the most crucial of these stages is the marriage of the client. As soon as the client reaches marriageable age his patron begins to exert pressure on him to marry. This is because a married man is more settled in the Quarter than a bachelor and is financially more trustworthy. He no longer spends money on prostitutes and he is more stable in character.

The landlord will try to marry the client off to one of the many girls of marriageable age who usually stay in his house. These are the foster daughters of his wives, or the daughters of his own relatives or of his wives' relatives. In Sabo, the key question in placing a girl when she is married, is from whose house was she taken, without great significance being attached to whether she is a real or a putative kinswoman of the land-lord. Indeed the client may even marry a daughter of the landlord, if the girl falls in love with him. I witnessed such a case in 1963 when the daughter of a porters' landlord fell in love with one of her father's clients, who worked as a porters' supervisor.

This is because marriage among the Hausa in Sabo is not involved in issues concerning status.[15] The landlords are not identifiable with any specific status grouping. Unlike the situation in Hausaland, Fulani or Habe descent is of no status significance in Sabo[16] though most of the population of Sabo are in fact Habe. In my field study I recorded cases of landlords who had lost their wealth and position and become simple clients, and of clients who, as a result of some circumstances, had gained wealth and risen to the position of landlord. In many Islamic societies the principle of equality in marriage between spouses, which is emphasized in the Shari'a, is jealously upheld and no girl is given in marriage to a man who is regarded as inferior to her father or brothers in social status.[17] But in Sabo this is not the case. There are no marked class distinctions in the Quarter in terms of appearance, standard of living or forms of conspicuous consumption, and there is nothing which can be described as 'class consciousness'. The main distinction is between 'Big Men', i.e., the landlords, and clients and, as indicated above, the line of demarcation is not rigid but is continually crossed by men moving to the one category or to the other. From the point of view of some of the clients with whom I spoke on this subject, the distinction between client and landlord is regarded as some kind of division of labour. I once asked a servant who was a descendant of a former slave and who worked for a landlord in Sabo without receiving any payment in cash, why he did not leave his master and take up a free job and earn money of his own. He exclaimed: 'Why should I do so? I am happy as I am. I do not have to worry and to struggle to earn my livelihood. I and my family are well accommodated, well fed and well clothed. And I am not over-worked.'

Whether the client marries a girl from the house of the land-lord or from outside the house, the landlord will provide him with the marriage payment[18] as a gift. The landlord will also give at least one room for the bride to live in.

The next stage in the development of the relationship between landlord and client will occur when the first child is born, and when, as is usually the case, it will be taken to be fostered by either the landlord or by one of his wives. This will create a new set of complex relationships between client and landlord. In one respect, this kind of fostering constitutes an indirect financial help to the client, as the landlord will feed, house, clothe, and educate the child. Secondly, as it is almost an obligation between close kin to foster the first-born child of one another, the landlord will be linked to the client as a kinsman by virtue of the fostering. Thirdly, fostering is always regarded as an act of friendship[19] between equals. Finally, the foster parent will inevitably benefit financially in the future when the fostered child begins to help in business. From the point of view of the client this last aspect of fostering is seen, not as an exploitation of his child by the fostering parent, but as an important measure of security in the future for the child. There are, thus, different and contradictory elements in the relationship created by fostering. The relationship signifies the superior status of the landlord but at the same time it emphasizes equality and friendship. It involves exploitation as well as benefit. These and many other elements involved in the relationship are closely interconnected and give the relationship a moral character with mutual obligations holding between the two sides.

At every one of these stages a new moral element is added to the relationship between landlord and client. Throughout the course of a few years the relationship becomes intense and highly personalized. In the process the client will be called by the community after the name of the landlord, in the same way that a son of the landlord would be called 'Umaru na al-Hajji Yahaya', i.e. Umaru (of the house of landlord) Hajji Yahaya.

As the relationship becomes stronger, the landlord will entrust more and more financial responsibilities to the client. The client's remuneration, i.e. his share of the commission (*lada*), will be increased. With more business to handle, the client will himself have assistants who will eventually become his clients and become directly responsible to him. He may also become responsible for running one of the houses for strangers, which will involve looking after the house and the dealers who are accommodated in it and providing them with food and company.

As the client becomes more senior he may even be taken, or sent, by the landlord to Mecca to perform the pilgrimage and to acquire the title *Hajji*, at the landlord's own expense. In 1963 I recorded four cases in this category. When a client reaches such a stage he will usually have a great deal of experience, connections, and assistants, so that with the death of the landlord he may have a good chance of starting off as a landlord in his own right, provided that he has acquired in the meantime at least one house for the accommodation of stranger-dealers.

Five of the thirty landlords who were operating in Sabo in 1963 had begun as landlords in this way. In two other cases, the landlords were, in effect, custodians of the property and business of their former landlords whose children were minors on the death of their father.

This brief account of the development of the landlord-client relation emerges from the detailed analysis of biographies of landlords and clients, and from the comparative study of the contemporaneous relationships between landlords and clients which are in different stages of development. There are of course variations from this model, depending on the magnitude and combinations of different variables. One important variable is that of the respective ages of landlord and client. In one case, mentioned earlier the landlord was a young man who, being an only child, had inherited the whole business house of his father. He also 'inherited' two of his father's most senior clients who had been associated with the father for about 30 years, and had for long been known in the Quarter after the name of the father. The two clients were much older than the new landlord and in conversations he referred to them as 'my fathers'. He consulted them on matters relating to the conduct, not only of business, but also of his own private life, and I have already mentioned that his intention to marry a Yoruba girl was vetoed by them.[20] I observed one of them one day settling an account of a transaction with the landlord. The client had sold a large herd of cattle and was now handing over the landlord's share of the commission. The commission totalled nearly £30, out of which the client was entitled to about £10. The client counted £15 which he gave to the landlord, saying: 'That is all; this is sufficient'; which meant that he decided to take for himself £5 more than he should have done. The landlord nodded in agreement. He later explained to me that his client was an honest and fair man, and that his assessment of his share from the commission was justified in moral, though not in contractual, terms.

The point which should be stressed about all this, is that the relationship which thus develops between landlord and client, cannot be measured in material or contractual terms alone. It is a relation which cannot be completely reduced to economic or political relations. There is an inescapable moral bond as well. This is a bond which is governed by an 'ought', by a categorical imperative, and is an end in itself, though, sociologically speaking, it serves as a means for achieving economic and political ends. To all purposes, the moral relation becomes a kinship relationship proper, serving multiple interests, and making use of primary kinship terms and patterns of behaviour. The landlord can thus be seen as the centre of a network of kinship relationships with his clients.

The relationship has also a political aspect. By virtue of his dominant economic and moral position, the landlord can rely on the support of his clients in any political dispute in which he will be involved. The power of a landlord is often measured by the number of his clients. People will say, for example, of a certain landlord that 'he is 60 men', meaning that he has that number of clients.

The Landlords in Politics

A landlord will need the support of his clients should he have to confront other landlords or the Chief of the Quarter who is also a business landlord. One frequent issue over which landlords have always struggled is housing. Houses are a source not only of economic, but also of political power, and because of their scarcity and of the ambiguity and complexity of the rights held in them, men have always quarrelled over them.

A frequent type of dispute arises between a landlord and the Chief of the Quarter. In 1963 the Chief had between 50 and 60 houses under his control.[21] Most of these houses he had 'inherited' from men who died without leaving heirs. Some of those deceased men had been clients of other landlords and in some cases a client had acquired the house from his landlord. When a client died, his landlord claimed that the house was originally his own property and demanded that it should be given back to him. In some of these cases even when the client's house did not belong originally to the landlord, the latter claimed that he was *morally* entitled to 'inherit' it, since the client, after associating with him for a very long time, had in fact become his kinsman. The Chief and his advisors did not accept these arguments. In a few cases which are recorded, the Chief explained that he had in fact bought the house from the deceased man just before the man had died.

Disputes of this type become complicated because the Chief occupies complex roles that cannot be easily separated. He is a landlord in his own right, he is a Chief, and he is the arbitrator in cases of disputes. In 1963 it was almost impossible to ascertain which of the houses he controlled were his own property and which were the property of the community. This has been particularly the case in recent years when there has been the fear that the Yoruba civil authorities will claim custody over houses left by settlers without heirs, so that there has been a tacit agreement in the Quarter that the Chief can nominally claim the houses as his own.

Some of the houses which the Chief controls serve to accommodate his own wives, married sons, business clients and their families, and other men and women who are related to him personally in one way or another. Three of the other houses serve as 'houses of strangers' to accommodate the scores of cattle dealers who come from the North to sell their cattle through the business house of the Chief. Another three houses are run as houses for strangers, to accommodate needy Hausa strangers, who apply to the Chief, in his capacity as Chief of the Quarter, to accommodate them. The other houses accommodate several hundreds of men and women, both settlers and migrants, most of whom work in various services in the Quarter, and are not related to the Chief in any way. But because the Chief does not charge them any rent they are regarded and regard themselves, and, when necessary, act as, the Chief's political clients. Indeed they form the core of the Chief's political support in the Quarter.

Thus, dispute over houses is directly involved in the struggle for political power between the landlords. This can be shown over and over again in the history of the Quarter.

Landlords within the same trade also compete with one another over business. This means that they compete for the stranger-dealers who come to the Quarter to trade. Generally speaking, a dealer has one landlord to whom he is accustomed to entrust his business in Ibadan. Often this is a strong relationship which sometimes continues to hold between the respective sons of landlord and stranger if the sons continue the business of their fathers. Landlords endeavour all the time to keep their dealers attached to them and they often give them presents and render to them services which have little to do with the particular trade in which they are engaged, in order to strengthen the relationship. But some dealers do, nevertheless, change their landlords and this often leads to one landlord accusing another of 'stealing' his stranger. A landlord who wants to be at peace with a landlord colleague will be very hesitant to take into his business house the regular stranger of the other landlord. This can be clearly seen from one of the cases which I witnessed during my field work. The landlord in that case was new, having set himself up as a landlord only three years earlier, and he did not want to incur the animosity of his colleague who was more senior and more powerful than himself. When the stranger applied to him, he went to his colleague and talked with him. He pointed out that he found himself in a difficult position as, on the one hand, he could not reject a stranger because this was his livelihood and any business coming to him was a gift from Allah. On the other hand he did not want to grab the stranger from a friend. As a way out of the dilemma, he offered to pay the colleague part of the commission which he would get from conducting the business of the stranger. The colleague agreed and did in fact eventually receive from the other landlord the promised payment.

But not all the landlords are in the same position as this landlord nor are they as considerate as he was and cases of disputes over strangers are therefore very frequent.

Landlords also compete to 'capture' the new, and hence uncommitted, dealer-strangers from the North, by sending emissaries to meet these dealers on their way to Ibadan, offering them presents and directing them to lodge with their masters. Within the cattle trade, one source of tension and sometimes of quarrels between a landlord and the Chief of the Quarter has been over this issue. Often, when a new cattle dealer comes for the first time to the Quarter and goes to the Chief for accommodation and advice, the Chief will persuade the man to entrust the sale of his cattle to the Chief's own business house. The Chief is thus frequently accused by his colleagues in the cattle trade of exploiting his public office to advance his own private business interests.

Landlords have also quarrelled occasionally over scarce titles which carry not only prestige and political influence but also economic benefits. The first and the most important of these positions is that of the Chief of the Quarter, and the records abound with accounts of factional disputes over this position. Associated with the chieftaincy, there are titles for the Chief's Advisors (*fadawa*) for the Chief Imam of the Quarter, Assistant Chief Imam (*naibi*) chiefs of different occupational groups, chief of the cattle market, and some other titles.

Landlords are thus in continual competition and strife with one another and with the Chief of the Quarter. But they can pursue these disputes only within certain limits. These limits are set by a number of factors.

To begin with, the clients of a landlord do not constitute a corporate group which is ever mobilized for corporate action. Each client is dyadically linked with the landlord but is not necessarily linked to the other clients within the landlord's house. There is of course a great deal of interaction between the various clients, as they have to co-operate in a number of ways in order to carry out their business duties. But there is also a great deal of jealousy and rivalry between them in which the landlord is directly implicated. This is because the amount of business, and hence income, which a client can get is allocated by the landlord. When cattle dealers come to a cattle landlord to have their herds sold, it is the landlord who decides which herds, or how many herds of cattle, should be marketed by which of his client-brokers. Similarly, in the kola trade, when a kola landlord receives an order from the North, it is he who decides which of his client-buyers will buy the consignment. As these clients receive commission in proportion to the business they are given to handle, their income is virtually decided on by the landlord. This total business which is carried out through the house of the landlord is limited, and therefore as the landlord has under him a limited number of clients, to give more business to one client means to give less to the other clients. I often heard clients complain that their landlord showed favouritism towards one or another of his other clients, for one reason or another, by giving those clients more business to handle. The house is further inhibited from developing as a corporate group by the multiplicity of ties between clients from different business houses as a result of interaction in small primary groupings in different fields of social life in the Quarter. Clients of the same age group interact, across house affiliations, as friends who worship, eat, and seek entertainment together. To all this should be added the fact that clients can, and occasionally do, 'change house' by offering their service to another landlord.

Thus tension within the house of the landlord, and the network of friendship between members of his house and those of the other landlords, limits the degree to which landlords can engage in serious disputes with other landlords.

Far more important than these factors which prevent landlords from indulging in serious disputes is that the landlords are under continual pressure to co-operate politically, both among

95

themselves and with the Chief of the Quarter, on fundamental political issues which affect not only their business, but also the welfare, and at times the very existence of the whole Quarter.

This is because the trade is conducted in the face of continual rivalry and competition with Yoruba business men who often mobilize political support within the Ibadan polity to harass the Hausa. Internal political strife within the Quarter can be sustained only in so far as it does not impair the corporate political stand of the Quarter against outside pressure.

The Nodal Position of the Landlords

To conclude this chapter, landlords may be highly individualistic men who possess charismatic traits and who are bent on the pursuit of wealth, prestige, and political power. But this is only one side of the picture. Structurally, they can be seen as nodal points at which different sets, or fields of social relations intersect.

Within the context of the total social field of long distance trade, they provide mechanisms for overcoming the technical problems of the trade. They provide a link through which business information is exchanged. They maintain a large establishment which makes it possible for men in different occupational specializations to co-operate promptly and efficiently and thus to speed up the transfer of the perishable goods. And through their political and other social roles they maintain a web of social relations within the Quarter which bind men by moral values and obligations and thus make it possible to create credit which is essential for the flow of the trade.

Within the context of Sabo, they maintain an institutional framework which ensures stability of structure despite the mobility of personnel. They control most of the housing in the Quarter and thereby ensure that most of the migrants who settle in the Quarter are those engaged in trade. They provide employment for the greater part of the population. Through the dyadic personal relationships which they develop with many men, they act as social landmarks for the regulation of marriage, and domestic life, and of a web of inter-personal relations. They also act as political leaders who support an informal administrative structure to regulate order within the Quarter

and to co-ordinate the activities of its members in political
dealings with outside groupings.

If we concentrate on these, largely unintended, consequences
of their activities, the landlords will emerge as social functionaries who maintain Sabo as an on-going social organization.
The continuous process of the rise, development, functioning
and fall of individual landlords can be interpreted in terms of
this organization. The bankruptcy of a landlord can thus be
seen as the failure of a social functionary in the co-ordination
and regulation of economic, political, and other social roles.
To put it differently, the social process in the Quarter requires
for its continual functioning men who can co-ordinate different
sets of relationships and different institutional activities. For the
landlord it is not enough to be a good businessman. He must
also be a politician, and the head of a complex domestic and
social establishment. Indeed it is for this reason that the Hausa
often refer to the landlords as The Big Men.

CHAPTER FOUR

The Politics of Long-Distance Trade
(1906–1950)

Some Sociol Processes Underlying Historical Events—
Role of the Thieves in the Struggle for Autonomy (1906–15)
—Indirect Rule and Hausa Exclusiveness (1916–29)—
Struggle Over the Commission (lada) *and the Integration of*
Authority (1930–42)—Battle of the Kola and Rebellion of
the Friday Mosque (1942–50)

The history of Sabo tells the story of the making of an ethnic polity in a town. It shows how in the course of successive confrontations with the Yoruba over the control of trade during the past 60 years, the Hausa have developed an ethnic politico-economic organization within the Yoruba city, and how the interrelations between the two camps became increasingly more strained and more 'retribalized'.

This development displays an opposite process to the one reported for the industrial urban centres in Central Africa.[1] In his study of the development of one of these centres—a town called Luanshya in Northern Rhodesia, now Zambia—Epstein shows how in a series of crises in industrial relations during two decades, the multi-tribal African labour force thwarted the attempts by their white employers to organize them and deal with them on 'tribal' lines.[2] In the process, the struggle of labourers against management was systematically 'detribalized'. Thus while the Central African case shows a process of 'detribalization', the Hausa-Yoruba case in Ibadan shows a process of 'retribalization', i.e. of a political cleavage developing on ethnic lines within a contemporary formal political set-up.

Some Social Processes Underlying Historical Events
From the discussion in previous chapters it should be clear

why the development of long-distance trade tends to lead to the development of an ethnic monopoly over all or some of the stages of the trade. As the articles of the trade are of a perishable nature, it is important to have speedy means of communication between the centres of supply and the centres of consumption for the continuous exchange of information about business conditions. If men from different ethnic groupings, speaking different languages, partake in the chain of the trade, such exchange of information will be greatly hampered by linguistic differences. There is no common national language in Nigeria other than English which is spoken mainly by the literate people in the towns and is rarely spoken by people engaged in indigenous trade.

In Sabo a man can obtain the latest information on trade conditions in any part of the North by paying a short visit to one of the two lorry parks of the Quarter where he can converse with Hausa traders, lorry drivers, and other passengers who stream through every hour of the day and of the night. Messages are continuously exchanged through lorry drivers and passengers between business associates from Sabo, the North, and other Hausa centres in the South. Two more strategic places for the exchange of business information are the Cattle Market, *Zango*, and the kola sheds at the railway station. In all these places Hausa men from different areas regularly meet and interact through the medium of the Hausa language.[3]

The importance of having one language in the trade is equally crucial in facilitating speedy communication and inter- action between men from different occupational specializations who should co-operate at many stages in the business. Thus kola traders, landlords, commission buyers, packers, measurers, carriers, transport agents, lorry drivers or railway porters, and various other occupational categories must co-operate and interact in the purchase, packing and despatching of the goods. Interaction is further facilitated by the ethnic factor in that these men not only speak the same language but also live near each other within the narrow confines of the Quarter, instead of being scattered throughout the large city of Ibadan.

Again, sharing the same language as well as living in close spatial proximity, is equally significant for the development of primary relationships of the type discussed in connection with the organization of credit.[4] Relationships of this kind will arise easily only between people who can communicate intimately with one another and who share the same body of cultural norms, values and symbols. For the same reason, dealers from the North will trust Hausa 'brothers abroad' more than non-Hausa strangers, and frequent interaction between them and the Sabo landlords is also characterized by primacy and intimacy.

Equally important for the systematic flow of the trade is the existence of an institutionalized arbitratory procedure for dealing with business disputes, whose machinery, rules, and underlying norms and values are understood, respected, and upheld by the people concerned. This, again, can be most conveniently realized when these people share the same cultural tradition.

I am not arguing here that there is a deterministic inevitability in the emergence of ethnicity in long-distance trade. Indeed there are many instances of men from different tribes exchanging business information, co-operating in the conduct of the trade and establishing relationships of trust. Nearly half of the Yoruba butchers who operate in the Cattle Market in Ibadan speak some Hausa and a number of Hausa brokers, especially the Ibadan-born ones, speak some Yoruba: and in this market there are extensive credit arrangements between Hausa and Yoruba. Both Yoruba and Hausa who operate within the market accept the rulings of the Hausa Chief, in his role as arbitrator.[5] What I am arguing is that there is a strong tendency towards ethnic specialization in long-distance trade. Traders try to maximize their profits by cutting down risks and costs and, under the political and economic circumstances of an underdeveloped country, this can be best achieved by the establishment of ethnic monopolies. In the same ways monopolies tend to develop and expand in capitalistic industrial countries, monopoly in long-distance trade can develop horizontally, in covering an entire stage in the chain of trade, like the monopoly by the Yoruba in Ibadan of the butchering trade, or vertically, in covering most of the stages in the chain, like the monopoly by the Hausa of most of the stages involved in the kola trade. The more extensive and effective the monopoly in both directions, the more economical, efficient, and hence profitable the trade.

This is the purely economic aspect. But to achieve such a degree of monopoly often requires that business men from other tribal groups be driven out. This is why inter-tribal politics is involved in the organization and development of long-distance trade. In due course the groups involved in such a struggle organize themselves for political action in order to co-ordinate the political activities of the group and to develop institutions of authority, leadership, and decision-making. The myth of cultural distinctiveness becomes the ideological basis of ethnic grouping. Finally, the group emerges as an autonomous polity with an internal political structure of its own.

This interdependence between economic and political processes can be analysed only when these processes are isolated from other social processes and this can be done if the study is first confined to a limited area. Here, the study will deal principally with Hausa-Yoruba interrelations within the city of Ibadan. Yet even after limiting the field in this way the complexities are so great that a study of the present situation will lead only to limited results. Therefore it becomes necessary to examine analytically as much of the history of the system of relationships involved as possible. For, this system has been continuously changing—economically, demographically, and politically—since the beginning of the present century.

These changes have occurred in a succession of events which have involved many individuals and groups. An analysis of a number of such extended events will make it possible to isolate processes and to examine their interdependence.

For this purpose I have chosen and treated events of this type in such a way that each event will deal with a particular stage in the history of the Quarter and will also be concerned with the analysis of a different sociological problem. I shall arrange the events in a chronological order, even though they are used *experimentally* for the purpose of isolating variables and studying their interconnections under different conditions. Whenever the records permitted, events have been chosen in which the same individuals are involved over long periods of time. In this way, biography and history are combined to provide a structural analysis of the changing social system.[6]

The history of Sabo will thus be divided for the purposes of this analysis into five periods:

(1) 1906–15, during which the Hausa cattle landlords, using the menace of the large number of Hausa thieves who operated in the city, as a means of pressure on the city's authorities, struggled to achieve an autonomous Hausa political

grouping and to prevent the encroachment of Yoruba men into the marketing of cattle in Ibadan.

(2) 1916–29, marking the formal institutionalization of Hausa autonomy in Ibadan with the establishment of a well circumscribed Hausa quarter, under the authority of a Hausa Chief of the Quarter, in accordance with the principles and practices of the newly developed British policy of Indirect Rule.

(3) 1930–42, which saw an internal struggle for power and authority within the Quarter, leading to the emergence of a unified political authority for Sabo, and thus making for a greater degree of political integration within the Quarter and for a more effective political action viz-à-viz the Yoruba.

(4) 1943–50, which was characterized by the development of Hausa monopoly over the trade in kola, and by a series of political disturbances within the Quarter, as a result of the assault by Yoruba political and economic groupings on the political autonomy of the Quarter.

(5) 1951–63, which ushered in a new era in the social organization of Sabo, as a result of the collapse of the British Indirect Rule system of government, and of the development of a nationalist movement in Nigeria which eventually culminated in independence. The political processes brought about by these developments subverted Hausa political autonomy and Hausa economy in Ibadan. Concomitant with these changes was the rapid reorganization of Sabo religion which now began to articulate Sabo political autonomy in terms of new symbols, myths, norms, values, and power relations.

The discussion of each one of these periods focuses on the analysis of one major variable, but this does not mean that that variable ceases to operate in the next period or that it did not operate in the previous period. Thus, for example, the political aspects of the development of the kola trade are discussed in the period 1943–50, but the kola trade began to intrude into and later to become part of Sabo social organization in the early 1930's, and continued to exist and even grew further up to the present. Also, in the analysis of a variable, events from previous and succeeding periods are often discussed together, in accordance with their sociological relevance.

In the description and analysis of a succession of events from 1930 onwards, I discuss at length the activities and different roles of Umaru, a leading cattle landlord since 1916, Chief of the Cattle Market since 1935, arbitrator in business disputes, a Shari'a judge, owner of scores of houses in the Quarter, and a shrewd leader who combined economic, political, ritual, and moral powers to become Chief of the Quarter from 1930 to 1943 and then, after a period of bitter struggle against enemies both within and outside Sabo, from 1949 to 1963.

Role of the 'Thieves' in the Struggle for Autonomy (1906–15)

In Ibadan today there are three different myths about the origin of Sabo.

The first is a 'classical' Yoruba version which states that, from the beginning of their settlement in the city, the Hausa have always been troublemakers and exploiters, and have harboured among themselves thieves, ex-convicts running away from the North, prostitutes, gamblers, and other types of undesirables. To keep them under control, the Yoruba chiefs of the city decided 'long ago' to segregate them from the rest of Ibadan by confining them within an enclosed area.

The second is a 'classical' Hausa version, which states that the Hausa observe different customs from those of the Yoruba and that therefore they have always sought to live on their own in a special settlement in which they can live under their traditional institutions.

The third myth is a more sophisticated version which states that the establishment of a Hausa quarter in Ibadan was part of the general policy of the British administration of Indirect Rule, and that Sabo was established in the same way in which special quarters (*sing. sabon gari*) were established for the settlement of southerners working in northern towns.

A study of the records shows that each one of these three myths tells part of the truth.

The Hausa Thieves in Ibadan have played such an important role in shaping Hausa-Yoruba inter-relationships and in the politics of the Quarter, that they should be regarded as part of the structure of Sabo polity.

During the first decade of this century a wave of burglaries swept the city of Ibadan, and a number of Yoruba chiefs held the Hausa responsible for them. In 1906, the Olubadan in Council resolved that all the Hausa had to be under the control of 'an approved headman of their race' who would be held responsible for his people, since those were scattered in different parts of the city.[7] In 1907 the Olubadan informed the Council—in which the British District Officer was a participant—that it was the wish of the Yoruba chiefs that the Hausa strangers should be forced to live in a special settlement which would be allotted to them and that they should be confined within that settlement 'from sunset to dawn' and that should any of them be found outside the settlement during the night they would be liable to imprisonment or banishment from the city.[8]

But the British officials vetoed these decisions. The Resident informed the Council that he had laid their wishes before the Governor who had disapproved of their resolution, which could not, therefore, be carried out.[9]

During the following six years the problem of the 'Hausa burglars' was discussed a number of times and some decisions were taken by the Olubadan in Council for the expulsion from Ibadan of 'notorious, foreign burglars (Hausa, etc.) ... particularly those who had been imprisoned more than once'.[10] It is not clear from the records, whether those decisions by the Olubadan in Council were duly approved by the colonial administration or whether any Hausa burglars were in fact banished from the city. But as from 1913 there are in the records entries indicating that the proposition for concentrating the Hausa in a separate settlement was renewed and finally in 1916 Sabo was in fact established.

To understand the sociological significance of these events one has to look at the activities and organization of the Hausa in Ibadan during that period. The scanty information in the records indicates that Hausa cattle 'traders' and butchers had settled in the city from the very beginning of the century. Akinyele mentions that the first Hausa migrants had settled in the compound of Oluyo.[11] It is clear both from the records and from old informants in Sabo that during the first decade of the century a few hundred Hausa men had settled in a number of Yoruba compounds in the city. An index to the scale of the trade in cattle in the city can be found in an order issued in 1913 by the Olubadan in Council to impose a tax on the number of cattle accommodated in Yoruba compounds, at the rate of 2/– per head a year, so that a man storing 50 cattle would have to pay a licence fee of £5 a year.[12]

The demand for cattle had been steadily increasing, for a

number of reasons. One was the expansion of the population of Ibadan. By 1911 it had reached 175,000. The railway between Ibadan and Lagos had been opened in 1901 and was later extended to Oshogbo by 1906 and then to Kano by 1912. Cocoa had been introduced into Yorubaland and had soon become a very significant source of income and wealth in the area. The British had already established sovereignty over the North, and by 1914 the whole of what came later to be known as Nigeria was given one administration, and Ibadan became one of its most important centres. At the same time the city was becoming an important marketing place.

Thus with more people in the city earning more, the demand for beef meat increased steadily, and the Hausa stepped in to supply it. Hausa cattle dealers brought herds of cattle and lodged in Yoruba compounds. They sold the cattle to Hausa migrant butchers and then returned to the North to bring more cattle. In time, a few of those dealers remained in Ibadan and had their associates or clients bring cattle for them to sell. Some of these settled men specialized in operating as brokers for other dealers coming from the North.

Brokers and their assistants, as well as dealers, lodged in Yoruba compounds that belonged to some local chiefs. These compound chiefs collected not only rent but also fees on the sale of the cattle. The cattle were kept near the compounds and were sold on the same spot to butchers. Figures for that early period are lacking but when the Quarter was founded in 1916, the records give names of 57 'cattle traders' and 21 butchers, though it is not clear how these men were organized or what specific roles they performed.[13] There is evidence that the butchers were organized within one 'house' under a Hausa Big Man who came to be known as Chief of the Butchers, and who was later described in many documents as one of the oldest Hausa settlers in Ibadan and as a powerful leader of the local Hausa community. There were also three cattle landlords under whom the other men who were mentioned as 'cattle traders' worked as client-brokers. In the meantime a number of Hausa migrants began to settle in the town to provide some services for the more senior Hausa settlers and to engage in petty trading. Together with these came also a number of Hausa prostitutes and some other Hausa men whose occupation was not at all clear, and among these were the thieves.

According to informants, the Yoruba landlords in whose compounds the Hausa were operating exacted from the Hausa the highest rent and sales' fees. These Yoruba thus developed a vested economic interest in their tenants and in the cattle trade to such an extent that some of the Yoruba chiefs in the Council of the city were reported to have objected to the idea of segregating the Hausa in a separate settlement. A number of Yoruba compound-heads began even to participate in the trade itself by buying and selling and some of them began to slaughter cattle on their own account and then sell the meat to other Yoruba.

The Hausa themselves began to agitate against the increasing payments demanded by Yoruba landlords and chiefs and, relying on the protection of the British administration against Yoruba harassment, began to demand a separate settlement where they could be their own masters. As a pretext for their demand they argued that their customs, religious practices, and their traditional way of life were very different from those of the Yoruba.

Meanwhile, the increasing numbers of cattle that were being brought for sale and slaughter within the town began to constitute a public menace, because of animals' droppings and of the interference of their movements with traffic in the streets. Some Yoruba chiefs, as well as the British officials in the town, advanced suggestions for restrictions on the movement of cattle within the town. In a meeting of the Native Authority Council in 1916, only a few months before the Quarter was established, it was decided that all the Hausa should be confined to a settlement and should not be allowed to stay in the town, that all cattle brought by the Hausa should be kept outside the town and that a market for the sale of these cattle should be held at a place outside the town, and that a penalty of £5 would be levied on those who infringed these rules. The Resident conceded that these rules would not apply to Yoruba settlers of Ibadan, who could buy cattle and bring them into the city.[14]

This problem of the traffic of cattle within the city has been present throughout these decades until today.

It was against this background that the few leading Hausa landlords took up the case for having an independent settlement in which no rent would have to be paid to Yoruba landlords and where they could monopolize the sale of cattle. To achieve this in the face of opposition offered by some of the Yoruba chiefs, they used the threat of the Hausa thieves as an indirect means of pressure.

Direct information on this aspect of the role of Hausa thieves during that period is scanty, but a survey of the activities of the thieves during the following decades throws a great deal of light on the political implications. Indeed from the records of subsequent years it becomes evident that the thieves have always constituted a significant structural factor in both the internal and the external politics of the Quarter.

Figures are of course lacking about the exact number of thieves operating in the city at any time, but a report by an official of the Administration on the situation in the 1940's states that four out of every five thieves who had been caught in Ibadan were Hausa.

In 1929 the Chief of the Hausa Quarter was dismissed from his office and banished from Ibadan, after it was alleged that he had knowingly kept stolen property in his house.[15] Again, in 1942, the Chief of the Quarter was brought to court, convicted of being in possession of stolen property, fined, and then duly dismissed from his office.[16] In 1933 the menace of the Hausa thieves reached such dimensions that the Native Authority Council had to legislate an Ordinance which stated that anyone coming under the jurisdiction of the Council, but who was not himself a member of the native community, and who failed to produce sufficient proof to the Native Authority that his means of livelihood and his occupation were sufficient to provide support for himself and for his family, would be asked by the Native Authority to leave the area 14 days after service of a notice of expulsion.[17]

In 1963, it was sufficient to spend only a number of months in the Quarter in order to recognize the professional 'thieves' and to learn details about their activities and organization. Many of the thieves frequented three gambling houses in the Quarter. The landlords of those houses employed 'middlemen' who recruited customers, mainly from among the strangers, from the lorry parks and from other parts of the Quarter. The landlords provided cards, but they did not gamble themselves. Their remuneration was a special 'cut' from every serving. Over 20 men who regularly attended gambling sessions were counted and I was told by some informants that those men had no source of livelihood other than gambling. Most of the professional thieves were also gamblers.

It was no closely guarded secret in the Quarter that the gamblers and the thieves had their own unturbanned chief, to whom I shall refer as Yaro. Yaro was a very forceful person and had a strange network of unorthodox connections with many people within and outside the Quarter. His role among the thieves was that of a protector and blackmailer at one and the same time. He exacted protection money from the three gambling houses, at the fixed fee of 5/- a week for each circle. He was an old settler and his name recurs in the records from the late 1940's. People in the Quarter said that he had connections with men of power and influence outside the Quarter to whom he regularly paid part of the 'fees' he obtained. He serves as what may be called 'Black Market Fixer'. A man who had problems within the City outside the Quarter, would first go to the Chief of the Quarter for help. But if the Chief failed in his efforts, or refused, the man would secretly contact Yaro, 'The Chief of the Thieves', as informants called him. While the Chief of the Quarter specialized in contacts with men from the traditional elite, Yaro specialized in contacts with other types of men of influence.

In 1949 Yaro was named by a northern political party as a police informer who made the police arrest Hausa prostitutes in Sabo, only in order to 'arrange' their release later, after extracting a price from them. During the following few years he played an important role in the political struggle within the Quarter in disputes over the chieftaincy, in the course of party political wrangling within Sabo.[18]

Again, in 1963 it was possible to learn about the organization of the thieves and about the specialists among them. One man was well known as a specialist in marketing stolen property, though I was assured by a number of informants that in the few previous years the thieves had been forced to change their methods of operation, by concentrating on stealing cash and abandoning as far as possible the stealing of goods in order to avoid being easily discovered. Among the professionals, some specialized in picking pockets in the markets or the streets, others specialized in shoplifting and others in housebreaking. Apart from the few highly professional thieves, there were many amateurs and part-time operators. All of them described themselves as 'petty traders' and some of them did actually peddle some goods for sale. I was told that men from some other occupations also engaged every now and then in 'living on their wits', as some kind of sport or second profession!

A visitor to the Quarter on any day can see practically hundreds of men who sit in the streets or on verandahs without visibly doing anything. Often one sees the same men sitting at leisure or walking through the Quarter day after day, and one wonders how they earn their living. When queried, informants would shrug their shoulders and say they did not know. Apart from these men there are also fluctuating numbers of Hausa men who do not stay in the Quarter but who sleep in the centre of the town, sometimes in mosques and markets, or even in the streets, and on several occasions in the past the District Officer advised the Council to announce to the public that men were to be prohibited from sleeping in public places.

The point which I want to stress from all this is that Hausa 'thieves' and Hausa 'men who live on their wits' have always been a force in the city, and that this has been of great significance for Hausa-Yoruba relations. Both the Yoruba Native Authority chiefs and the officials of the British administration were very sensitive to matters affecting law and order in the city. The Yoruba chiefs had to prove to the Administration that they were capable and had enough authority to maintain social order, and the British officials in the city had to prove to their superiors that they had the people in the town under control.

The Hausa landlords and, later, the Hausa Chief of the Quarter, have always been well aware of the sensitivity of the authorities towards this problem and time after time they exploited it in their political and economic manoeuvring with the Yoruba. In letters to the Yoruba chiefs and to the District Officer the Chief of the Quarter often reminded them that 'You have appointed me here as your eyes and ears . . . I know these men well . . .' In other words, he was saying that only another Hausa could tell which Hausa was a thief and which was not and that those thieves could therefore be effectively controlled only when the whole Hausa population in Ibadan were to be accommodated in one place, under some kind of Hausa authority.

This contention by the Chief and the leading landlords of the Quarter was consistently upheld during the following decades. When during the 1940's some Hausa migrants began to settle in the centre of Ibadan and to compete in business with the Hausa in Sabo, these 'floating Hausa' were described by the Sabo landlords in one petition after another as 'thieves, pickpockets, and undesirables' who chose to live outside the Quarter in order to evade the surveillance by the Hausa Chief and the payment of taxes. The landlords of Sabo insisted that it was in the interests of peace and order in the town that the 'floating Hausa' be forced to live within the Quarter.

Thus, when earlier in this period the Yoruba chiefs wanted to confine the Hausa within a restricted settlement, they might have done so on the suggestion of the Hausa landlords, who were using the bogey of the thieves as a means of pressure to achieve their own end of gaining autonomy.

Events during that period and during subsequent decades raise the question whether the thieves were in any way working for the landlords or whether they were at all in collusion with the landlords in exerting pressure on the authorities. What is important sociologically is that the thieves were there, that they were a source of anxiety to the authorities, both Yoruba and British, and that both Hausa leaders and the authorities believed that the thieves could be controlled by forcing the Hausa to live in a separate area, under the authority of a Hausa chief. From the records, as well as from conversations with informants, it is certain that the Chief of the Quarter has nearly always been able to exert a great deal of control over the activities of the thieves. His major weapon against them has been the threat of exposing them and having them arrested or expelled. This control by the Chief was exercised in varying degrees at different periods, depending on political conditions and tactical manoeuvring with the Yoruba and the British. Thus, the least that can be said about 'collusion' is that the Chief actively manipulated the thieves by intensifying or relaxing the pressure on them. When he wanted to exert pressure on the authorities he relaxed the control over the thieves.

The Quarter provided shelter for many of the thieves as it made it easier for them to mingle with the hundreds of Hausa strangers without exposing themselves unnecessarily. But the settlers of Sabo tolerated the thieves provided that these did not go so far in their activities as to endanger relations between the Quarter and the authorities and also provided that they did not operate within the Quarter itself. At the time of my field-work there was a kind of gentlemanly agreement which, I was told, had been maintained for many years, that the thieves would not operate in the Quarter and that the thieves' leaders would expose to the Hausa any of their followers who did not honour the agreement. But this was by no means the case all the time. When the Quarter became politically united and the Chief enjoyed the support of the majority of the population, the thieves were under effective control. As is natural in every community, however, there were cleavages within the Quarter which frequently led to factional disputes. In such disputes each faction accused the others, in front of the authorities, of harbouring thieves, and the thieves did then operate within the Quarter.

At one period during the early 1950's a series of thefts occurred within the Quarter and the victims were Hausa strangers who were conducting business in the Quarter. For the settlers this was a grave development as it endangered their very livelihood. For, if word spread in the North and in the Hausa diaspora in the South that Sabo was not safe for trade, traders would not come to the Quarter but would go instead to neighbouring Hausa settlements.

A swift and violent reaction soon followed when, according to informants, about 60–70 men (mostly clients of landlords) gathered together in the central school building of the Quarter and decided that the only way for them to deal with the thieves was to assault them physically. Generally, massive physical violence is unknown in Sabo. In recording the history of the Quarter over a period of about 60 years, I have come across only two incidents involving collective violence, and this was one of them. The meeting was called on the spur of the moment after a rumour had spread that the thieves had gathered in the racecourse adjacent to the Quarter, and had been gambling there with money which they had stolen on the previous day from Hausa strangers. Informants say that the attackers assaulted the thieves with sticks and that many men from both sides were injured. Soon the police were called and scores of arrests were made. Informants stated that many settlers who did not actually take part in the assault went to the police and declared that they had participated in the attack and asked to be arrested. They did this in order to give moral support to those settlers who had already been arrested and to demonstrate that they had done a job which the police should have done.

From all this it is clear that the thieves have always been part of the power structure of Sabo and that a delicate balance between them and the settled population had to be maintained. Indeed, any analysis of the political organization of the Hausa Quarter will have to treat the thieves as part of the structure of Sabo.

During the period 1906–15 the association between the thieves and Hausa business landlords was even stronger than in later periods, because the Hausa in Ibadan were then few in number, and only few men 'without visible means of livelihood' could come to the city without the patronage of some important Hausa. From the records one gathers that in fact some of the thieves at that time were the regular clients of Hausa landlords who operated in the town. The landlords must have known about the activities of those thieves.

Thus when in the early 1910's the Hausa were pressing for a separate settlement of their own it is quite possible that they used the thieves as a source of pressure on the Yoruba chiefs and on the British administration. And as indicated earlier, some of the Yoruba chiefs had been driven by the menace of the thieves to demand that the Hausa should be segregated.

But at this time, the Yoruba chiefs were not unanimous in favour of granting a 'tribal' autonomy to the Hausa, because some of the chiefs had in the meantime developed a vested economic interest in the Hausa as tenants in their compounds both in the form of taking rent and of sharing commission from the sale of cattle with the Hausa landlords. Details about disputes between Hausa and Yoruba during that period over the commission from the sale of cattle in Ibadan are few, but in the records for other towns such disputes are abundant. Indeed in the case of the town of Oyo one dispute went on for decades and lasted well into the early 1960's.

Thus while the Hausa at this period agitated for a separate settlement, the Yoruba chiefs were divided so that some of them were in favour and others were against. The final decision, however, was in the hands of the British. But during the earlier years, the British had been rather shocked by the 'undemocratic' excesses contained in the resolutions of the Olubadan in Council 1906–7 to keep the Hausa in a settlement under curfew 'from dawn to dusk'. A stalemate developed, until a new British policy with a new ideology had been evolved. In 1916 the British planned and with a great deal of determination set up the Quarter, against the opposition of some of the Yoruba chiefs. The Hausa were glad to co-operate.

Indirect Rule and Hausa Exclusiveness (1916–29)

During the first few months of the year 1916 Hausa ethnic distinctiveness in Ibadan was formally institutionalized with the establishment of Sabo, as a Hausa 'village' on the edge of the town. A few months later the District Officer submitted to the Resident a list containing the names and occupations of 394 Hausa men and women who had already settled in the village.[19] Towards the end of the year the Resident sent a letter to the District Officer instructing him to ask the Olubadan the reason why nearly 10% of the Hausa were still living in the town.[20] One also learns from the same letter that orders had been given for all Hausa in the town to move to the settlement. In a document a few years later an inquiry was made as to why *one* Hausa man was still living in town. The residential exclusiveness of the Hausa thus seems to have been complete.

It is evident from the records that in 1916 the British administration had completely reversed their policy of a decade earlier and were now in full support of Hausa separatism. A new set of administrators had been installed who implemented a new policy and it was a British engineer and a health inspector who planned and supervised settlement in the village.

This change in British policy did not develop directly from the logic of the situation between Hausa and Yoruba but was part of a new high-level administrative policy, indeed a new political creed—Indirect Rule. In 1912 Lord Lugard had returned to Nigeria to become Governor-General in 1914 and was to bring the southern and northern protectorates and the colony of Lagos together under a unified administration. The British were to rule as little and as cheaply as possible. Expediency was soon turned into a form of government, which was acclaimed as a model for the whole British Empire. The administration had to seek to understand native institutions, to preserve native groupings, to look for the native 'natural rulers' in these groupings and to appoint those rulers as agents of the central administration. Where rulers were not obvious they had to be found. The British officials were to enhance the prestige of those chiefs and to interfere as little as possible with their rule. The system was to cushion the native communities against radical social change and thus save them from the rapid disintegration of their tradition and their society.[21]

During the following three decades, the British did their best to implement this policy, often in the face of great difficulties. Throughout these decades the British officials in Ibadan tried to keep the Hausa as exclusive as they could, even in the face of mounting opposition from the Yoruba hosts.

A major source of trouble for the administration in Ibadan was that, in conformity with Indirect Rule, the British had to support the authority of the Yoruba chiefs of the town and to subordinate the Hausa Chief of the Quarter to the authority of the Yoruba. But the Hausa continually resented this and sought, whenever possible, to deal directly with the British. The British had frequently to intervene on behalf of the Hausa, though officially they tried to maintain the fiction that the Yoruba chiefs were the masters of the situation, and on numerous occasions the Yoruba had to give in, against their own wishes.

The British drew clear boundaries for Sabo and maintained that only Hausa should be allowed to build houses and live within the Quarter. Up to the mid-1930's Sabo remained exclusively Hausa.[22] Later on, a number of cases arose which threatened to disturb the tribal character of the Quarter. There were two cases, one in the late 1930's and the other in the early 1940's of two influential Yoruba men erecting buildings in Sabo. Later, other cases arose of Hausa men who, before returning to the North, sold their houses to Yoruba men, apparently without opposition from the Hausa Chief of the Quarter.

In a number of letters to the Yoruba chiefs, during the 1940's, the British officials expressed their opposition to this trend. The Yoruba chiefs, on the other hand, maintained that they were not prepared to intervene to prevent the Yoruba from buying houses from the Hausa. In one letter on this issue the Olubadan pointed out that there was no law forbidding non-Hausa from acquiring property in the Hausa settlement and that the Council did not intend to legislate such a law. The Council assured the British, however, that the Yoruba landlords would not be allowed to live in Sabo themselves, but would only be allowed to let rooms in those houses to Hausa tenants. The problem seems to have been left at that with the British officials accepting the position that Yoruba individuals could own houses in Sabo but that only Hausa should be allowed to live in those houses as tenants. This stand was consistently maintained until the early 1950's.

The number of houses acquired by the Yoruba in the Quarter up to the present has been very small. Indeed, as I indicated earlier, the Hausa themselves allowed, and probably themselves wanted, some of the houses in their settlement to be owned by Yoruba, so that prostitutes and other 'undesirables' could live in those houses without the city authorities holding the Hausa community or their leaders responsible for accommodating them. As early as 1939 the Superintendent of Police in the Province complained in a letter that a certain influential Yoruba man who had bought a house in Sabo had been letting rooms to 'undesirable characters from the North'.

As from the late 1930's, when the Quarter had become congested, some Hausa began to live in the centre of the town. The Chief of the Quarter as well as the leading landlords, wrote numerous petitions to the Olubadan and to the District Officer demanding that the 'Hausa floating population' should be compelled to move to the Quarter, alleging that those Hausa had been harbouring thieves and evading the payment of taxes to the local authority by being outside the control and supervision of the Hausa Chief. The British did not want in this case 'to compel people to live where they did not want to live', but advocated instead that the Council should persuade Yoruba landlords in the town not to let rooms to Hausa, and to ordain that no Hausa should be allowed to sleep in public places such as mosques and markets.[23]

On the whole, the British did their best to preserve the tribal identity and exclusiveness of the Hausa Quarter. The issue was clear: to populate Sabo only by Hausa.

Hausa autonomy in Sabo, however, depended not only on territorial exclusiveness, but also on the development of a Hausa political authority within the Quarter. From the very beginning, it was officially arranged that the Hausa Chief should be directly responsible to the Olubadan[24] of Ibadan. Formally, the Chief of Sabo was appointed, and ceremonially installed, by the Olubadan. He also received a salary of £24 a year from the Council. He derived his authority directly from the Yoruba chiefs. In official letters he always addressed the Olubadan as 'Our Father'. He was not supposed to have any direct dealings with the British officials. If he wanted to communicate with the British he had to do so through the office of the Olubadan. And when the British officials wanted to communicate with him they had to do so through the Olubadan. Even in those cases when the most cherished private interests of those officials were involved this procedure was followed. Thus in one letter in 1931, the District Officer wrote to the Olubadan and Council: 'Please inform Seriki Gambari [i.e. the Chief of the Hausa] that cattle are not allowed on the new Golf Course!25

This arrangement was in conformity with the general policy of Indirect Rule. The Olubadan and the Council were the recognized authority in Ibadan and the British had to uphold that authority and to enhance the prestige of the Yoruba chiefs in their own city. The Hausa in Ibadan were a small minority and their affairs had therefore to be left to the Ibadan chiefs.

Strictly speaking, however, this was contrary to the tenets of Indirect Rule policy which ordained that people should have their own 'natural rulers' administering their affairs. The Yoruba chiefs could by no stretch of the imagination be regarded as natural rulers of the Hausa. In fact on numerous occasions the Yoruba chiefs took decisions against the Hausa and acted in what was, for the Hausa, an arbitrary and hostile manner. The British were of course fully aware of this and they always tried to strike a balance between the necessity of upholding the authority of the Yoruba chiefs and of protecting the interests of the Hausa. They did this in a variety of ways, though officially maintaining the fiction that the affairs of the Quarter were the domain of the Olubadan alone. They often discussed matters directly with the Hausa Chief, arrived at decisions, and *then* put these matters through the proper, formal, channels. They also prevented the Ibadan Council from taking decisions hostile to the interests of the Hausa and on many occasions vetoed decisions already taken by the Council in connection with the Hausa. The Hausa on their part understood the game and often shrewdly manoeuvred their way and even played the British and the Council off against each other. On occasions, the Yoruba themselves had to ask the British to intervene to put matters right between themselves and the Hausa.

These anomalies in the relationships between the British, the Yoruba, and the Hausa, were dramatically reflected at times of crises over the Chieftaincy in Sabo. This was particularly the case during a disturbed period in Sabo's history, between 1943 and 1949, when the struggle between Hausa and Yoruba over strategic positions in the kola trade was at its zenith.

With the establishment of a Hausa Quarter and the setting up of a Hausa chief in it, Hausa ethnic exclusiveness in Ibadan was in fact formally institutionalized. This was a product, partly of a new British policy, partly of the desire of some Yoruba chiefs to contain the threat of the Hausa thieves, and partly of the endeavour of the Hausa to live on their own in order to protect their trade. But, once established, formal Hausa exclusiveness became a new factor which assumed importance in its own right and enabled the Hausa, not only to consolidate their trading enterprise, but also to gain more and more ground. It enabled them to gain complete control of the trade in cattle and, later, to capture business in the kola and in some other trades.

The monopoly over the marketing of cattle followed very soon after the setting up of the Quarter. The removal of the Hausa from the centre of the town into Sabo meant that the Yoruba landlords with whom Hausa cattle traders and brokers had been lodging, lost not only the rent which the Hausa had paid, but also parts of the commission (*lada*) which the Yoruba had been extracting from the Hausa. Yoruba land-lords also lost the fees which they had been collecting for keeping cattle within enclosures on their land. Soon after the establishment of the Quarter it was officially ordained that all cattle should be kept out of town, near to the Hausa Quarter. A single fully fledged market for cattle, which came to be known as 'Zango' was soon established, and one of the leading Hausa brokers became its Chief, who, since then, has been known as Chief of the Cattle Market (in Hausa, *Sarkin Zango*). This Chief became responsible for order in the market, and for many years to come he collected a special market toll. A large enclosure for keeping cattle overnight was established near Zango and was in time placed under a Fulani chief[26] (known until today as *Sarkin Fulani*) who was appointed by the Hausa Chief and was assisted by a number of Fulani drovers. This has always been a technical speciality for which the Hausa have no talent and has remained until today a Fulani concern. Today the Chief of the Fulani is the head of a small community of about 50 Fulani men and a few women. He runs a house for strangers to accommodate some of the Fulani drovers who accompany herds of cattle from the North to the South. Drovers accompanying 'marching cattle' remain with the herds until the animals are sold, but cattle brought by train are looked after by Fulani drovers who are permanent settlers in the compound of the Chief of the Fulani. The Fulani Chief is entitled to 6d. (in 1963) a night for each head of cattle that is kept with him after it is bought. This fee is paid today by the Yoruba butchers, since they are the buyers. In addition to the Market and the Enclosure, an abbatoir was established on a nearby plot. A few years after the establishment of the Quarter, the District Officer ordained in a document that 'all cattle must be sold only in the Cattle Market'. Hausa monopoly over the marketing of cattle in Ibadan was thus complete.

Exclusiveness eventually helped the Hausa to capture a great deal of the lorry transport business between the North and the South. Sabo soon became an important transport centre for the tens of thousands of Hausa who migrate annually from the North to southern Nigeria and to Ghana. Scores of 'houses for strangers' were set up to accommodate them and scores of 'travel agents', working on commission basis, began to earn substantial income from giving various kinds of service to them. Some of these agents specialized in obtaining travel certificates for those transients who were going to Ghana.[27]

As a result of the concentration of the Hausa in a separate settlement, hundreds of Hausa men and women have been able to earn their living by providing services for the population of the Quarter. If the Hausa were scattered throughout the massive city, many of those services would have been provided by the Yoruba. Even beggars, thieves, and petty traders, who operate in town greatly consolidated their position and captured new grounds by using Sabo as a base.

Quite apart from all these economic gains, the Quarter became in time a fundamental vested economic interest for the Hausa in another respect. Originally, Sabo was established as a separate village on the periphery of the town.[28] But soon the city grew so fast that Sabo was outflanked and its location has now become part of the town. This means that the land on which Sabo stands has greatly appreciated in value. This is of course in addition to the accumulating capital asset in the buildings.[29]

Tribal exclusiveness has thus become a means of keeping this economic position. On several occasions the Council adopted schemes to remove the Quarter from its present site to a new area on the outskirts of the city, but the Hausa have consistently and strongly opposed them. At one time there was a scheme to remove them to a much larger area, with a great scope for expansion, but massive Hausa protests and requests were presented to the authorities and the scheme was abandoned.

The Quarter has also enabled the Hausa to devlop social institutions which have served as a stable framework to ensure continuity of structure despite the mobility of personnel. The Hausa developed their own religious organization and their own social groupings, and proximity of residence has intensified informal social interaction within the Quarter, while residential exclusiveness has greatly inhibited such interaction with the Yoruba and thus prevented the development of loyalties across the lines of ethnic distinctiveness.

Finally, as a result of these different processes which accompanied the establishment of the Quarter, the Hausa acquired such a degree of ethnic distinctiveness that it became possible for them to develop collective political functions and to create an integrated system of political authority which soon became a powerful weapon in the struggle to capture further economic fields.

Struggle over the Commission (Lada) and the Integration of Authority (1930–42)

Concomitant with the developing tribal distinctiveness of the Hausa was the integration of Hausa authority in the Quarter. Without organized authority to co-ordinate the political effort of the community distinctiveness would have been useless. Indirect Rule formally gave the Hausa a chief with certain powers but in order to function at all the Chief had also to have power and authority from within. Thus the continual confrontations between Hausa and Yoruba in competition for economic benefits from trade, together with the rapidly increasing population of Sabo and the developing complexity of its social life, led to the emergence of a unified 'tribal' administration and leadership. But this was achieved only after an intense struggle for power and authority within the community.

In December 1929, the incumbent of the position of Chief of Sabo was found, by the city authorities, guilty of being in possession of stolen property and of accommodating in his houses 'thieves and ex-convicts', and was therefore dismissed from his office. He was told by the Council that there had been enough evidence to send him to jail for a long period but that, instead, he would be given two weeks' notice 'to pack up his load and leave Ibadan for his own country'. He was warned not to try to bribe any chief in an attempt to have the decision revoked. In passing, the Council also observed that Sabo had become too big for him to look after.[30]

A few days later two of the most senior men in Sabo at the time, Shuaibu, Chief of the Cattle Market (*Sarkin Zango*), and Yakubu, Chief of the Butchers (*Sarkin Pawa*) were summoned by the Council and were told that the Hausa should decide among themselves on a new Chief and should suggest candidates for consideration by the Council. In the meantime, these two men, being the eldest settlers in Ibadan and enjoying the respect of the community, would be responsible for their village and for keeping it free from thieves. The Council Minutes record that the two men promised to do so.[31]

The Hausa were eventually invited to come to a Council meeting in January 1930 and, according to the Minutes, 230 of them attended. The Council and the District Officer discussed the appointment of a new chief and considered that it would be best to have one of the senior members of the community for the vacant position. The Olubadan suggested Shuaibu, Chief of the Cattle Market, as candidate. But Shuaibu who was present in the hall declined to accept, saying that he preferred to remain Chief of the Cattle Market. As an alternative candidate he suggested his eldest son, Gambo. The Olubadan seconded this nomination.[32]

A number of Hausa seniors said, however, that they would support the candidature of a cattle landlord called Umaru, who was said to have been living in Sabo since it had been established. The Council, apparently prompted by the District Officer, sought to ask the opinion of the Hausa who were present. The Minutes record that 'the followers of Gambo were put on one side of the Hall and those of Umaru on the other' and it was found that Gambo had only 28 followers while Umaru had nearly 200. It is significant that Shuaibu himself supported Umaru, and not his own son, explaining that Umaru was indeed senior to his son.[33]

That meeting does not seem to have been decisive because the records describe another meeting, two weeks later, when 350 Hausa men came before the Council and, according to the Minutes 'practically every Hausa voted for Umaru'. Gambo, the rival candidate, was also present and was formally informed that Umaru would become the new Chief. Umaru was asked by the Council to go to see the Resident.[34]

Umaru thus became the new Chief of Sabo. He was later to become a most powerful and most controversial figure who dominated the political life of the Hausa, not only in Ibadan, but also in many other towns in Yorubaland, from that time until the present (1963).

It is clear from the records that until 1930, the Chief of Sabo had not enjoyed full authority within the Quarter. Both the Chief of the Cattle Market and the Chief of the Butchers were powerful men in their own right and exercised a great deal of influence in the Quarter.

The Chief of the Cattle Market received a large income from market tolls and from arbitration in cases of disputes within the market. At the same time he operated as a cattle landlord in the Market, accommodating northern dealers and collecting commission from the sale of their herds. He had been in Ibadan since the beginning of the century and enjoyed the confidence and patronage of some of the Yoruba chiefs.

The economy of Sabo at the time was based principally on cattle and butchering and the position of the Chief of the Cattle Market was associated with a great deal of economic and political influence. Even today, after the diversification of Sabo's economy, and especially after the development of the trade in kola and the emergence of many other occupational groupings in Sabo, the position of Chief of the Cattle Market is associated with a great deal of power. Indeed, in all those Hausa communities in Yoruba towns where cattle markets are in operation, the Chief of the Hausa Quarter is at the same time the Chief of the Cattle Market.[35] This should explain, therefore, why in 1930, when these two positions were separate in Sabo, Shuaibu preferred retaining the chieftaincy of the Cattle Market to getting the chieftaincy of the Quarter.

The Chief of the Butchers, Yakubu, was an equally powerful man and a senior settler. Although he was called 'Chief of the Butchers', most of the butchers who followed him were in effect his own clients, living in his many houses and paying allegiance to him. Elderly informants in Sabo emphasize that the man was so powerful that he, rather than the Chief of the Quarter, used to 'inherit' the houses of his deceased clients and that in time he thus came to control a large number of houses. In 1963, one of his three sons, Momo, was still in possession of seven houses which he had inherited from his father, almost two decades after the Hausa had lost the butchering business in Ibadan.

Thus, in 1930, there were three strategic economic and political positions in the power structure of the Quarter: Chief of the Cattle Market (*Sarkin Zango*), Chief of the Butchers (*Sarkin Pawa*), and Chief of the Quarter (*Sarkin Sabo* or *Sarkin Hausawa*). Each position had its own sphere of power, but was closely connected with the other positions. It is evident from the records on this period that although there was one official Chief of the Quarter, power and authority were in fact divided among these three positions. In effect, the three chiefs had formed a kind of collective leadership in Sabo and in the official documents for that time the three men were often referred to as 'the chiefs of Sabo' or as 'the Hausa chiefs'.

No detailed data is available to describe how the men in those positions had operated in the Quarter during the period 1916–29. The dismissal of the incumbent of the position of Chief of Sabo in 1929, without any trace of protest from Shuaibu, Yakubu, Umaru, or any other Hausa senior, is perhaps indicative of the fact that those men were only too pleased to see him go. In the light of subsequent developments, they might even have themselves plotted against the man.

However data on the relations between these three men from 1930 onwards are abundant, and reveal relations characterized by continual strife, rivalry, machinations and political subversion. No sooner had Umaru become Chief of the Quarter than he, in collaboration with Yakubu, began plotting against Shuaibu in order to cut him down to size. Within only four years Shuaibu was in fact stripped of much of his power and authority and the way was paved for Umaru to gain complete control of the Quarter.

The issue over which the battle was fought was that of the collection and distribution of the commission (*lada*) on the sale of cattle. This commission was in fact the major source of income for Sabo and the basis of its economy.

Umaru became officially Chief of the Quarter in February 1930, but already in July the same year he, together with other cattle landlords, complained to the Council that the Chief of the Cattle Market had been 'receiving money from strangers who brought in cattle for sale'. According to the Minutes, Shuaibu was warned that action would be taken against him by the Olubadan and Council if this practice continued.

A month later two separate complaints were lodged in writing to the Council against Shuaibu, one by Umaru and the other, dated only a day later, by Yakubu. Both complained of the burden of the commission they had to pay to the Chief of the Cattle Market. Umaru pointed out in his complaint that the cattle traders had been hard hit by the economic depression which had affected Nigeria—indeed the whole world—at the time.

I have to point out here that the nature of the commission (*lada*) which has been the basis of the economy of the Hausa communities in Yorubaland, had for long vexed the patience and the understanding of the British officials in Nigeria and had on many occasions during the colonial period made them take decisions and issue orders which proved later to be impractical and even ridiculous. The Yoruba chiefs were also occasionally confused over the subject but were better informed than the British. Part of the difficulty has been the result of the ambiguity of the term used. *Lada* is a Hausa word, originally derived from the Arabic word *el'ada*, meaning 'the custom'. The connotation of the word in Hausa is 'the customary payment'. But there are different 'customary payments' for different services in different trades and at different times and places.

In the sale of cattle, *lada* stands for payment for one or more of the following services: (i) accommodation for cattle dealers;

(ii) boarding for cattle dealers; (iii) fee for the broker who concludes the sale of cattle; (iv) insurance to the dealer that credit given on sales to butchers would be honoured (v) 'banking services' provided by the landlord's house in the collection of debts by the landlord's clerk and in keeping safe the cash in the landlord's house, at the landlord's own risk, until the dealer asks for it at his own convenience; (vi) market toll; (vii) keeping herds of cattle within enclosures adjoining the Cattle Market; (viii) special fee for the Chief of the Hausa Quarter for patronizing the market; (ix) patronage, or 'protection', ostensibly by local patrons.

Within Ibadan the term has stood for different payments at different times. In 1963 the rate was 13/- on each head of cattle sold in the market and was collected in cash by the broker from the buyer. Out of this amount the broker deducted for himself 3/- as his commission on the transaction and he handed over the remainder to his landlord. The landlord then paid 2/- to the northern dealer in order to remunerate him for waiting for his money, usually for a period of about four weeks. The landlord paid also 1/- to the clerk, who would later collect the money and to the 'boys'[36] who looked after the cattle on the premises of the Market. The landlord finally retained for himself the remaining 7/- to cover his expenses on accommodating and feeding the dealer, to cover his risk-taking in insuring that the credit would be eventually paid by the buyer and, when the money was collected, in keeping the money in his house until the dealer asked for it. In 1963, no money was paid to the Chief of the Cattle Market or to the Chief of Sabo (the same man, Umaru, had succeeded to the position of the Cattle Market on the death of Shuaibu in 1935) and only 6d. was paid by the buyer on each head of cattle which was kept for a night within the Cattle Enclosure which was run by the Fulani Chief (*Sarkin Fulani*).

In contrast to these arrangements in Ibadan, the commission in the town of Oyo—which is only 30 miles from Ibadan—was in 1963, 5/- on a head of cattle. Oyo is a much smaller town than Ibadan and because it is so near to Ibadan, the northern cattle dealers do not lodge with the local landlords, but only stay in the market for a few hours and then proceed southward. And because the scale of the business is so small, the landlords themselves conduct the sale on the market and do not, therefore, have to pay client-brokers or a client-clerk. Only 50% credit is given on sales, as compared with nearly 100% in Ibadan, and there is thus less charge for interest or for risk-taking. The cattle dealer receives half the pay, and then proceeds with the rest of his cattle to the South and when he returns back he collects the rest of the money on the way. Previously there had been an endless dispute between the Hausa and the Alafin of Oyo over the payment of *lada*. It lasted until 1962 and was terminated only in court. Scores of documents bear witness to the confusion in the dispute. At one stage the British officials conducted a survey to examine the practice in different places. There had been a period of many years when the Alafin had collected 1/– on each head of cattle and at one time even installed an agent in the Hausa Quarter to collect the money. At another period that same fee had been collected by the Hausa Chief of the local Cattle Market, and at yet another period it had been collected by the Chief of the Hausa Quarter.

In Ogbomosho, another Yoruba town about 60 miles north of Ibadan, the commission was in 1963, 12/– per head of cattle, out of which 1/6 was paid to the Chief of the Hausa Quarter, who was also the Chief of the local Cattle Market, 2/– was paid to the dealer, and the rest of the commission went to the cattle landlord.

In Lagos in 1963, the commission was £1 per head and was thus higher than in Ibadan principally because accommodation and board in the Capital of the Federation cost more.

Turning back to Sabo in 1930, the Chief of the Cattle Market collected 1/6 on each head of cattle sold in the Market. The money was paid out of the lump commission which the cattle landlords received. This means that the money was partly paid by the cattle landlords and partly by the butcher-buyers. Thus, both Umaru and Yakubu were financially affected, the first because he acted as landlord and the second because he acted as butcher. This meant that the cost of supplying beef in Ibadan was unnecessarily high, at a time when the demand for beef had been at a low ebb as a result of the world depression. A reduction in the costs of supply could stimulate the demand or at least could increase the dwindling margin of income for the landlords.

Umaru and Yakubu were fully supported in their stand by

the other cattle landlords and by the butchers. For Umaru, the question was not only economic but also, and probably largely, political. The payment of a special sum to Shuaibu on all sales in the Market meant the recognition of his authority over the Market which was the basis of Sabo's economy. This invested Shuaibu with a great deal of power and political influence in the Quarter and enabled him to establish important connections with Yoruba chiefs outside Sabo. There is evidence that his relations with the Yoruba chiefs were very strong and both he, and later his son and grandson, were rumoured in the Quarter to be 'bad Muslims' because of this close association with the Yoruba. Had he wanted, Shuaibu could eaily have become Chief of the Quarter and even if he was not interested in occupying the position Shuaibu's son, Gambo, unlike his father, had strong ambitions to become Chief of the Quarter. Both father and son constituted a subversive element for the authority of Umaru. Indeed, Shuaibu had maintained his own 'kingdom', because as Chief of the Market and as cattle landlord, he was patron to many men in the Quarter and he enjoyed a great degree of autonomy within his 'business house'.

Umaru, who, as his career in the following three decades shows, was a very ambitious and rather ruthless man, could not tolerate such a 'pocket' of power outside his authority within the village of which he was head. As the dispute over the commission went on, it became clear that he wanted to destroy Shuaibu completely, and by attacking Shuaibu's monopoly over the market toll, Umaru with his supporters were in fact trying to dislodge Shuaibu from the position of Chief of the Cattle Market altogether. In Umaru's petitions to the District Officer and to the Council he suggested that Shuaibu should be content with the commission which he collected from marketing the cattle of his own dealers who used to lodge with him. The District Officer eventually conducted an enquiry about the practice in other towns in this respect and discovered that at least in Ilorin the Cattle Market Chief acted as an ordinary cattle landlord and received commission only from his role as landlord.

Shuaibu was duly warned by the District Officer not to interfere with the sales conducted by the other landlords. He was also asked to recognize the authority of the Chief of the

Quarter and was warned that 'any person disobeying the Chief of Sabo would be ordered to leave the town'.

A letter from Shuaibu to the Council, dated a few weeks later, shows that Umaru and Yakubu had already stopped making payment to Shuaibu on cattle sold in the Market. And when the District Officer was asked by the Council to comment on the letter, he boldly declared: 'We are not prepared to enforce *lada*; the collection of *lada* is illegal'.

About a year later Shuaibu tried desperately to reassert his authority as Chief of the Market by submitting a petition to the District Officer and the Council, requesting permission to move from Sabo and to settle in a place near the Cattle Market, farther away from the Quarter.

This was followed by a long counter-petition signed by fourteen Hausa men, among them Umaru, Yakubu, the Chief Imam of the Quarter and the Chief of the Barbers, both objecting to the removal of Shuaibu and also asking that he should be banished from Ibadan altogether because he had gathered around him thieves and trouble makers. The petitioners claimed that they were expressing 'the decision of the whole Quarter'.

The District Officer discussed the matter with the Hausa leaders and then wrote to the Council that he objected to the removal of Shuaibu because he was a 'debtor' to many dealers who conducted their sale of cattle through him and if he left the Quarter his creditors would not be able to collect their money from him, presumably because he would then be out of the control of the Chief of the Quarter and of the moral pressure of the community.

Shuaibu then sank into insignificance in the records and died three to four years later. At the same time, the records indicate that Umaru was collecting market toll himself and that in fact he himself had assumed the role of the Chief of the Cattle Market in addition to his role as Chief of Sabo.

In the meantime, Yakubu, Chief of the Butchers, had been rapidly losing ground, both economically and politically. The Hausa hold over the butchering industry in Ibadan was being lost to the Yoruba as a result of a number of processes. Ibadan had been steadily expanding both in population and in territory and, because of the consequent increase in the demand for beef, more slab houses in different parts of the town were set up, each serving one segment of the town, and each having its own local network of distribution to market stalls and to consumers. Thus at the time when the Hausa had been concentrated in Sabo, on one side of the town, the network in which beef was distributed had been extending and ramifying continuously in all directions. Distribution to retailers required extensive contacts with Yoruba individuals and with market authorities. It also called for different credit arrangements which necessitated close personal contacts. The Hausa were incapable of solving these problems.

Another process was the rapidly growing bureaucratization of municipal administration which made the butchering industry subject to special licensing and regulations. In 1963 a butcher's licence cost something like £60–£70, after various kinds of formal and informal expenses were met. This amount is roughly equivalent of the average annual income of a gainfully employed man in Ibadan. In that year only one Hausa had a licence which he had obtained under unusual circumstances. He did not use it himself because he was not a butcher by profession but 'let it' to another Hausa who used it in his name for the payment of regular rent.

Thus exploiting the dispersion of the industry, making use of extensive local networks of relationships between people, and seeking the protection of the all-Yoruba City Council, the Yoruba captured the bulk of the butchering industry in Ibadan from the hands of the Hausa. Within a very short time, the Yoruba butchers organized themselves effectively and efficiently within a strong association under a Yoruba Chief of the Butchers. Apart from this all-town organization, the butchers in each of the eight slaughter houses organized themselves locally under an elected head to deal with their specific problems.

In the 1950's and up to the time of my field work in 1962–63, the Yoruba butchers formed a solid front within the Cattle Market to oppose and counter any manoeuvre by the solid front of the Hausa cattle landlords.[37]

These processes which led the Hausa in Ibadan to lose their hold on the butchering industry, had already been in operation in the latter years of the 1930's. Indeed Yakubu's alliance with Umaru, early in the decade, against Shuaibu had been the result of the growing difficulties which Yakubu and the other Hausa butchers were encountering in the conduct of their business in town. By the beginning of the 1940's Yakubu had already lost much business and his influence was waning.

Thus by that time Umaru emerges in the records, as well as in the accounts of informants, as the most powerful man in Sabo. He had succeeded in acquiring a large number of houses, and with his money he had started many of his clients off as traders or as agents working for him. The number of men living in his houses, and therefore paying unquestionable political allegiance to him, increased tremendously. His praise singers were loudly active on every occasion and he had gathered around him a number of influential men to act as his advisors and retainers. He had official messengers through whom he communicated with the Olubadan and with other officials in the city. His sources of income included not only his trade and activities as business landlord but also his role as arbitrator in cases of financial disputes, when he exacted 10% of the amounts involved in the disputes. He also collected fees for his service in solemnizing marriages and the naming of newly born babies and also for witnessing divorces. But he also spent lavishly by making regular payments to his advisors and other supporters. He gave money also to malams and to the needy. He maintained houses for Hausa strangers and also paid the expenses of the funeral and burial of every Hausa stranger who died in the province. His people feared him but they also respected him: they saw in him a shrewd leader who was capable of manipulating both the colonial administrators and the Yoruba chiefs to guard the interests of the Quarter's business.

Through his various roles within the Quarter, he became the centre of a widespread network of social relationships which provided Sabo with a political organization and coordinated the processes of communication, deliberation, decision-making, and action. Through his contacts and connections outside the Quarter, he served as an effective channel of co-operation with the heads of the other Hausa communities in Yorubaland for concerted action against the Yoruba in both the cattle and kola trades, and in time he became the head of the whole Hausa diaspora in Yorubaland.

Battle of the Kola and Rebellion of the Friday Mosque (1942–50)

By the early 1940's many Yoruba business and political groupings had begun to realize that Hausa political autonomy in Yoruba towns was an instrument for the development and expansion of Hausa business enterprise and monopoly at the expense of Yoruba traders. There was a great deal of agitation, in the Yoruba papers and in a series of petitions to the Ibadan Council, against alleged insulting behaviour on the part of the Hausa Chief of Sabo towards the Olubadan, against the Hausa Chief for having his own uniformed messengers and against the building up of a large central mosque in the Quarter. In a document in 1941 the chiefs of the Ibadan Council insisted that the District Officer should make the Hausa realize that, however long they might remain in Ibadan, they would always be regarded as strangers and that on no account would they be allowed in the future to 'express self determination' of any kind.

In 1942, Umaru, like his predecessor 12 years earlier, was brought to a civil court, and accused and convicted of having been in possession of stolen property. This was duly reported in the daily papers. A few days later an Ibadan (Yoruba) political association known as the Ibadan Band of Unity, presented a formal petition to the authorities demanding the immediate dismissal of Umaru from his position as Chief of Sabo.[38] Having no other alternative, the District Officer gave in, and Umaru was officially informed by the Ibadan Council that he was dismissed.

The Council eventually informed the District Officer that it was their wish that Gambo, son of the former Chief of the Cattle Market, the late Shuaibu, should be appointed as Chief of Sabo, and justified their choice on the grounds that he had been born in Ibadan and that his father had been known to them since the beginning of Hausa migration to Ibadan. But the District Officer insisted that the matter should be left to the people of Sabo to decide.

The Hausa, however, were almost unanimous in their demand that Umaru should be reinstated and solemnly declared that they would not recognize Gambo as Chief. This was supported by a massive, well-organized, campaign of petitioning. In one day,[39] ten petitions were submitted to the Council, with copies to the District Officer. Each petition was signed by one landlord or by one of the occupational chiefs and by scores of other men described as 'his followers'.

The dismissal of Umaru proved to be the beginning of a particularly turbulent period in the continuous strife between

Hausa and Yoruba. For, in the course of the previous decade, Sabo and scores of newly established Hausa communities in different Yoruba towns and villages, had become the base for a new, rapidly developing Hausa monopoly—that of the kola trade.

The kola nut is consumed widely and in large quantities by men, women and even children of West African savanna. While its major centres of consumption are in the North, the nut is grown only in the forest zone, where the necessary climatic conditions prevail. Until the end of the nineteenth century, the peoples of northern Nigeria depended for their supplies on imports brought in by very expensively operated caravans from the Gold Coast and from other neighbouring countries. With the opening up of the Lagos Kano railway line, an ever-increasing volume of imports from those countries came by sea to Lagos, to be despatched by rail to the North. These imports, however, dwindled very rapidly as farmers in Southern Nigeria, principally those in the Western Region, with much guidance and encouragement from the authorities, greatly expanded kola cultivation, as a subsidiary product, on their cocoa farms. A dramatic turning-point came with the world financial depression of the early 1930's when imports rapidly dwindled to a negligible quantity. Soon the imported nut was everywhere being replaced by the Nigerian nut whose flavour proved to be highly popular with the northern consumers. Today northern Nigeria depends heavily for its supplies on the South.

The Ibadan District developed into an important centre of supply, and in 1934 the Ibadan Native Authority Council decided to establish a special kola market on a plot adjacent to the Hausa Quarter, in order to facilitate the trade. The Council assumed that supplies would be bought by enterprising Yoruba traders from Yoruba farms in the bush and then brought to the market to be finally sold to the Hausa traders. In what seems from the records to have been a wave of enthusiasm, the Council announced that the market, which would be called 'Aleshinloye', after the Olubadan, would be opened with an official ceremony. Notices announcing the opening were to be posted in railway stations 'as far as Kano and in all the principal towns'. The Chief of Sabo was instructed to send his messengers to the northern provinces in order to announce the establishment of the market to the great merchants in the major towns, and he was to see to it that those merchants should attend the opening ceremony.

But the records covering the following years indicate that the market was a complete failure. The Hausa kola traders were not in attendance there. Dispensing with the services of Yoruba traders and middlemen, they went straight to the sources of the kola, penetrating deeply into the forest, to buy their supplies from the Yoruba farmers. At first the Hausa collectors operated from the existing Hausa communities which they used as bases, leaving in the morning and returning later in the day with the purchased supplies. But within a relatively short period they established new Hausa stations, within Yoruba settlements near the farms, which served as outposts from which Hausa commission buyers operated, with the help of locally settled Hausa guides and brokers. In a few years' time, some of these outposts developed into fully fledged and well-organized Hausa communities. The demographic, economic, and political processes involved in this development were similar to the processes which have already been discussed in relation to the growth of Sabo.

Thus in the course of the following two decades scores of such communities sprang up in Ibadan, Shagamu, Abeokuta, Agege, Ifo, Ijebu and some other districts, with each community serving as a centre of Hausa trade. Each community developed a core of permanently settled Hausa population who maintained an institutional framework which made it possible for other parts of the population to move periodically from one province to another, according to the different kola seasons.

In this way the Hausa established an elaborate, large-scale, complex, organization through which they managed to control the kola trade, to overcome the technical problems involved in it, and finally to dictate prices to the Yoruba farmers.

As Hausa monopoly over the trade tightened, the Yoruba kola traders organized for counter-action. As from the early 1930's, they began to present to the Council one petition after another, demanding that the Hausa 'strangers' should be prevented from going direct to the farms and should be forced to buy their supplies from the formally established markets in the towns. In 1940, the Council discussed the matter in a number of its meetings and reached an almost unanimous decision that a rule should be officially laid down 'that no one other than a native of Ibadan and its villages should buy kola in the Ibadan District except in the kola markets'. But the British Resident vetoed this decision on the ground that it involved direct interference with the freedom of trade.

The matter was again discussed in several meetings during the following few years when the Yoruba chiefs advanced a proposal to establish rural kola markets from which the Hausa were to be forced to buy. But here again, the District Officer objected, ruling that no one should be forced to buy or sell anywhere.

Representatives of the Yoruba kola trade, who were present in some of the sessions of the Council, also objected to the proposal, and maintained that there was no need for such markets and that all they wanted was a ruling to prohibit the Hausa from going direct to the Yoruba farms. The representative of the kola farmers, who was also present in those sessions, declared, on the other hand, that the farmers on their part were quite satisfied with the current arrangements by which the Hausa buyers came direct to their farms, since those arrangements solved for the farmers the problem of labour shortage, as otherwise large numbers of men would be required to carry the kola from the farms to the markets. The Hausa buyers brought with them their own carriers, together with the lorries which carried the kola away.

The traders' representatives were shocked by the attitude of the representative of the farmers which they later described as 'treachery'. They stated to the local authorities that the attitude of the farmers' representative was detrimental to the interests and progress of 'his own kith and kin' (meaning the Yoruba) and only helped the Hausa strangers to thrive. They claimed, furthermore, that in Hausaland the authorities prevented southern strangers from going to the villages to sell kola unless those strangers were accompanied by local Hausa brokers who extracted their commission from the strangers on the spot. In Yorubaland, on the other hand, they went on, the Hausa went to the villages, bought the kola, packed it and loaded it on their lorries and went straight to the North, evading the payment of taxes and cheating the helpless farmers.

In the end, however, the Hausa won the battle and captured

the field of middlemanship between the Yoruba farmers and the Hausa kola landlords.

But this battle was not confined to the issue of the collection of the produce. It also strained the relationships between the Hausa buyers and the Yoruba farmers, and at some stages in the continuing fight both Yoruba farmers and Yoruba kola traders joined forces against the Hausa. This was particularly the case over the payment of commission. From the start, the Hausa claimed that it was only proper and 'in accordance with the accepted custom' that the Yoruba sellers (i.e. the farmers) should pay the commission (*lada*), which amounted to 10% of the purchase price, to the Hausa commission buyers. When a Yoruba seller refused to comply with this demand the Hausa boycotted him collectively until he was forced to pay. The Yoruba were indignant and vociferously pointed out that the Hausa held a double standard in their business 'tradition', since while they insisted that sellers should pay the commission in the case of kola, they had been equally insistent that the buyers should pay the commission in the case of cattle, so that in both cases the payment was extracted from the Yoruba.

This issue of the payment of commission continued to be a sore point in Hausa-Yoruba relations and on numerous occasions the Yoruba agitated against this 'injustice' and 'bad practice'. At some stages in the dispute the Yoruba organized for action but with little success.[40] The odds against the farmers' position have been many. The farmers are many in number and, being individual producers, are scattered over a wide region with few occasions for interaction and communication among themselves. They have made many attempts to organize effectively but their associations have been mainly local and ephemeral. Those associations have come into being only during a particular, immediate, crisis, at the end of which their unity disintegrated.

As against this, the kola landlords are much fewer in number, possibly not exceeding 200 (in 1963) in the whole region. Although they are based in particular localities, they regularly and frequently meet together. As different areas have different types and different seasons for kola, a landlord buys supplies from different areas. His business interests are thus not confined to his local settlement but cover a very large part of the region. They often meet at the kola sheds of the railway stations and in the lorry parks. In addition to this interaction between the landlords, thousands of Hausa commission buyers, carriers, packers, and porters circulate, in accordance with the seasons, between the various centres, and they are also followed in this movement by men and women from different occupational categories to provide the necessary services for them. Quite apart from all this interaction, there is the organized system of communication and co-ordination of collective action which is maintained on the political level between the various Hausa communities through their respective chiefs.

Thus the attack in 1942 on Hausa 'expansionism' in Ibadan was in fact an attempt to break the tight organization of political co-ordination not only within Sabo but also between Sabo and the other Hausa communities in the area.

When the overwhelming majority of the Hausa of Sabo refused to accept Gambo as chief, a deadlock developed and lasted for 11 months during which the Quarter was thrown into turmoil. For the chieftaincy was essential to mobilize and direct the Hausa struggle against the Yoruba and it was also essential in maintaining order within the Quarter. Business began to suffer and eventually even the business landlords who had been very friendly to Umaru, after having been alarmed by the impending ruin of their business and of the economy of Sabo generally, came to realize that it was better to have Gambo as Chief than to have no chief at all.

Finally, the majority of the landlords and of their clients informed the authorities that the Quarter had now agreed to accept Gambo as Chief. Gambo was duly installed, but a few months later he suddenly died and was said to have been 'murdered' by the black magic of Umaru. The demand to reinstate Umaru as chief was revived but in view of the opposition of the Yoruba chiefs and probably as a result of guilt feelings on the part of those who had actively caused trouble to the deceased man, Sabo accepted Bashiru, the son of Gambo, as successor, who eventually remained in his office until 1947.

But, although Sabo accepted Gambo, and later Bashiru, as chief, most of the landlords and their clients continued to support the leadership of Umaru and to seize on every opportunity to demand his reinstatement. This was dictated not merely by the personal joint interests which many had with

Umaru, but because the majority believed that the man was particularly fitted for the job and that, apart from all his other qualities and of his services to the Quarter, he was also very firm and fearless in his dealings with the city's Yorubu authorities and with the British administration.

The resistance of the pro-Umaru majority to Gambo and to Bashiru, and their passive defiance of the authority and the stand of the Yoruba Council revolved around and was symbolized by the central mosque of the Quarter which Umaru had built, at his own expense, in 1939–40. Umaru, who was now not bound as Chief of the Quarter to lead his people to the city's central mosque for prayer on Friday, began to perform that prayer in the mosque which he had built, under the ritual leadership of the Chief Imam of the Quarter. This precipitated a major dispute with the Yoruba over ritual issues, since the Friday Prayer is in fact a strategic political occasion of the first order.

In Islam, the five daily prayers can be performed individually and in private. But the Friday midday prayer must be performed publicly and collectively. The prayer contains less ritual elements than the ordinary weekday, noontime prayer (*salāt el dhuhr*) but it has as a central feature a sermon which contains exhortations to piety and a special blessing for the ruler of the land, for the congregation and for the community of Islam.

According to the Maliki School of Islamic theology, to which the Hausa, the Yoruba and nearly all other West African Moslems subscribe, the prayer must be centralized in each local community.[41] All the men within the local community must perform the prayer together, in one central mosque, which is known as the 'Friday mosque' (H. *Jami'i*) under the ritual leadership of the Chief Imam and in the presence of the local ruler and the leaders of the community. A division of the Friday ritual congregation is believed to be fraught with mystical dangers which can bring about the annihilation of the whole community.

In the history of many Islamic communities, the Friday prayer has been an issue, as well as an occasion, for serious factional disputes, sometimes involving a great deal of violence, over seemingly trivial theological grounds. On analysis, these disputes turn out always to be involved in political divisions of a serious nature. This is because under the pre-industrial conditions which prevail in most of these communities, where institutional differentiation is not highly developed, the Friday prayer is, in effect, a regularly recurring social situation where political and religious issues interpenetrate and affect one another.

The prayer has therefore many political potentialities. In the first place, it tends to occasion the concentration in one place of all the men of the local community. This aspect of the prayer has always been manipulated in political struggles of various sorts in countries where public meetings are prohibited or are not institutionalized. I myself have seen on a number of occasions in different Islamic lands Friday Prayer congregations turning to serious political demonstrations for one reason or another.

Secondly, the men gather together in order to form a ritual community which requires a high degree of harmony and co-operation between its members and its groups. Individuals or groups who are enemies in ordinary secular life are required to enter the mosque and go through the prayer with pure hearts. However, under certain circumstances enmities can be so deep that the face-to-face confrontation in the prayer between factions may lead to an outbreak of violence.

Thirdly, because of the presence of the ruler or leader of the community and of the symbolic reference to him in the sermon (*Khutba*), every Friday prayer in fact signifies a renewal of allegiance to the existing political order. But this again may, under certain circumstances, lead to instantaneous or to pre-arranged political action and more than one ruler has been assassinated on this occasion. In fact the prayer has always been an ideal strategic occasion in Moslem countries for staging rebellion, as, in the presence of all the men of the community in one gathering, it is possible to assassinate the ruler and to present the community with the fact: the King is dead, long live the King.

Finally, the prayer is an occasion for reconditioning men's moods and attitudes and for what Turner has described as the 're-charging of religious symbols with significata'.[42] For in the last resort, it is within the psyches of men that the secular and the mystical interact. Men are reminded of the ultimate values underlying their political order and are also confronted with the thoughts of creation and death, reward and punishment, this life and the life to come.

These various elements which constitute the Friday prayer are differently emphasized in various Islamic communities or at various periods within the same community, even if the formal structure of the prayer is the same everywhere. Generally speaking, the prayer is emphasized and elaborately celebrated in centralized societies. Thus, for example, Mitchell reports that among the Yao important chiefs establish Friday mosques in their central villages in order to enhance their authority.[43]

Thus the decision by the pro-Umaru faction to hold a separate Friday prayer within the Quarter was in fact a political decision of great significance. Gambo, and later his son, continued to go to the Yoruba central mosque for prayer together with a new Sabo Chief Imam appointed by Gambo to replace the former pro-Umaru Imam. Within a short period the majority of Sabo men performed the Friday prayer in the Sabo central mosque. Umaru went from his house to the mosque for the prayer in an impressive demonstration, riding on his very expensively maintained horse[44] and preceded by drummers, praise singers and a large following.

There were strong and incessant protests against this defiance all through this period by Gambo and Bashir, by different Ibadan political groupings, and by the Yoruba Imamate. But nothing could be done as long as the official Chief, and the official Chief Imam of the Quarter, attended the prayer in the city's Central Mosque.

From one letter by the Yoruba 'Ibadan Band of Unity' one learns that the authorities tried to use force to quell this rebellion. 'The Olubadan', the letter tells the District Officer 'sent police and one messenger from the Chief Imam to stop the prayer on Friday but the ex-chief [Umaru] ordered the people to ignore the message . . . To pray separately, within one town has always caused the desolation of that town . . . Nothing like this is ever allowed to take place in the North . . . We demand that Umaru should be banished . . .' In one among scores of letters against Umaru, Gambo concluded: 'You appointed me king of Sabo, but [Umaru] is still King in the Quarter.

There can be no two kings in one kingdom . . .'

Umaru was summoned by the Council, by the Olubadan in

private, and by the District Officer, all of whom tried to persuade him to leave the city, but he refused, pointing out that
Ibadan was now his home town in which he had his trade which
was his only source of livelihood. The Yoruba chiefs were
inclined to banish him by force but the District Officer said
that would be against the law.

The rebellion, which centred on and was symbolized by, the
Friday prayer, continued. One anti-Umaru letter to the
Olubadan stated: '[Umaru] is only deposed nominally. He
still assumes all of his former prerogative unquestionably. He
still receives reward on marriages solemnized. He inherits the
property of the deceased. He has professional singers who
perform in the Quarter taunting songs and libellous parodies
on all who do not follow him and you know your honour that
those songs are more injuring than daggers. [Umaru] has a
large number of followers and supporters. Please have him
expelled.'

In 1947, and on the advice of an English friend, Bashiru,
son of Gambo and grandson of Shuaibu, submitted his resigna-
tion from the chieftaincy of the Quarter. In his letter giving
his decision he wrote that he was resigning because of 'the
constant unrest of mind, malice, hatred and ill will . . . manufactured by my people'.

A few months later, after further disorders and pro-Umaru
agitations, the Olubadan wrote to the District Officer that
Umaru was 'the wish of the people' and that there would be no
peace unless he was re-appointed as Chief. The District Officer
replied that under the circumstances he no longer had any
objections to Umaru's return to office.

Umaru was duly turbanned by the Olubadan as Chief and
informants speak of a whole week of feasting in the Quarter to
celebrate this victory. On Friday of that week Umaru dutifully
and devoutly led his people in a procession for the Friday
prayer at the city's Yoruba Central Mosque and continued to
do so until 1952 when he stopped for totally different reasons
which will be discussed later.

These events throw into relief the nature of the interconnectedness between the organizational requirements of
long-distance trade and the development of a distinctive tribal
polity. With the growth of the trade in cattle, the Hausa
agitated for a separate village for themselves, using their

cultural difference from the Yoruba as an ideology, and the menace of the Hausa 'thieves' as a means of pressure. On the other hand, when, largely as a result of the introduction of Indirect Rule policy by the colonial government, they were formally recognized as a distinct polity based on territorial separateness and on a system of authority of their own, they used this formal recognition not only to consolidate what they had already achieved in trade, but also to capture new economic fields in the collection of kola, in transport, and in services for settlers and for transients. The Chief of the Quarter, using some of the power which he formally derived from the Administration, helped in the co-ordination of Hausa political activity against the Yoruba on both the local and the regional levels. The Yoruba for their part soon recognized this inter-dependence between Hausa political organization and Hausa monopoly in trade so that in their reaction they attempted to attack the Hausa on both fronts.

This system of relations underlying Hausa unity and exclusiveness continued to function on these lines as long as the colonial government continued to uphold the policy of Indirect Rule. But when this policy collapsed in the early 1950's, formal recognition of Hausa distinctiveness was virtually withdrawn and Hausa political autonomy was seriously threatened by a number of disintegrative processes both from within and from without.

CHAPTER FIVE

From a Tribal Polity to a Religious Brotherhood (1951-63)

Limitations of Party Politics—The Rise of the Tijaniyya Order—The Localization of Ritual—Rituals of Social Exclusiveness

The 1950's brought about two major processes of change into the social organization of Sabo, one political and the other religious. The first came when the collapse of Indirect Rule began to undermine the political autonomy of Sabo. The second came with the dramatic and massive adoption by the Hausa of the Tijaniyya mystical order. On the surface, the two processes seem to have been independent of one another, but in fact they were closely interconnected. Within a short period after adopting the Tijaniyya, the Hausa in effect transformed their community from a tribal polity to a ritual community. In the process, their formal political organization, which was undermined by the rise of Nigerian nationalism, became informally articulated in terms of religious ideologies, symbols, myths, attitudes, loyalties, ceremonial, and power structure.

Limitations of Party Politics

Between 1916 and 1950, Hausa autonomy in Ibadan had depended directly on the principles of Indirect Rule. Their ethnic distinctiveness and the authority of their chief were formally legitimized and upheld by the colonial power. But with the rise of the Nigerian nationalist movement and with the rapid transfer of power from Britain to the new nationalist leadership, the system of Indirect Rule began to disintegrate. The unity and exclusiveness of Sabo, and indeed of the whole network of Hausa communities in Yorubaland, were now undermined.

The Hausa soon reacted to this threat by attempts to re-organize themselves in terms of the new formal political structure by manoeuvring their course in the arena of party politics. The early 1950's saw an upsurge of intensive political activities on the local, regional, and federal levels throughout Nigeria. Constitutional reforms, the re-organization of the administration, and imminent independence brought about a great struggle for power. Between 1951 and 1960, several federal, regional and local council elections were held. Offici-ally, this competition for power on all these levels was con-ducted on party, and not on tribal lines. But in fact the three national parties that dominated the political scene were largely tribal in character, with each party deriving its power from the support of one of the three major ethnic groups in Nigeria. Thus, the Northern People's Congress (N.P.C.) represented the interests of the Hausa-Fulani majority in the North, the Action Group (A.G.) represented the interests of the majority of the Yoruba of the Western Region, and the National Council of Nigerian Citizens (N.C.N.C.)[1] represented the interests of the Ibo of the Eastern Region of Nigeria.[2]

For the people of Sabo, however, this form of political ethni-city was of no great help in solving their problems, because it operated on the national, not the local, level. Their main concern was to find a substitute for the support which the now withdrawing colonial power had given to their autonomy. Previously, power and authority for all political groupings, on all levels in Nigeria, were formally derived from one foreign political source, which presumably stood over and above local, tribal, and other sectional interests. When the British began to relinquish their exercise of power in the country, however, they could not hand it over to one political entity, but had to distribute it on different levels and among different groupings.

At first, the people of Sabo found it only natural to support, and to seek the support of, the Hausa-dominated Northern People's Congress (N.P.C.). Already in 1949, when the N.P.C. was only a cultural association, its newly founded branch in Lagos, in collaboration with some Sabo agents, presented a series of petitions to the Ibadan District Officer protesting against alleged persecution of the Hausa in Ibadan and against the bad conditions prevailing in Sabo. One of the major demands made in those petitions was the setting up of 'mixed courts' in Ibadan, parallel to those that had existed in the North, to which cases involving Hausa in the Yoruba city should be referred. The petitions pointed out that the interpreters who were employed in Yoruba courts which dealt with cases that involved Hausa, did not understand the Hausa language well and that this was often detrimental to the Hausa in those cases. In one of the petitions a demand was made that the proposed mixed court should be headed by a Hausa man, and the Chief of the Quarter, Umaru, was proposed as a candidate.

There were also bitter complaints against what the petitions described as 'police persecution' of the Hausa of Sabo. In one complaint it was stated that the local police were arresting masses of Sabo prostitutes only to release them later, after collecting bribes from them. One letter named Yaro, 'Chief of the Thieves,' as a police informer who collaborated with the police against the prostitutes.

More petitions were presented in 1950 and 1951 by the newly founded Sabo Branch of the Northern People's Congress. Among other things, they complained of cases of Hausa migrants being taxed both in the North and the South. The petitioners also demanded permission to hold a separate Friday midday prayer in the Quarter. One of the most significant demands was that the Hausa community in Sabo should be placed under the protection of the Nigerian (i.e. federal) police, and not the regional (i.e. Yoruba) police. To this last demand, the Superintendent of the Police retorted in a note to the District Officer that the Hausa should be informed that as long as they chose to live in Ibadan they were within the jurisdiction of the Ibadan Authority.

In the course of this campaign of petitioning, a number of new Sabo leaders, posing as officials of the local branch of the Northern People's Congress, secured lengthy interviews with British officials during which various complaints and requests were discussed.

But the Hausa of Sabo soon learnt that within the new political structure in Nigeria, their 'natural' allegience to the Northern People's Congress was of no use in solving their political problems. Indeed some of the Hausa leaders thought that such allegiance would be harmful. I was told by informants in the Quarter that a Hausa federal minister in Lagos had advised a Sabo delegation, who had gone to him for support, that it would be in their own interests to seek the patronage of the local southern parties instead of that of the N.P.C. which, within the Ibadan context, could give them little help. The people of Sabo also learnt quickly that their support of the Northern People's Congress was of no practical consequence for that party itself, because the Hausa in Yorubaland were dispersed in many electoral constituencies and their votes would be squandered to no purpose if those votes were given to the party.

The Hausa were thus led by circumstances to take the stand that it was in their best interests to support and to get the patronage of the party in power in Ibadan. But although they followed this policy consistently in subsequent years, many of them insist that they have remained 'at heart' loyal to the Northern People's Congress. The N.P.C. branch in the Quarter continued to function and active members met from time to time to collect money to help to repatriate Hausa prisoners and to help other needy Hausa strangers.

The N.P.C. is particularly supported in the Quarter by the kola landlords who, on many occasions, have publicized their support for the party and the monetary contributions which they have made to it. The cattle landlords, in contrast, have consistently publicized their support for whichever party happened to be in power in Ibadan. This difference in orientation and in tactics between the two occupational groups has been dictated by the nature of economic organization. The cattle landlords are always apprehensive about the thousands of pounds which they give in credit to Yoruba butchers. The kola landlords on the other hand have to prove continuously to their northern customer-dealers that they are true Hausa, into whose hands, therefore, these dealers can entrust their money.

However, the general stand of the Quarter as a whole, as expressed by the landlords collectively and by the Chief, was to secure the patronage of the party which was in authority in Ibadan. Yet it was not as easy and as straightforward to carry out this policy as it sounds, because the Yoruba had for a long time been torn by internal cleavages. It is true that during the 1950's the Action Group developed into a party representing the Yoruba, but some of the cleavages within the Yoruba camp drove some of the groupings involved to forge an alliance with the N.C.N.C. 'foreign' party in order to emphasize their opposition to the other Yoruba groupings who identified themselves with the A.G. This was particularly the case within the city of Ibadan, where, because of a deep traditional division in the population, the N.C.N.C. proved to be a serious contender for power and authority against the Action Group.[3]

Thus during the early 1950's the Hausa of Sabo witnessed two southern parties contending for power in their city and it was difficult for them to decide which of the two parties to support. They would certainly have liked to wait and see which side would win the elections. But the parties themselves, in their struggle with one another, sought the support of the Hausa in the Western Region and so each party in its turn demanded support from Sabo. Thus according to well-corroborated accounts by informants, an eminent N.C.N.C. leader called on the Chief of Sabo one day early in 1952, and asked him to instruct the people of the Quarter to support his party. The Chief replied that he should first deliberate over the issue with his people, and promised to do his best to persuade them to give their support.

The next day, as the news had spread that the N.C.N.C. were about to capture the allegiance of the Hausa, the Chief of Sabo was called to a meeting by one of the most eminent Yoruba chiefs of the city, who was also an important leader of the Action Group party. The Yoruba leader asked the Hausa Chief to promise that his people would give their support to the Action Group, and when the Sabo Chief said he had been asked to support the N.C.N.C., he was reminded that the Hausa had an obligation to support the Action Group, on the grounds that this was the true party of the Yoruba, which represented the very hosts on whose land, and under whose protection, the Hausa had been living and earning their livelihood. The Sabo Chief gave his promise of support, but requested that one of the Action Group leaders should come to the Hausa Quarter and speak to the people to explain to them the aims and the organization of the party.

A few days later, Chief Obafemi Awolowo, the head of the Action Group, came to the Quarter with some of his party assistants and addressed the Hausa gathering through a microphone. It must be remembered that both the A.G. and the N.C.N.C. attached so much importance to Hausa support not only because they believed that by gaining the affiliation of the Ibadan Hausa community they would also gain the affiliation of all the tens of thousands of Hausa in the Western Region, but because they thought that they would thereby also score a great propaganda success in the North, where they were out in force in an attempt to gain the support of the masses in opposition to the ruling class which dominated the N.P.C. According to eye-witnesses, after Awolowo finished his speech the Hausa men present came forward, one after the other, and became members of the Action Group.

Later in the same year the Action Group party won the regional election and Awolowo became head of government. But soon, in 1954, the N.C.N.C. won the local election in Ibadan and the very N.C.N.C. leader who had asked the Sabo Chief for support, became the Chairman of the Council and of all of its standing committees. As a result the Hausa found themselves in a difficult situation, and for the whole duration of the N.C.N.C.'s reign in Ibadan their Quarter was ridden with serious divisions and a great deal of subversive activity. For as soon as the victorious N.C.N.C. were in office in town, they sought to get rid of Umaru, the Chief of Sabo, and to have a Hausa supporter of their own appointed in his place.

The local branch of the N.C.N.C. in the Quarter became the headquarter for the mobilization of forces that were opposed to Umaru and his faction. Any Hausa who had a personal grudge against Umaru was recruited. At the head of this developing opposition movement were Yaro, Chief of the Thieves, and Momo, son of Yakubu, former Chief of the Butchers. An important cattle landlord who had just quarrelled with Umaru over the ownership of a house in the Quarter joined in, together with all of his clients. The N.C.N.C. group within the Quarter soon launched a campaign of petitioning against Umaru and demanded his dismissal. One petition claimed that the Chief had imposed the Action Group on his people against their wishes. Another gave details of several houses in the Quarter which the Chief was said to have unlawfully inherited. One of these petitions was signed by nearly a hundred men.

Umaru reacted to this by having his own followers, who included most of the leading landlords in both the cattle and the kola trades, submitting counter-petitions, alleging, amongst other things, that the rebels were in fact well-known thieves and trouble makers.

The Chieftaincy Committee of the Council gave an interview to the spokesmen of the rebels and then decided to summon both factions, together with Umaru, to a meeting, so that the charges and the counter-charges could be made on the spot. But perhaps because the Council was dominated by the N.C.N.C., Umaru declined to attend on three successive occasions despite the official invitations which he had received to each meeting. The Committee were outraged and at the third meeting decided that 'the Assistant Local Government Inspector should be informed that on several occasions [Umaru] refused the call of the Chieftaincy Committee . . . which will not be responsible for the consequences that might result from the demand for his removal'. In another meeting, held a month later, the Minutes record that the Hausa Chief had dishonoured the invitation of the Committee, that the members were concerned about this attitude of disrespect, and that they resolved that a stipend of £2 per month which had been paid to him would be stopped immediately.

In the face of this mounting commotion, Umaru pleaded that he had been ill on all those occasions when the meetings of the Committee had been held and agreed to attend the next meeting in which he promised to face his opponents and to answer their accusations.

Two meetings were duly held in which the two Sabo factions met in the presence of the Committee. Umaru was accused of neglecting his duty as Chief, of instructing his drummers, trumpeters, and singers to chant insulting lines against his adversaries, of keeping stolen property in his houses in order to send it to the North to be sold, and of committing a host of other, minor, wrongs against some people in the Quarter. Umaru refuted the accusations one by one and was supported in this by the landlords whom he had brought with him. He finally pointed out that the spokesman of the N.C.N.C. faction, Yaro, was in fact a well-known professional gambler. Yaro was asked if this allegation was true and he admitted it. This made a bad impression on the Committee who later decided that the grievances against the Chief were not serious enough to warrant his dismissal and that it was sufficient to admonish Umaru to be more cooperative with his opponents.

This factionalism on party lines within the Quarter continued, though with diminishing intensity, until the declaration of the Emergency Situation in the Western Region in 1962, when all party activities were banned and the Region was put under a federal Administrator. When the emergency was later lifted, Awolowo, the Action Group leader, went to detention to face trial while Akintola, formerly also a leader in the same party, returned to Ibadan as regional Prime Minister to form a new party, the U.P.P.

Thus at the beginning of 1963 there were three southern parties operating in Sabo: A.G., N.C.N.C., and U.P.P. The N.C.N.C. influence had in the meantime diminished, and for several weeks the Hausa tried to make up their minds whether to remain loyal to the Action Group party or to transfer their allegiance to the U.P.P. At this stage I witnessed the curious phenomenon of three A.G. Hausa leaders in the Quarter paying a visit to Awolowo in detention in Lagos to express their continued support for him, then hurrying back to Ibadan to join in a Hausa delegation that went to welcome Akintola back as Premier, then returning back to the Quarter to hoist the A.G. flag on the branch office of the A.G., and finally sitting down in the same office to plan the establishment of a branch of the U.P.P.—now anti-A.G.—in the Quarter. When the men observed that I was baffled they laughed and one of them pointed out to me that the Hausa, being strangers in Ibadan, must be careful in declaring their loyalties and must always support the party that held power. As the situation was not clear at the time and no one could tell the outcome of the new A.G.–U.P.P. cleavage they had to be on the safe side and so woo both camps until the issues became clearer.

It is evident from all this that the Hausa of Sabo have not been able to re-organize their ethnic polity in terms of the new major organization of power in Nigeria. The most that they were able to do was to have a Sabo man elected as member of the Ibadan City Council. Informants say that when early in the 1950's Awolowo went to Sabo to urge the Hausa to join the A.G., the Hausa promised their support if they would be allowed to send a representative to the Council. Awolowo is said to have agreed, but to have made it a condition that the Hausa councillor ought to know English. But as no Hausa in the Quarter at the time spoke English the Hausa sent an English-speaking young man from among the Kaka Gida group of the Quarter as their representative. At the same time about ten Hausa young men, including the son of Umaru and the sons of some other leading landlords, began to study English intensively, under an Ibo teacher, to prepare themselves for the new opportunities. In the next election a Hausa young man from this group was elected and continued in this position until 1962. But he was very much of an outsider within the Council and throughout his career in the Council he did not succeed in achieving anything for the Hausa. He was affiliated to the A.G. and was always inhibited from betraying any traces of 'tribalism' which has always been regarded by all the parties as an enemy of progress.

The Hausa also failed to get real support for their exclusive polity from the party in power. Even when the Hausa supported the A.G. and when the A.G. was in undisputed authority in the city and in the Region, the support which the Hausa could get was limited and very often questionable. This is because the Action Group had to defer to Yoruba pressure-groups within its confines, and among these groups were the Butchers and the Kola traders and farmers. And when disputes between Hausa and Yoruba over trade arose, the A.G. had to support the Yoruba side.

But a more serious development was the subversive process that party politics brought into the social structure of Sabo. In the first place, the new party political activities brought about interaction between Hausa and Yoruba, in meetings, in negotiations, and sometimes even in social gatherings. This interaction occurred within modern groupings, under new myths, ideologies, and symbols that were inimical to ethnicity. And because the Hausa were only a minority, numbering a few thousands in a city of about three-quarters of a million, there was the danger that the Hausa would become less 'tribal' in their sentiments and would even in time become to some extent assimilated. This interaction between Hausa and Yoruba would have coincided with an even more intensive interaction in the field of Islamic learning and Islamic ceremonial.

Interaction of this sort was dangerous to the myth of Hausa distinctiveness. In business terms this meant that Hausa northern dealers would be reluctant to entrust their money and goods into the hands of half-Hausa or assimilated Hausa. On the other hand, if the distinction between Hausa and Yoruba became blurred there would be no way of preventing Yoruba from infiltrating into the trade and would in time put an end to Hausa monopoly. Above all, Hausa collective action would be greatly weakened as the very principle holding them together would have been broken.

Party politics was disintegrative of Hausa autonomy in yet a more serious way in that it greatly weakened the authority of the Chief of the Quarter. This was the result not only of the withdrawal of formal support under Indirect Rule, but of the growing ability of the secretaries of the Sabo branches of the major parties to mediate between Hausa individuals and the authorities. The increasing power of Yaro, derived from connections outside the Quarter, became a disturbing challenge to the Chief's authority and there was a time when it was rumoured that he would replace Umaru as Chief. This increasing weakening of the authority of the Chief affected the very distinctiveness of the Hausa in that the Chief was finding it increasingly more difficult to force individuals to observe collective action that was necessary for the continuity and functioning of Sabo as a distinctive polity.

The Rise of the Tijaniyya Order

It was during this period of intensive, but frustrating and disintegrative party political activities, that the Hausa of Sabo adopted the Tijaniyya order. In the course of only two years, 1951–52, the overwhelming part of the Hausa joined the order. In 1963, 85% of the men in the Quarter were Tijanis. About 10% were not affiliated to any order, either because they were still too young to join or because they were undecided as to whether to settle in the Quarter or to return to the North. Only about 5% of the men belonged to the Kadiriyya order, which had been the main rival order to the Tijaniyya throughout West Africa for many decades.

Of the eight mosques in Sabo, only one is associated with the Kadiriyya. This is a mosque which was especially built for the followers of the Kadiriyya by Momo, son of Yakubu, former Chief of the Butchers. Momo was by now very bitter against Umaru, the Chief of Sabo. He believed that Umaru had deprived his father of his former position, enterprise and wealth, and had in the end killed him by black magic. In 1963,

Momo was lying ill in bed, fully convinced that his illness was due to the evil magic of Umaru. One day, during the period of my fieldwork in the Quarter, he saw a black bird, with a ring round its neck, perching in his yard. He was greatly agitated, jumped out of his sick-bed, ran out of the house, and then into the Chief's Office and shouted at the Chief: 'You will never succeed in murdering me'. Momo eventually died, only a few weeks before I left the field towards the end of 1963.

Thus, when party politicking began, Momo not only organized the N.C.N.C. party grouping against Umaru, but also established the Kadiriyya group in the Quarter. The Tijaniyya developed into the formal order of the Quarter to the extent that the people held the attitude that 'you do not become one of us if you are not a Tijani'. The Kadiriyya on the other hand developed into a pocket of extreme defiance and antagonism against the Chief and his 'establishment'. Its members included a few of the settlers who were hostile to Umaru, for one reason or another, and whose occupations did not require much co-operation within the Quarter. A larger element within the Kadiriyya consisted of new migrants who had been Kadiris before migrating to the South and who had not yet decided to remain in the Quarter. On the other hand, settlers who before their migration had been Kadiris changed their allegiance to the Tijaniyya.

The Tijaniyya order was founded in North Africa towards the end of the eighteenth century.[4] Throughout the nineteenth and the present centuries it advanced in many parts of West Africa. This advance occurred in waves at various times and in some places that were characterized by serious political upheavals. Towards the beginning of the 1950's a very large number of Islamic communities, in many West African countries, adopted the order. Although no reliable monographic studies or surveys about the spread of the order in these communities are available, some writers think, on the basis of impressions, that the order made many recruits in the Hausa-Fulani North during the 1950's. Crowder makes the interesting observation that in northern Nigeria, the Tijaniyya has become particularly strong in Kano province and has thus emerged as a rival to the traditionally dominant Kadiriyya in Sokoto, the seat of the Fulani emirs. Thus many people in Kano have become Tijanis in order to give expression to their opposition to the hegemony of Sokoto.[5] A number of writers have also pointed out that the Tijaniyya has been advancing among the Yoruba.[6]

From the evidence which I collected, however, it is clear that the Tijaniyya came to Sabo neither from the Yoruba nor from the Hausa in the North. The Hausa of Sabo had known about the Tijaniyya long before this period through various contacts, but the order had never gained a foothold in the Quarter. The first two Tijani ritual masters (*mukaddams*) ever to operate in the Quarter were appointed late in 1950. One of them was a father's sister's son of Umaru. They received their ritual instructions from a total stranger to this part of West Africa, a shaikh of the order from the Senegal, who had come by sea to Lagos and then proceeded northwards and visited Ibadan. Later, the same shaikh also visited northern Nigeria and appointed masters there. The Hausa adopted the order in the 1950's because the Tijaniyya provided solutions to some of the political problems they faced as a result of the coming of party politics. The process was of course neither rational nor intended by individuals. It was 'vehicled' in a series of countless small dramas in the lives of men. This process will be discussed later in greater detail. It is not important for the present to consider what were the motives of individuals in joining the order, or whether the Tijaniyya was adopted as a result of spontaneous decisions taken by the Hausa of the Quarter or as a result of cultural diffusion from either the North or from the Yoruba. What is analytically significant here is what the Tijaniyya has done to Sabo and how it has interacted with the other social institutions of the Quarter.

The Tijaniyya introduced a number of far-reaching changes in the organization of ritual in Sabo.

It greatly intensified ritual activity, for in addition to the usual five daily prayers that are ordained by orthodox Islam, it enjoins two ritual duties a day, one is the *wirds* (the Hausa call it *wurudi*) which consists of the recitation of the following items: (1) The formula of penitence—'I beg forgiveness of God'—100 times; (2) *Salat el-Fatih*, a special prayer in praise of the prophet Muhammad, 100 times; (3) 'There is no God but Allah', 100 times. The *wirds* can be observed individually. The second ritual is known as the *wazifa* and consists of reciting the following formulae: (1) the formula of penitence—'I ask forgiveness of Allah, etc.'—30 times; (2) *Salat el-Fatih*, 50 times; (3) 'There is no God but God, 100 times and (4) the special distinguishing prayer of the order known as *Jawharat el-Kamal*, 12 times.[7] The *wazifa* is held in the evening and is performed collectively.

The Tijaniyya also collectivized ritual in the Quarter. In orthodox Islam a man can perform all the five daily prayers privately on his own. But a Tijani must perform at least the evening prayer in a group under his own ritual master. This has led to the formation of a new kind of ritual grouping in Sabo.

The Localization of Ritual

The Tijaniyya also localized the daily ritual within the Quarter. Formal Islam is universalistic and a man can perform his daily prayers anywhere he chooses. But a Tijani must have at least the evening prayer and the evening ritual duty of the order, the *wazifa*, under his own ritual master, the *mukaddam*, from whom he gets his ritual 'instructions', unless of course he happens to be travelling away. Thus one of the most impressive scenes an observer can witness in the Quarter is the massive gatherings of all the men, at about seven o'clock in the evening, in groups which fill every yard or verandah in the area, for the performance of the ritual. Even the ordinary weekday, midday prayer (*Salat el-Dhuhr*) is attended by large gatherings of men, some of whom halt their business in the centre of the town and make a two or three mile journey to the Quarter for that purpose.

The localization of Sabo's rituals was completed in 1952, when the Hausa finally seceded from the Yoruba-dominated Friday midday prayer (*Salat el-jumu'a*) in the Central Mosque of Ibadan, and began to hold that prayer in the central mosque of the Quarter, the very mosque that Umaru had built in about 1940 and in which he had organized his rebellion during the 1942–48 period. It all started with a dramatic suddenness when one day early in 1952 a number of important Sabo malams came to the Chief of the Quarter to tell him that it had come to their knowledge that an important Yoruba Imam in the city had been allowing his wives to go out of their house in daylight to trade in the market-place. The Hausa Chief called a meeting with his advisors, the business landlords, and the leading malams. A decision was unanimously reached to secede from the Yoruba Central Mosque of Ibadan and to hold the prayer in the Quarter.

A bitter polemic ensued between Sabo's malams and the leaders of Yoruba Moslems. The city's Imamate wrote practically scores of protests, which they addressed to the Olubadan in Council and to the colonial administration, auguring grave mystical calamities that would befall the city if the heretical Sabo movement was allowed to succeed. In those protests the Yoruba Imamate pointed out that in the Hausa towns in the North only one Friday mosque was allowed in each town and this was confirmed in correspondence between the Ibadan District Officer and many District Officers in the North. Meetings were arranged between Yoruba and Hausa malams, in which the Yoruba side argued against the separation of the Friday ritual community on various theological grounds. The Olubadan summoned the Hausa Chief and talked to him on the subject but the Chief was reported to have shouted rudely at the Olubadan, telling him that the Hausa were free to worship Allah as they chose and that freedom of worship was one of the principles upheld by the new constitution.

This secession from the Yoruba Central Mosque was of great consequence because it meant that the Hausa had excluded themselves from the growing masses of Yoruba Moslems in the city. Today, the only ritual co-operation between them and the city's Moslems is their nominal attendance at a general communal prayer-ground, the *masallacin idi*, on the two major feasts of Islam.[8]

Otherwise, Sabo is completely separated from the city's Islamic organization. One of the most significant manifestations of this separation is that the Quarter starts feasting and fasting on directives from the North, and not from the city. Islamic feasts and the fasting in Ramadhan have no fixed dates in the calendar, but follow the appearance of the new moon in certain lunar months. Thus the new moon may be seen by people in Ibadan and the city's Yoruba Moslems would then start ceremonial, but Sabo would wait for a word from Kaduna, capital of the Northern Region, to be given to the Chief on the telephone. On such an occasion which I witnessed in 1963, messengers from other Hausa centres in the vicinity of Ibadan had travelled to Sabo and sat near the Chief's office waiting to carry the news back to their communities, even though the awaited news was being given on the radio.

The Yoruba Moslems in Ibadan are in no way less orthodox or less learned than the Hausa, and a few Sabo malams with whom I talked privately on the subject acknowledged this. But the prevailing myth in the Quarter is that the Yoruba are not good Moslems and that the Hausa must therefore stand apart to preserve their ritual purity and religious enlightenment and many men seemed to be quite genuine in holding this view.

On the face of it, Sabo's secession from the Yoruba Friday prayer in 1952 was not a novel development because something similar had occurred in the 1943–48 period.[9] But in that earlier period secession was not formal and was not made in the name of the whole Quarter. It was a secession by a large political faction within the Quarter and it served as a symbol, and as an organizational mechanism, for resistance against another faction and against interference in the affairs of Sabo from without. When Umaru was thrown out of office at the time he had the economic and the political power to dominate the Quarter, but he did not have legitimate formal authority, and by organizing and manipulating the Friday prayer he gained moral support which gave him, in the eyes of his followers, legitimate authority within the community. Furthermore, the prayer had also served as a weekly occasion for his supporters to meet and to renew their allegiance to him. Indeed, informants in 1963 emphasized that during those days men in the Quarter were not at all religious and that they had been given to drinking beer and to spending most of their free time gambling or in the company of prostitutes. They did not even observe the simple religious duties. The impression one gets about that period is that many men who had not been religious, attended the Friday prayer in answer to the political call of Umaru. Umaru could not then have organized political meetings or rallies to fight his political battle against his opponents because the city's authorities would have banished him and stopped the meetings. But gathering for the performance of a prayer was something else, even though this was a prayer held in defiance of the city's Yoruba Imamate. Indeed, Umaru's opponents at the time realized that that prayer was political in nature and at least on one occasion the local police were sent to stop it, while on another occasion Bashiru's faction staged a physical assault on Umaru's congregation.[10]

But in 1952, the Prayer symbolized the ritual separation of the whole of Sabo from Yoruba Islam in the city. What the prayer now signified was the assertion that, despite the principles of Nigerian nationalism, which were formally opposed to tribalism, and despite Sabo being submerged within the large Yoruba city, the Hausa remained distinct as a ritually delineated community of pure and superior Moslems. In this way the Quarter could still maintain, though implicitly, the motto: Our way of life is different; we Hausa are different—a myth whose continuity is essential for the maintenance of Hausa autonomy and Hausa monopoly in trade.

Rituals of Social Exclusiveness

One of the most significant political aspects of the intensification, collectivization, and localization of ritual in the Quarter is that men are on the one hand inhibited from developing much intimate social interaction with the Yoruba and are on the other hand put in situations which are conducive to the development of intensive, spontaneous, social interaction within Sabo.

The Tijaniyya created permanent ritual groupings in Sabo. Initially a ritual group would be brought together mainly through the dyadic relationship between an initiate and his ritual master. But as soon as the different initiates begin to gather together as a ritual group every evening, the gathering becomes transformed into a permanent social group, whose members interact with one another intensively. Men come to the ritual some time before it begins and linger on in company long after it ends. Through the social interaction occasioned by the performance of the ritual, members of the ritual assembly develop small, intimate, primary groupings of various sorts, which are characterized by intense sentiments of loyalty, affection, co-operation, and mutual help. The grouping truly develops into a brotherhood[11] and members call one another by the term 'brother'. Even men who, before becoming Tijanis, called one another 'brother' begin to understand the term in a new sense and a new dimension. When I questioned informants as to what they meant by the term 'brother', they often referred to various forms of close friendship, to bonds holding them together in a foreign country, or to bonds resulting from common province of origin in the North—all depending on the context of the conversation—but many added, 'We are brothers in religion'.

One form of such primary groupings is that of 'the dining company'. Nearly all the men of the Quarter eat their meals outside the house in company with other men. The dining men meet in the same group regularly, in a verandah, or on the side of the road, and the food is brought to them from their homes by small children. The food of each man is brought in one or two covered bowls. Then the men start eating from one another's food.

Another kind of grouping is that of seeking company for entertainment. After the evening ritual, numerous small groups of men can be seen drifting to various kinds of amusements until the late hours of the night.

During my fieldwork I concentrated for a few weeks on the close observation of the social interaction between 32 men who were informally associated together in what they referred to as 'The Group'. Twenty-four of them were Tijanis, initially under the same ritual master. Of the remaining eight men, two were at that time in the process of being considered for admission to the order by the same master, four were recent migrants, and two were adamant for joining. Of the 32, 28 formed four separate dining sub-groups, each having a special place for eating, 25 formed two praying sub-groups, the members of each praying together four times a day, and 8 attended a special daily Arabic class under the master. Fifteen members formed three small sub-groups with particularly close 'brotherly' attachment, such that any member would represent any other member in his betrothal ceremony or in the naming ceremony of his child, since in these ceremonies he is not allowed by custom to be present but should be represented by a close 'brother'. The sub-groups cut across one another so that a member of a praying sub-group had some different associates in the dining-sub-group, and so on. All the members of 'The Group' made contributions to help in the wedding of a member and they also assisted one another in times of need. Only two members were related to each other as actual brothers, two others were related as first cousins, but the remaining 28 were not related to one another by kinship or by affinity, or by place of origin, or by trade. The Group grew principally out of the ritual Tijaniyya grouping under one master. Those members of the Group who were not Tijanis had been brought into the Group as friends by the Tijani members. All the members spent their leisure time within the Quarter and did not have Yoruba as friends. They sought entertainment in the company of one another. Above all, the members formed a reference group, with special norms, values, and rules to which individual members deferred in their conduct. Members seemed to be constantly concerned with whether their conduct in different situations would be approved or disapproved of by 'The Group'.

There were many other groupings of this type in the Quarter. Membership was not exclusive, so that some of the members of a group interacted with members from other groups, although each group tended to have a core of members who spent most of their free time in interaction within the group.

The person-to-person relationships that arise in such close and intensive interaction are moral relations and are therefore governed by categorical imperatives, by intrinsic values and norms. They are supported by myths, symbols, and ceremonials that are derived from the 'blueprint' of Hausa traditional culture, which is carried as 'mental luggage', as Forde puts it[12] by the migrants from the North. Many of these types of relations are new and have risen in the Hausa diaspora, under circumstances that are different from those prevailing in Hausa societies in the North. But because of the structural opposition with the Yoruba these new relationships are expressed in the idiom of Hausa culture whenever possible. If moral relationships of this sort were formed in the course of primary social interaction between Hausa and Yoruba, other cultural idioms would have been developed. If relations with the Yoruba were particularly cooperative and friendly, some Yoruba customs might have been adopted.[13] The Yoruba side on the other hand (other things being equal) might have also adopted some Hausa customs. As a result of these processes the cultural division between the two sides might have been blurred.

Thus one of the unintended results of the ritual changes that the Tijaniyya brought into Sabo was the renewed emphasis on traditional Hausa values, norms, beliefs, and practices and the exclusion of Yoruba customs from the diaspora culture.

A second result is that the intensification of social interaction within the Quarter has brought about a homogenization of Hausa diaspora culture. The different brands of Hausa culture which migrants from different parts of Hausaland brought with them are blended in a new milieu and the outcome is a new Hausa culture which is peculiar to the settlers.

This homogenizing process brought by the Tijaniyya has operated not only within one Hausa community but within the entire Hausa diaspora in Yorubaland. Indeed the Tijaniyya ritual groupings have become the institution of stability-in-mobility par excellence for the whole Hausa diaspora. When men from one Hausa community move to another Hausa community they immediately join one of the ritual groupings for the performance of the rituals of the order and as soon as the ritual is over they begin conversation with other Tijani brothers and within a short period become socially incorporated within one or another of the groupings. As a result, there is a standardization in culture between the various communities. Rouch observed that the Hausa migrant communities in Ghana share a distinct brand of Hausa culture.

Thus on the one hand intensive social interaction which the Tijaniyya brought, creates strong moral obligations between members of the same community and between them and members from other communities in the Hausa diaspora, while on the other hand it inhibits the development of similar moral obligations between Hausa and Yoruba. The political consequences of such a situation are far-reaching. Political action is the result of decisions taken by individuals and, as recent research about the nature of small social groups has shown, is greatly influenced by moral obligations even in highly differentiated and bureaucratized industrial societies.

Thus with the rise of the Tijaniyya, Hausa identity and exclusiveness which were imperilled by the coming of party politics, are now cast in a new form and validated in terms of new myths. Brotherly relations which were based on tribal affiliation within a foreign land are now based on affiliation within a mystical order. Political obligation in the Quarter is now rooted in intensive moral relations and ritual values.

These changes created a new power structure in Sabo and effected a reorganization of the authority of the Chief of the Quarter, without which the Quarter's distinctiveness cannot be maintained.

CHAPTER SIX

The Ritualization of Political Authority

The Composite Nature of Authority—The Mobilization of Ritual Power—Malams in the Process of Political Communication—Malams in the Process of Decision-Making —From Witch to Hajji—Ritual and Moral Sanctions— New Ritual Mechanics—A Religious Blueprint for Political Change

The Tijaniyya effected a reorganization of the system of political authority within the Quarter, as articulated in terms of new beliefs, symbols, values, and power structure. Without a system of authority, the distinctiveness and political autonomy of Sabo could not have been maintained. Authority is necessary to apply pressure to individuals to fulfil their obligations to the collective interests of the community and to maintain mechanisms for political communication, for formulation of problems, deliberation, decision-making and co-ordination of action.

Authority is also essential for the maintenance of a number of administrative functions that are necessary for the continuity of the community, especially when that community is, like the Hausa Quarter, several thousand strong. The Chief of Sabo acts as a Shari'a judge, regulating marriage, divorce, inheritance and custody over children. He also arbitrates in disputes and generally seeks to uphold what the community regards as just. He appoints occupational chiefs who uphold professional standards and discipline and who serve as a link between members of the occupation and the Chief. He runs a number of public services, maintaining mosques and a cemetery, helping the needy, taking care of the funerals of Hausa strangers who have died and looking after a number of houses for strangers,

where Hausa transients who come to him for help are accommodated. He also officiates in marriage and in naming
ceremonies.

The Composite Nature of Authority

To be effective, authority always rests on power. Indeed
authority is simply the legitimate exercise of power. The power
behind authority is always composite, as it is derived from
different kinds of social relations: political, economic, ritual and
moral. Even in societies which are ruled by unpopular dictators,
the authorities make use of power derived from networks of
moral and ritual relations.

Thus the Chief of Sabo has always relied for the maintenance
of his authority on all these forms of power, some of which have
been personal, relating to the incumbent of the office, while
others have been of a more public character, being associated
with the office itself. But the different sources of power are
combined in different proportions in various societies, or at
various periods within the history of the same society. Thus
during the Indirect Rule period, the Chief of Sabo derived a
great deal of power from the backing of the Olubadan and,
ultimately, from the colonial administration. He was then
authorized to arrest thieves and other offenders and hand them
over to the police. In criminal cases that were not within his
jurisdiction he was always asked to give his views by the police
and by the court and these views were very often crucial.
Informants who were settlers in the Quarter at that time consistently repeat that in practice the Chief had far more
authority and far more supporting power from the Olubadan
and from the British administration than he was entitled to
formally. It is evident that it was a routine practice on the part
of the Chief to resort to pressure when the need arose, by
threatening to report them to the authorities, or to withold his
help as an intermediary between his people and the authorities
when these people needed it. For, at the time, he was almost
the sole mediator between his people and the authorities.

With the coming of party politics, Indirect Rule collapsed,
and the Chief lost a great deal of this coercive power. The
traditional chiefs of the town from whom he had formally
derived his authority had now themselves lost most of their
power and were reduced to ceremonial figures. On the other

hand the local Sabo secretaries of the political parties, as well as some special 'political brokers', like Momo, began to fix things for people in the Quarter because those secretaries had easier access to the newly emerging political and administrative elite than the Chief. Furthermore, the development of party factionalism within the Quarter and the inevitable identification of the Chief with one faction or another, weakened his political authority in other respects.

The Mobilization of Ritual Power

It was this vacuum in the power structure behind the authority of the Chief that the Tijaniyya soon filled and it thereby changed the whole character of authority in the Quarter. The Tijaniyya did this by creating a new ritual power structure. It intensified, routinized, and institutionalized the dependence of laymen on the ritual powers and services of the malams.

In orthodox Islam there is no priesthood and every believer can have direct access to God. Indeed in every one of the five daily prayers ordained by orthodox Islam there is a phase, known as the time of sanctification[1] when the worshipper enters into communion with God. The Tijaniyya, however, emphasizes the principle of intercession according to which the sacred emanation of Allah, often referred to as *baraka*, is mediated to members of the order through a chain[2] of ritual masters and saints. A Tijani man is, therefore, ritually dependent on his master who initiated him into the order and who is thus his direct link to the chain of mediators.

The order concentrated ritual powers in the hands of the malams in a number of ways. Unlike most of the other Islamic orders, the Tijaniyya is exclusive in that it does not allow its members to pay allegiance to any other order. In most Islamic countries a man can belong to many orders simultaneously and Ahmad al-Tijani, the founder himself, belonged to many orders in the course of his religious career. A Tijani, however, can belong only to the Tijaniyya.

The Tijaniyya in Sabo is a highly puritanical movement and one of its major missionary efforts has been directed towards freeing Islam from the remnants of pagan beliefs and practices. One of its most important missions in West Africa has been its crusade against the bori cult. Despite at least a century and a half of Islamization, the Hausa, in the North as well as in the South, have believed in and practised this cult. According to the cult, most of the afflictions from which people suffer are due to the activities of a wide array of different types of spirits.[3] Cure is obtained through the performance of elaborate rituals to the spirit. Islam had always been opposed to the cult which, in time, ceased to be a folk cult, and became a specialization confined to select groups which performed the rituals on behalf of ordinary people. Informants in Sabo are unanimous that until about the middle of the 1950's there was, in the Quarter, a strong and large body of bori initiates who attended to the needs of the population. They were well organized and had their own chieftainess who was officially recognized by the Chief of the Quarter. But the Tijaniyya in Sabo directed a relentless attack against the cult. In the ceremony of initiating a man into the order, the initiate makes a solemn promise to have nothing to do with the cult. Today there is only a handful of bori practitioners whose sessions are held in secret. With the death of the last bori chieftainess in the Quarter in the mid-1950's no other woman was appointed and the position practically ceased to exist.

However the belief in the spirits continues under a different guise. In their crusade against the cult, the malams did not deny the existence of the spirits but they identified these spirits with the different categories of *jinns* whose existence is acknowledged in the Koran. In Islamic theology, however, the wicked *jinns* and their master, Satan, are not independent mystical entities but are the creation of God, in accordance with His own designs which no one can comprehend. But there are secret ritual formulae and special prayers, which the malams know, and through which the afflictions of men can be cured. Some malams are said to have a number of *jinns* under their control. Thus today, people who would have taken their problems to the *bori* practitioners before the Tijaniyya came, now go to consult the malams.

The dependence of laymen on malams became institutionalized after the coming of the Tijaniyya. When men are initiated into the order, at about the age of twenty, they become permanently linked to their ritual master, not only for ritual purposes but also in matters relating to daily life and to general social conduct. A man is initially accepted into the order only when the master is satisfied that the man is of good character and that he can be relied on to lead a life of purity and to refrain from such practices as drinking alcohol or smoking. Thus, apart from their continual ritual dependence on their malams, men's general social behaviour is also subject to the seniority of their masters. In this way, men's religious, moral and social perceptions are guided and reshaped by the malams. A man's ritual master is usually also the malam who officiates in the ceremonies of the life cycle of the man and of his family. The man's child usually gets his education in the 'Arabic School' run by the master and the man himself attends daily 'Arabic classes' for adults given by the master himself, when texts of Islamic learning are discussed and interpreted in terms of practical daily life.

Malams in the Process of Political Communication

By their various activities, the malams have become the principal channel through which political communication is effected in the community, as they have become the link between chief and subjects, landlords and clients, one age group and another. In their capacity as diviners they receive messages of distress from people and pass these messages to the malams of higher position within the ritual hierarchy.

The threat of the coming of party politics was felt first and foremost by the thirty business landlords who controlled most of the housing and employment in the Quarter. But quite apart from this threat, they have always suffered from many subversive processes that are inherent in their position itself. As described above, most of their wealth is contained in housing and in cash, but ownership of the houses is not documented and the cash is usually kept in simple wooden chests inside the houses, guarded against theft mainly by ritual charms. Part of the money is frequently given to assistants to act as agents in the North or in other parts of the Hausa network of trading communities, without any documents, receipts, or detailed accounts playing any part and it frequently happens that these agents do not honour their obligations to their patrons who, in this way, sometimes lose large sums of money. Furthermore, it is in the nature of their business in long-distance trade, that landlords guarantee dealers from the North against the loss of the money or goods from these dealers.

Because of the pre-industrial conditions prevailing in the country, debtors sometimes default and goods are sometimes lost in transit and the landlords involved thus have to pay for these losses.

These and many other processes have always made the position of the landlords highly vulnerable and in my field study I recorded cases of landlords losing their wealth and position and becoming simple clients, and of clients rising to the position of landlord. The landlords are thus perennially ridden with grave anxieties and rely heavily on the mystical services of the malams.

In Sabo belief there seems to be no limits to the mystical powers of the malams in effecting dramatic changes in individual fortunes and in interpersonal relationships, and the popular stories about their exploits are countless. Malams are, therefore, power; and the landlords are always on the look out for particularly 'big' malams in order to attract their service. For they believe that without the power of malams a landlord cannot meet his numerous problems. Even the most enlightened of the Hausa of Sabo assured me that much of the power and wealth of the Chief of the Quarter is derived from the mystical support given to him by the Chief Imam and some other big malams. Informants were also emphatic that the Sardauna of Sokoto, the Premier of Northern Nigeria until the coup in 1966, owed all of his powers and influence to a hundred powerful malams who worked day and night for him on various missions in the mystical world and who thus helped him to overcome problems and to defeat his enemies.

A man in Sabo will not undertake any enterprise before asking his malam to divine the prospects for him. If you want to get a loan from a wealthy man you must first ask the help of your malam. The malam will offer a special prayer and write a special formula in order to soften the heart of the wealthy man so that he will be favourably disposed towards giving you the loan. Or, if your property has been stolen, your malam will consult the mystical world and will find the thief for you. If you want a certain girl to fall in love with you, or if you want to pass an examination, to get a special political office or even to inflict harm on an enemy: in all contingencies you go to your malam for help.

The Hausa of Sabo believe that a great part of the power of

the malam consists in *knowing* the right formula for the purpose. In the Koran and in the books of Islamic learning there is a formula for everything. A powerful malam is thus first of all a man who knows a wide range of formulae for a wide range of problems. But, informants qualify, this is not enough, as any man who can read Arabic books can learn a great number of formulae. Indeed there are books sold in Sabo market, written in Arabic and published mainly in North Africa, in which you can find classified formulae for almost every contingency in life and the men who can read Arabic in the Quarter often buy these books and spend long hours of their spare time in formulae hunting, in a spirit of treasure hunting. One of my informants confided to me that he had even found a formula for birth control. Formulae alone, however, are useless unless one also knows the secret prayers which accompany them and these prayers are not recorded and are known only to the malams. Yet even these prayers can be imparted and taught to laymen, but their efficacy, in conjunction with the formulae, is still not guaranteed as it is essential to satisfy a third condition which only few can do: that is to have 'purity of heart', to which the Hausa refer by the Arabic word *tahara*. This is a quality which few men possess and those few do not go out of their way to show it. A true malam is a devout man who does not directly seek worldly pleasures and who uses his mystical powers only for morally approved ends.

The malams in Sabo differ greatly in satisfying these conditions. They differ in the amount of knowledge they have of formulae. The Hausa of Sabo say that a good malam does not say he knows all the formulae. Some malams would tell a man that they know the correct formula for the solution of his particular problem when in fact they do not know the formula or the secret prayer which should accompany it. A good malam is also very modest, is not after wealth or power, and is devoted to learning and teaching only. But it is nevertheless the case that worldly comfort and even wealth are criteria by which the greatness of a malam is measured. This is because the more powerful a malam is the more sought after he is by people and the more presents he gets. On the other hand, the wealthier a layman is the greater are his chances of attracting to his service powerful malams. A malam in Sabo needs housing to accomodate not only himself and his family but also the many pupils who are sent from other Hausa communities to learn under him. He also needs space to teach small children, with the help of his assistants, and to hold daily classes for adult men. A malam also needs a steady income to support himself, his family and his senior pupils. In Northern Nigeria, most malams combine religious service with a trade. In Sabo, on the other hand, only a fraction of the 119 local malams are engaged in trade on the side. All the rest devote their entire time to religion.[4] They are able to do so because they are patronized by the wealthy men of the Quarter. The wealthier a man is the more powerful the malams he can accommodate and support. Malams do not ask payment for their services but they are given presents for every piece of help they provide, and the wealthier a man is the more presents he can give to the malams.

There is a great demand for malams in Sabo and people say that lucky is the man who can accommodate and support a powerful malam in his own house. Because the business landlords control a great deal of housing and of wealth they have the means of patronizing the most important malams of the Quarter. A big malam is thus one who is patronized by a big landlord. On the other hand a man becomes a big landlord and sustains that role as a result of the support of big malams. Thus in Sabo a very close association has developed between landlords and big malams. This association has been of crucial political importance for Sabo society and for the continuity and functioning of the network of Hausa trading communities in Yorubaland. The malams link landlords and clients, chief and people, one age-group and another. They mediate between the categorical imperatives of the universal religious dogma and the changing conditions in the local community. Through their services as diviners, and as teachers and interpreters of the principles of Islam, they guide the behaviour of laymen in the interests of the community as a whole. The Hausa of Sabo say that a man who does not follow closely the advice of his malams will end disastrously, and this they often support by recounting numerous dramas from the history of the Quarter in the last few years.

Malams in the Process of Decision-Making

Any threat to the community is generally manifested in increasing difficulties and anxieties experienced by individual landlords and clients. These anxieties are conveyed to individual malams in the course of divining and serious consultations. Through their interaction with one another, the malams 'pool' their observations, and a pattern, or patterns, of general stress are developed. Through their own 'research' a general policy is developed and is offered in the form of ritual diagnosis and ritual solutions in sessions between malams and laymen. In the process, clients are given guidance in the conduct of their lives in ways which are in the interests of the landlords, of the Quarter as a whole, and of the network of Hausa communities in Yorubaland.

This, however, does not mean that the malams' main function is to give support to the precarious position of the landlords. The malams are by no means blind or willing tools in the hands of the landlords, even if, in fact, they are financially supported by them. The malams have their own groupings and their own interests and point of view. As a group, they have a great deal of autonomy and their devotion to the service of the order and of Islam in general cannot be questioned.

Many malams are ignorant and some cannot even understand or comprehend their so-called 'Arabic learning'. Other malams know more, and some are very learned. But one of the malams' main characteristics is continuous learning. The malams have their own circles, the junior ones learning under the senior ones. Before the coming of the Tijaniyya order into the Quarter, it was possible for a relatively ignorant malam to acquire a high ritual reputation by sheer luck. Even today if an ignorant junior malam helps a man in a situation of great affliction and succeeds, his fame will earn him, at least for a short period, a ritual status far higher than that merited by his learning and devotion. But accidents of this sort are not frequent. This is due directly to another principle which the Tijaniyya brought into the organization of the Quarter's religion. The Tijaniyya brought a scale of grading malams on the basis of their learning and religious devotion. This is the scale instituted through the arrangement by which the so-called 'instructions' of the order are imparted from a senior malam to a junior one. The most senior of the malams in the Quarter, i.e. the ritual masters (*mukaddams*) of the order, receive their instructions from more senior malams of the order outside the Quarter. The chain of these ritual links extends ultimately to the Shaikh of the order, outside Nigeria.

Thus the malams constitute an autonomous order in themselves which cuts across the patron–client relationship within Sabo. Their ritual functions and the links which they maintain with the higher positions within the hierarchy of the order endow them with a political authority in their own right. They influence Sabo polity in the spiritual interests of the order as much as in the interests of the landlords, the clients, the Quarter as a whole, and the other Hausa trading communities in the area. The position of the malams intersects the interests of all these groupings.

Today, political authority in Sabo is legitimized by a system of beliefs and practices which are rooted in men's ideas about the ultimate order of the universe and of the meaning of life in it. It is rooted in the anxieties of men, in their day-to-day afflictions and in the ritual activities associated with these ideas and anxieties.

From Witch to Hajji

This change in the nature of political organization of Sabo, i.e. the change from a polity based on the support of the colonial power to a polity based on men's religious loyalties, effected a change in the character and status of the Chief of the Quarter and also in that of the leading business landlords. In 1955 the Chief dramatically decided to go on a pilgrimage to Mecca, taking with him, at his own expense, two of the leading malams of the Quarter, one of them the Chief Imam. He announced his decision in a meeting held at a central building to which all the men of the Quarter had been invited. An important malam, who had been especially brought down from the North, addressed the gathering, saying that if any man had a grudge or complaint against the Chief, he should bring it out there and then. The malam explained that the Chief must have the full forgiveness of everyone of his people for any wrong he might have committed against them. The Chief's departure and subsequent return were marked by much public festivity and ceremony in the Quarter. During the following three years all the thirty landlords went on pilgrimages, some taking with them their malams. During this short period, eight of the malams became *Hajjis*, all, except one, at the expense of one or another of the landlords. At the beginning of the decade there were only 6 Sabo men who had been to Mecca, but by the end of the 1950's the number rose to 45.

The pilgrimage is, as is well known, one of the five pillars of Islam, and is therefore a religious duty. There is no doubt that the Chief and the landlords were genuine in their religious fervour and piety in performing it. But, seen within the context of the social history of the Quarter, it was very much connected with recent political developments. Today people in Sabo make a clear distinction between the character of the Chief before the pilgrimage and after the pilgrimage. Previously, the Chief is said to have been cruel and brutal, though very shrewd and capable of leading the people. He used to 'murder' his rivals ruthlessly by pagan black magic. After the pilgrimage, however, the Chief became a virtuous and pious man. He still relied heavily on the mystical support of the malams, but he never used those malams for evil ends.

Thus the pilgrimage to Mecca by the Chief, the landlords, and the leading malams, was in many respects the rite of passage of these men into new roles in a new polity. Today when the Chief wants to deliberate over an issue he simply tells his messenger: 'Call the *Hajjis*', i.e. the leading landlords and the leading malams. In ordinary conversations between people in the Quarter these 'Big Men' are often referred to as 'the *Hajjis*'.

Ritual and Moral Sanctions

An important aspect of these changes in the structure of political authority is a change in the nature of sanctions. The different kinds of power on which authority is based are associated with different kinds of sanctions: physical, economic, moral and ritual.

During the period of Indirect Rule, the Chief of the Quarter enjoyed a great deal of coercive power, indeed well beyond the formal limits of his authority. He could easily frame people, arrest them and hand them over to the police, by denouncing them as thieves or 'undesirables'. In some cases he even ordered his messengers to manhandle or assault people whom he regarded as deviants. Potentially, he could also mobilize other members of the community to stage physical assaults on individuals or groups. As he was the only formal link between the community and the authorities, he could withhold, or threaten to withhold, his support of individuals who were not loyal to him. However, with the coming of party politics he lost much, if not all, of this use, or threat of the use, of coercion. Today he can still blackmail people by threatening to denounce them to the authorities or to withhold his goodwill and support, but to a much lesser extent than before.

In the field of economic sanctions, little change has taken place, because now, as before, the Chief is the principal referee in the Quarter for the creditworthiness of settlers. This means that he can always affect the business reputation of a man and determine to some extent the amount of business that the man can have. Also, as the Chief has always been the accepted business arbitrator in the Quarter, and even outside it, his general approval and goodwill is sought by every man, since the Chief can consciously or unconsciously sway his judgement this way or that and thus affect the fortunes of people. The Chief derives similar power from his role as a Shari'a judge who handles matrimonial and inheritance cases.

Quite apart from all this, the Chief exercises a great deal of economic pressure by means of the scores of houses which he 'owns', or controls, presumably on behalf of the community. Several hundreds of people live as tenants in these houses, free of charge. The Chief can eject them at any time he wants to and indeed I recorded a number of cases of people actually being evicted in this way. This is a strong sanction as it may mean that those people will either have to spend a great deal of money on renting a room[5] if they are lucky enough to find one, or, if they do not find a room, they may have to leave the Quarter altogether. Furthermore, the Chief continually invests money by giving some capital to men and by setting them up in business. These are always men who have proved their loyalty to him and are thus reaping the fruits of that loyalty.

It is in the field of moral sanctions that there have been great changes. The increasing social interaction within small primary groupings, which the Tijaniyya brought about, has subjected individuals to the continuous pressure of groups and to the norms and values which govern the relations between members of these groups. As a result, men have become more sensitive to collective pressure. These primary groups are interlinked in a variety of ways which have truly made the order into a 'brotherhood'. A man will run the risk of losing membership of these groups if he acts against the political interests of the Quarter. Disobedience to the Chief reverberates immediately and becomes an infringement of the norms and values of the small groups. A man's friends are also his ritual 'brothers', with whom he may also have direct or indirect economic relations. They are his comrades in political confrontations with the Yoruba.

One of the most severe sanctions in the hands of the Chief of the Quarter is that of 'public scandalizing'. This is a sanction, or threat of a sanction, which he uses only in serious cases of dispute and only as an ultimate measure against an important man whom he cannot threaten or punish effectively in other ways. I did not myself have the opportunity of witnessing this sanction being actually used against anyone, but I recorded from accounts by informers a number of cases, one of which had occurred only a few months before I began my study in the Quarter.

The scandalizing takes place at a special meeting held at a specific time, in front of the house of the accused man. Days before the meeting the Chief of the Quarter sends his messengers to the Big Men of the Quarter (i.e. the landlords and the leading malams) to ask them to attend. Other men also gather. At the meeting, the Chief tells the gathering of the wrongs committed by the accused man. The accused, who would have been inside his house listening to the charges brought against him by the Chief, has no alternative but to come out of the house and confront the Chief and the gathering in order to defend himself. Should he not appear, the gathering concludes that the charges are true and the man's reputation will most certainly suffer a great deal, but even more serious will be the adverse effect on his creditworthiness in business. This is because the gathering consists, not only of his friends, his malams, his ritual brothers, his business associates, and his political allies but also of many Hausa strangers who happen to be in the Quarter, amongst whom will be some of the dealers who conduct their business through him. The meeting may last for hours, during which all aspects of the issues involved are aired and various opinions expressed about a settlement. The advisors of the Chief, who are often described as 'the men who understand Arabic', who are originally learned malams, illuminate the issues in the light of Hausa customs and Islamic norms. The accused appeals to some of the men present to give evidence to prove some of his contentions. In the end a kind of consensus is achieved about a compromise.

Although scandalizing in this dramatic form is not a daily occurrence in the Quarter, men are conscious of its threat all the time. Scandalizing meetings on a much smaller scale, are, in fact, held informally in a number of ways when men are called upon to answer charges that are made in public. One of the cases on this scale which I witnessed occurred within 'the group' which I mentioned in the previous chapter. Three members accused a fourth of a breach of promise in sharing profits in an ad hoc business deal in which they had taken part. The accusations were discussed in a gathering of about ten members of the group and the accused argued his case. There was a great deal of pressure on him from various associates to honour his obligations. In the end a compromise was found and the matter was settled.

The Chief is assisted in exerting moral pressure of this type by making use of the social networks of landlords, malams, and occupational chiefs. He also makes use of various other techniques. One of his weapons in this respect is his control of the musicians[6] of the Quarter. The Musician's Chief, is in fact, the official announcer[7] for the Chief of the Quarter. These musicians are essentially praise-singers but they can also sing offensive songs which can be directed against specific people. During the period 1942–49, all the musicians of the Quarter, together with their chief, remained loyal to Umaru when he was dismissed from the Chieftaincy of the Quarter. Umaru's control over this medium of communication was so complete that when Gambo, shortly after his appointment as Chief, prepared for the wedding of his son, no musician in Sabo was ready to play for him. In a letter which Gambo sent to the Council in relation to the incident, he stated that in order to avoid trouble he had to bring musicians from Ilorin. Throughout that troubled period in the Quarter's history, Umaru effectively used the musicians to sing his own praises and to scandalize about Gambo, and later Bashiru, and all the leading men who supported them.

Magical attacks are of course not easy to observe, and they may be fantasies; but there are endless stories about the deadly efficacity of the ritual powers of the Chief and of the malams who support him. Informants in the Quarter are unanimous that, up to the middle of the 1950's, the Chief used to practise black magic but that after going to Mecca he stopped doing so. He is credited with the 'murder' of several enemies, one of whom was Gambo.² Today, the Chief is believed to be still able to 'murder' people 'by juju' but he is said to refrain from doing this. On the other hand, the Chief Imam of the Quarter is often described as the 'Chief's bodyguard', and is said to be continuously supplying the Chief with ritual charms to protect him from enemies and to enhance his health, wealth, and power. A learned informant told me solemnly that the Chief would not survive for one day without the ritual support of the Chief Imam. One of the many themes that recur in the numerous stories of the Chief's ritual capacities is that of men who sued him at the Yoruba civil courts but died mysteriously one or two days before the case was due to be tried. The Hausa regard with abhorrence and shock any attempt or threat by a Hausa man to take the Chief to a Yoruba court. This is regarded not only as treason but also as a sin. Men often say that anyone who does not obey the Chief is not a true Moslem, no matter whether the Chief has faults or not.

In discussing these forms of sanctions I have been mentioning the Chief as if he were the only political authority in the Quarter. But, as I mentioned earlier, the political 'establishment' of the Quarter today includes not only the Chief but also the *Hajjis*, i.e. the landlords and the leading malams, who participate in the processes of communication, decision-making, and co-ordination of political action, so that they also, both in general and each within his own sphere are capable of exerting a great deal of pressure, through reward and punishment, to make people conform to the norms and values of the community.

New Ritual Mechanics

The new structure of power has been routinized, institution-alized, and legitimized by the development of new ideologies, myths, values, loyalties, and attitudes. New symbols have been introduced and old ones reinterpreted and the whole social order is now conceived by the people in terms of the will and the schemes of Allah.

All this necessitated intensive discipline, training, and indoctrination. Ritual activity therefore became intensive and more frequent. This was made the more necessary for the additional reason that Islam is categorically opposed to the employment of any material ritual symbols or such accompaniments of rituals as singing, music or dancing. Thus the supreme, dominant symbol in all Islamic rituals, the word 'Allah', must, according to orthodox Islam, be only abstractly conceived. Indeed there is a whole theological science in Islamic tradition, called *tanzih*, whose sole purpose is to do away with anthropomorphic or any other materialistic attributes of Allah.

This abstract nature of Islamic dominant symbols has always constituted a problem in the practice of orthodox Islam because a ritual symbol can affect men and motivate them to action only if it appeals also to their emotions and not just to their intellect. This point has been recently illuminated by the analysis of ritual symbols by Turner.[9]

Turner points out that a dominant ritual symbol has two poles of meaning; one ideological and the other sensory or emotional. At the ideological pole there is a cluster of meanings referring to moral values, principles of social organization, rules of social behaviour, the ideals of corporate groupings—in short all the obligatory elements in social conduct. At the sensory or emotional pole, on the other hand, there are gross sensations, desires and feelings. The norms, values, principles and rules which constitute the ideological pole are abstract and remote and merely their perception by the participant in the ritual act is not sufficient to induce him to act in response to them. Psychologists recognize three phases or elements, in a human action: cognition, affection, and conation. For example, a man is walking in the street and suddenly perceives a car coming towards him. This agitates him emotionally. He is frightened. The emotional energy which is thus released will drive him to avert the danger. Thus the man will act in accordance with intellectually perceived ideals and principles only if somehow his emotions are aroused. In the performance of ritual this is achieved by the sensory pole. As Turner points out, in the action situation of ritual, the ritual symbol effects an interchange of qualities between its poles of meaning. Norms and values, on the one hand, become saturated with emotion, while the gross and basic emotions become ennobled through contact with social values. The irksomeness of moral constraint is transformed into the love of goodness. Ritual thus becomes a mechanism which periodically converts the obligatory into the desirable.[10]

Islamic ritual symbols, however, have little sensory pole and the question is, how do Islamic rituals overcome this technical difficulty.

Like all symbols, the word 'Allah', has no specific definition. It stands for a variety of meanings. It conjures up different meanings to different people, or to the same people at different times. In the Koran alone there are many scores of alternative names for Allah, each name emphasizing one or another of His limitless qualities: the self-sufficing, the all-encompassing, the all-powerful, all-knowing, the absolute creator, the recorder, exalter, honourer, abaser, compassionate, thankful, forgiver, patient, watcher, the giver of livelihood and of wealth, the giver of life and the taker of life. There is no power in the universe which is outside his domain. He is the creator of the angels and also of the devil and of the devil's associates. Both the good and the bad which come to man originate from His will, in accordance with designs which only He can know and comprehend.

On the lines of Turner's analysis, we find in these qualities of Allah, two features of the ritual symbol. First, the condensation of many meanings within the single formation of the symbol. Secondly, the unification of such disparate meanings as life and death, good and evil, riches and poverty, within the single verbal symbol.

It should be obvious that even those qualities of Allah which are known cannot be fully and simultaneously remembered by the worshippers all the time. Different qualities of Allah are stressed in different social situations.[11] There are also wide variations in the range of meanings of the symbol. Furthermore, the various meanings are usually so vaguely stated that laymen require the help of the ritual experts to understand them in terms of current social issues and conditions. Symbols are continually interpreted and reinterpreted in the light of empirical experience, or, as Turner puts it, symbols are continually charged and recharged with significata. In Sabo this is done in a variety of ways, through divination sessions between malam and layman, when the malam diagnoses and offers remedies in terms of the will of Allah. It is also done in 'Arabic classes' for adults in which the Koran and some other religious texts are read by the pupils and interpreted by the malam, and in preaching sessions of all sorts.

The important point which must be stressed here is that the effective meanings of the symbol 'Allah' are not fixed but continually change in accordance with social conditions and events. As Turner points out[12] while a 'sign' refers to a definite meaning which is fixed and can be clearly conceived, a symbol has no definite reference and many of its connotations are rooted in the unconscious mind. The symbol is continually charged with those significata that are situationally relevant. Under some conditions the number and range of significata may be reduced. For example, in a modern Islamic country where a clear-cut secular code of law is adopted, the quality of Allah as the 'law-giver' will not be emphasized. Similarly, in Sabo society before the coming of party politics when the authority of the Chief of the Quarter was directly supported by the Native Authority and was ultimately backed by the colonial power, those significata which refer to Allah as the upholder of the political order were not charged into the symbol. But after the coming of politics, when the Indirect Rule system collapsed and Sabo political autonomy and the structure of authority within it were articulated in terms of religious reorganization, many of the significata which were not charged into the symbol before, were now so charged. In other words, under the impact of recent political circumstances the symbol is now loaded with more significata than before. And because these significata are so numerous and because they are also highly abstract in nature, and therefore elude the grasp and the retentive capacities of the human mind, it is necessary to repeat the symbol in rituals so that the necessary conditioning of men's social behaviour will be maintained. Hence the importance of a ritual like that of the *dhikr*, when the word Allah is recited, at varying paces and in varying pitches, over a thousand times. For ordinary men, to honour political obligations without the threat of the sanctions of organized force, requires a great deal of determination and discipline. But men are usually so immersed in their day-to-day problems that they easily lose sight of the ultimate principles and values which govern their social life. It is in solving just this problem that frequent and intensive rituals are fundamental.

This is like writing a note to yourself: 'Remember to buy a dictionary'. It may take you weeks to bring yourself to buy the dictionary, as this is not a pressing problem. But then you may write: 'Remember to exercise every morning and remember that if you want to achieve anything in your profession you have to write 1,000 words a day'. Here you are dealing with pressing points and you therefore need to have a glance at your notes several times a day. The more you load the list with things you should remember to do the more frequently you need to refer to the list. Similarly a Hausa in Sabo today has to remind himself of all the things he is ordained to do by Allah, as it is on such discipline that the continuity and functioning of the political autonomy of the Quarter, and consequently of the Quarter's economy and of his own economic interests, depend.

There are of course various 'informal' processes through which worshippers tend to associate an abstract symbol with some material objects. For example, among the Tijanis the rosary which a man uses to count the right number of times for repeating a prayer, becomes in time associated with the notion of the sanctity of Allah, acquires *baraka*, and is often used by the Hausa as a source of comfort and medical relief. In the same way, bodily movements that accompany the performance of ritual and the use of colour symbolism, the very frequent use of invocations of Allah in connection with such physical events as eating, drinking, sleeping, all these tend to compensate for the mechanical weaknesses in Islamic rituals.

But the most important association in Sabo ritual is between the worshipping group itself and the symbol 'Allah'. A whole complex of emotional feelings of different types is also generated in the course of the daily and weekly ritual, by the multiplex relationships which link and cross-link the men who make up the ritual group. For this is not an impersonal gathering of strangers who come together for the formal performance of ritual activity, but it is a group of men who are members of the same face-to-face community and who are thus related to one another in secular life in a variety of ways. The confrontation of these men in the ritual thus gives rise to feelings which are associated with these relationships, and these feelings in their turn become associated with the general meanings of the ritual symbols and thus affect the functioning of these symbols. Indeed there is a school of anthropologists who hold that a major function of ritual is to bring together people who are in secular life forced into potential dispute by conflicts of interests and of social principles, in order to emphasize general social interests and moral exigencies of co-operation to enable their social group to continue as an ongoing concern.

A Religious Blueprint for Political Change

These different processes of change, the mobilization, routinization, and ritualization of power relations, operate through countless minor episodes in the lives of individuals and groups. The emerging contemporaneous political organization, which is analytically presented by the sociologist as a neatly worked out system, is mostly unintended by individuals. A great deal of structural 'trial and error' or rather of adjustment and readjustment, of harmony and discrepancy between the constituent processes, have been going on all the time. This is true of all social change.

But parts of the processes are nevertheless directed and to some extent planned consciously by leaders. More economy in time, in stress, and in social tension can be effected when the leaders of the rapidly changing community adopt a suitable 'blueprint' for the change. In Sabo the Tijaniyya provided such a 'blueprint', for it presented a ready-made system of norms, myths, beliefs, rituals and organization which offered solutions to fundamental current problems.

There were many other 'blueprints' in the immediate cultural area of Sabo. But the Quarter's freedom of choice was not unlimited. It was not possible for the community, for example, to articulate its reorganization in terms of an elaborate kinship structure because the Hausa are bilateral and Sabo was, in any case, a community of migrants who had originated in different places of origin. Within the field of religion the choice was also limited. Sabo could not, for example, adopt a separatist Christian church as other non-Hausa communities were doing. The Hausa had already been committed to Islam whose beliefs and practices they shared with their communities of origin in the North and with all Hausa communities in the diaspora.

But even within the confines of Islam there were numerous possibilities to choose from, in the form of mystical orders[13] many of which were known in the Quarter. Itinerant malams, or malam-traders, representing one order or another circulate in Moslem communities throughout West Africa. There are many similarities between these orders. But there are also fundamental differences between them, so that one order can 'fit' better than others to the structural conditions of a certain community or a certain category of communities. Evans–Pritchard shows how out of the many orders known in Cyrenaica, the Sanusiyya fitted best the structural 'need' of Bedouin society in a certain phase of its recent history.[14] Similarly, the Tijaniyya fitted the requirements of Sabo better than the other orders, for a number of reasons. One of these reasons is that the Tijaniyya was the only mystical order within Islam which did not preach asceticism and the renouncement of earthly gains. An ideological strain of this nature would not fit the ethos of a community of ambitious traders. But the fitting of the Tijaniyya was not, of course, perfect. The order added a heavy ritual burden on the people of Sabo on top of the ordinary rituals of orthodox Islam. What is more, all these added ritual duties did not make the Hausa of Sabo into better Moslems. In fact, from the orthodox point of view, a Tijani is a rather bad Moslem, because the order makes some extravagant theological claims about the place of the founder, Ahmad al- Tijani, within the chain of saints and prophets. Furthermore, the specific prayer of the order,[15] which is said to have been imparted to the founder by the Prophet Muhammad in a daylight vision, and which is repeated twelve times a day, contains a grammatical error. In Islam, which regards Arabic as a sacred language, this is tantamount to sacrilege. However, ordinary Tijanis in Sabo, and indeed many of the malams, are hardly aware of such points. They know very little about the history of the order or even about its distribution in West Africa. They do not think of the Tijaniyya as a system; they live it. The leading malams of the Quarter who do know about these theological points either dismiss these 'discrepancies' lightly or point out more serious weaknesses in rival orders.

Systematic and detailed monographic studies on the spread of the Tijaniyya are still lacking. But from the current literature and from my own limited enquiries in a number of small communities in Southern Nigeria and in Ghana, it is evident that towards the beginning of the 1950s a very large number of

Islamic communities, in many West African countries, adopted the order. Many scholars have reported that in recent years the Tijaniyya has been replacing other Islamic orders, particularly that of the Kadiriyya, in many areas. Between 1947 and 1950, an important Shaikh of the order made a grand tour of West Africa, visited numerous Moslem communities, including Sabo, and wherever he went appointed local ritual masters who duly initiated people in their communities.[16] I believe that this success of the order in the 1950s is significantly connected with the structural changes which had been taking place at about this time in many of the new states in the area as a result of the collapse of British Indirect Rule.[17]

Political Ethnicity in Contemporary African Towns

The Making of an Ethnic Polity in Town—The Economics of Ethnic Groupings—Ethnic Grouping as a General Political Process—The Political Dimension of Ethnic Groupings—The Informal Nature of Political Ethnicity—Social and Cultural Strategies in Political Ethnicity: A Comparative Scheme; (1) The Problem of Distinctiveness (a) Myths of Origin and Claims to Superiority (b) Descent and Endogamy (c) Moral Exclusiveness (d) Endo-Culture (e) Spatial Proximity (f) Homogenization; (2) The Problem of Communication; (3) The Problem of Decision-Making; (4) The Problem of Authority; (5) The Problem of Ideology; (6) The Problem of Discipline—The Challenge to Social Anthropology Today

I discussed in the previous chapters some of the processes involved in the development and functioning of an ethnic polity, which is based on corporate economic interests, within a contemporary setting in a West African city. Underlying these processes, is a general process which has been called 'retribalization'.

The Making of an Ethnic Polity in Town

Sabo developed in conjunction with the growth and organization of Hausa monopoly in long-distance trade in kola and cattle between northern and southern Nigeria. The Hausa have been able to overcome the technical problems which are involved in this trade by the development of an ethnic monopoly over the major stages of the trade. This has involved the development of a network of Hausa migrant communities in the Western Region of Nigeria. Sabo thus came into being as a base for control over parts of the southern end of the chain of the trade.

But in the process of achieving such control, the Hausa have come face to face with increasing rivalry, competition, and opposition from various Yoruba individuals and groups. From the very beginning, economic competition led to political encounters with members of the host society. The Hausa, confronting mounting pressure from the Yoruba majority, were forced to organize themselves for political action. With the growth of the trade, the increase in the number of settlers in the Quarter, and the expansion of the host city, Hausa political organization became more complex and more elaborate, in two different, but closely related, spheres. First, the Hausa developed and maintained their tribal exclusiveness. Second, they built an internal organization of political functions: communication, decision-making, authority, administration, and sanctions, and also political myths, symbols, slogans, and ideology. The principal aims of the whole system are (a) to prevent the encroachment of men from other ethnic groups into the trade, (b) to co-ordinate the activities of the members of the community in maintaining and developing their economico-political organization, and (c) to maintain mechanisms for co-operation with other Hausa communities in both the South and the North, for the common cause.

During the period of Indirect Rule by the British many of these functions were officially recognized and constituted part of the formal organization of power which had been set up by colonial rule. The Hausa were recognized as a distinct 'tribal' group and were given a well-defined residential base and a recognized 'tribal' chief. The authority of the chief was ultimately supported by the power of the Administration.

This formal recognition of Hausa political organization enabled the people of Sabo, not only to consolidate their gains in the control of trade, but also to capture more economic fields, and the actual Quarter itself, with its buildings, sites and strategic position within the city, became a vast vested interest for the community.

With the coming of party politics in the 1950's, as the Nigerian nationalist movement arose and later with independence, the whole formal basis of Hausa distinctiveness was undermined. Sabo was no longer officially recognized as an exclusive 'tribal' grouping and the support which had been given by the power of the government to the authority of its Chief was withdrawn. The weakening position of the Chief affected not only the organization of the functions of communication, decision making and co-ordination of action, but also the very distinctiveness of the Quarter because it was no long possible for the Chief to force individuals to act in conformity with the corporate interests of the community.

In the meantime, the ethnic exclusiveness of Sabo was being threatened by increasing social interaction between Hausa and Yoruba in two major social fields: in party political activities and in joint Islamic ritual and ceremonial. Interaction of this kind was likely to result in the creation of primary, moral relations between Hausa and Yoruba, under new values, norms, and symbols.

The adoption of the Tijaniyya by the Quarter brought about processes which halted the disintegration of the bases of the exclusiveness and identity of Sabo. The reorganization of the Quarter's religion was at the same time a reorganization of the Quarter's political organization. A new myth of distinctiveness for the Quarter was found. The Quarter was now a superior, puritanical, ritual community, a religious brotherhood, distinct from the masses of Yoruba Moslems in the city, complete with its separate Friday Mosque, Friday congregation, and with a separate cemetery.

The localization of ritual in the Quarter inhibited the development of much social interaction with the Yoruba.[1] On the other hand, the intensification and collectivisation of ritual increased the informal social interaction within the Quarter, under Hausa traditional values, norms, and customs.

The principle of intercession which the Tijaniyya introduced, and the concentration of all the mystical forces of the universe in Allah, vested a great deal of ritual power in the malams. The malams became the sole mediators between laymen and the supernatural powers of Allah. Through their services as teachers, interpreters of the dogma, ritual masters, diviners, magicians, spritual healers, and officiants in rites of passage, the malams developed multiple relations of power over laymen and, through the hierarchy of ritual authority instituted by the Tijaniyya, this power is finally concentrated in the hands of the Big Malams.

Through their manifold relationships with the business landlords and the Chief, the Big Malams have become part of the 'Establishment'. They act as advisors to the landlords and to the Chief and they formally participate in the formulation of problems, in deliberation, and decision-making, and in the co-ordination of action in matters of general policy. They also play significant roles in the processes of communication and co-ordination in the course of the routine administration of the Quarter.

The Hausa of Sabo are today more socially exclusive, or less assimilated into the host society, than at any other time in the past. They thus seem to have completed a full cycle of 're-tribalization'. They speak their own language even in their dealings with the Yoruba, and they dress differently and eat differently from their hosts. Hausa customs, norms, values, and beliefs are upheld by a web of multiplex social relationships resulting from the increasingly intense interaction within the Quarter. On the other hand, the absence of inter-marriage with the Yoruba, and the ritual exclusiveness brought about by the Tijaniyya, have insulated the Hausa from much social interaction with the Yoruba and thus inhibited the development of moral ties and loyalties across the lines of tribal separateness. Finally, with the withdrawal of the British from Nigeria, the two ethnic groupings came into a sharp confrontation and the cleavage between them became deeper and more bitter.

Sabo has acquired more social and cultural distinctiveness as a result of marked social and cultural changes among the Yoruba in Ibadan. During the past few decades the Yoruba have developed cash crops, trade in European goods, and some light industry. They have adopted a relatively great measure of Western education and developed a fair degree of occupational differentiation and specialization in their society. The adoption of the city as capital of the Western Region, and its development as an administrative centre, together with the building of a large university[2] and a university hospital in it,[3] have brought further differentiation within its population. The formation of different kinds of voluntary associations,[4] the intensified activities of political parties, the emergence of a Western oriented elite[5] and of a new economically privileged class in it, have created a web of links and cleavages cross-cutting one another, and have thus changed the structure of Yoruba society.

In sharp contrast with all this change among the Yoruba of Ibadan, Sabo society and culture remain basically unaffected, like an island of continuity in a sea of change. Its economy remains stable and is today not much more sophisticated in its organization than it was twenty years ago. Its education remains purely 'Arabic' almost untouched by Western education.[6] The ambition of a Sabo man is success in trade, higher Islamic learning, and, as the crowning of success in both endeavours, pilgrimage to Mecca. While many of the Yoruba are culturally oriented towards European or American civilization, the Hausa of Sabo remain oriented towards the North and the North East, towards the interior of Africa and the civilization of Islam.

The Economics of Ethnic Groupings

This 'conservatism' on the part of the Hausa is not the result of their situation as migrant strangers in the Yoruba city. Other migrant strangers in Ibadan have changed socially and culturally along with the Yoruba. This can be clearly seen among the Western Ibo who began to settle in Ibadan in the early 1920's and who in 1964 numbered 2,000–2,800.[7] They, too, were originally regarded as strangers and were concentrated in a special residential area.

But, as Okonjo shows, their residential segregation has completely broken down and today ethnic mixture in the compounds where they live 'is the rule rather than the exception'.[8] They do have a tribal association, 'The Western Ibo Union, Ibadan', but it is a weak association, meets once a month, and has often suffered from the embezzlement of its funds and from frequent quarrels among its members.[9] Like many other tribal associations in Africa, the Western Ibo Union in Ibadan has aimed not at the development of ethnic exclusiveness, but on the contrary at promoting the successful adaptation of its members to modern urban conditions.[10] Indeed some writers show that affiliation to such tribal associations is often only a temporary measure taken by new migrants to the city to get help to integrate within the new social milieu.[11] Second-generation Western Ibos in Ibadan speak Yoruba 'without accent' and have Yoruba as their playmates.[12] As Okonjo shows, the Western Ibos in Ibadan can be found scattered in places of work all over the town. They are occupationally differentiated, ranging from university lecturers, through mechanics, clerks, and printers, to workers of all sorts.[13]

This integration of the Western Ibo in Ibadan on the one hand, and the apparent insensitivity of the Hausa of Sabo to the great changes that have been taking place around them in the town on the other, has been attributed by some writers to strong 'achievement motivations' among the Ibo (and the Yoruba) and to particularly 'conservative' and 'traditional' traits in the basic structure of the Hausa personality.[14] Thus in a comparative study of 'achievement motivations' among the Hausa, Yoruba and Ibo in Nigeria, LeVine writes: 'Hausa traders are everywhere in West Africa . . . but their pattern of trade is traditional and no matter how long they stay in modern cities like Accra and Lagos, they remain conservative with regard to education, religion and politics and aloof from modern bureaucratic and industrial occupations. . . .' According to LeVine, this traditionalism among the Hausa, as against the spirit of being 'go-ahead' among the Ibo and the Yoruba, is the result of '. . . conservatism versus modernism, authoritarian versus democratic ideology, and Islamic obedience versus Christian individualism. . . .'[15]

I do not intend to discuss here the methodological and theoretical assumptions in these arguments, nor is this the occasion to question the value and the validity of comparing large ethnic stocks, like the Hausa, Yoruba, and Ibo, in this way when the multiplicity and complexity of cultural, historical, and social variables have not yet been sufficiently analysed. What I want to point out is that if a comparison of this sort is to be attempted at all between members of these different ethnic groups, it must be carried out within the same, or similar, situations, such as those that I have been discussing in this book where Yoruba have confronted Hausa over the capture of strategic positions in the organization of long-distance trade.

It is quite true that Hausa organization of long-distance trade is 'traditional', but what LeVine seems to overlook is that in the present circumstances this organization is the most rational, the most economic, and hence the most profitable.

This is not a 'petty trade' of the type indulged in by masses of men, women and children all over West Africa, including Ibo and Yoruba; it is serious business involving large sums of money and yielding wide margins of profit and steady incomes to the men who are engaged in its far-flung organization. If it were not so profitable, the Yoruba competitors would not have gone to such a great deal of trouble, during all these years, in order to gain a foothold in it. So far it has been economically more viable than the numerous small-scale modern enterprises which have sprung up everywhere in Southern Nigeria following independence,[16] and have ended in bankruptcy after a short time. The Hausa landlord knows of the existence of banks, and sometimes even makes use of their services, but he will still keep large sums of cash money in his house and thus run the risk of losing it through theft, not because of the blind force of custom or of ignorance, but because of a number of practical, rationally calculated considerations.[17] Similarly, the Hausa cattle dealer knows of the advantages of having his cattle transported from the North to the South by rail, instead of having them driven on the hoof. The journey on the hoof takes about 40 days and by the time the cattle arrive at the southern markets they will have lost much weight, contacted disease and thus depreciated in value. On the other hand the journey by rail takes only two days after which the cattle arrive in a healthy condition and thus fetch a higher price. Nevertheless, the dealer will often move his cattle rather than send them by rail. Here again he does this not in a blind adherence to tradition but only because, after the calculation of costs and risks, he finds that driving the beasts will be more profitable than sending them by rail. The Hausa is here making a choice between alternative courses of action and his decisions are rational and are aimed at the 'maximization of profits'. If this were not the case, i.e. if there were more economical methods of organizing the business so as to reduce costs and raise profits, then the question should be asked why have the more 'go-ahead' Yoruba not adopted them and thus succeeded in throwing the Hausa out of business. Indeed an attempt of this kind was made a few years ago by a number of enterprising Europeans who intended launching a modern organization for securing beef supplies for southern Nigeria and for export, by slaughtering cattle in the North and then transporting the meat to the South by air. The experiment failed and the whole enterprise was given up as un-economic, and the Hausa continue until today to dominate the trade and to run it in the 'old ways'. The Hausa are not ignorant about the possibilities of air transport or air travel and anyone who has travelled on the internal West African air lines would have noticed the steady traffic of Hausa traders using this method of transport daily. But they have not used it for transporting meat because they can deliver the meat more cheaply by the traditional ways. They understand the operation of the widely spread network of relations in which the trade is conducted, between breeders, dealers, middlemen, brokers, financiers, speculators, drovers, and scores of other intermediaries in different communities of the network which extends from the remote expanses of the savanna, where the Fulani raise their cattle, down to the southern parts of the forest belt, where the beef is finally consumed. To rationalize the trade and to put it on modern bases will require a complete social and economic revolution covering almost every stage in the chain of the trade and this at present is not feasible.

Thus in the field of long distance trade, the Hausa cannot be said to be inferior to the Yoruba in 'achievement motivations'. Indeed, as I have shown earlier in the book, the Hausa can be said to have out manoeuvred and outwitted the Yoruba in many situations. This is not a matter of superior or inferior psychological make-up, but is a question of political developments and political organization. And this brings us back to the phenomena of ethnicity and to the process of ethnic political grouping.

Ethnic Grouping as a General Political Process

The Hausa in Ibadan are more 'retribalized' than the 'Western Ibos', not because of their conservatism, as LeVine suggests, and not because of special elements in their traditional culture, as Rouch and others contend, but because their ethnicity articulates a Hausa political organization which is used as a weapon in the struggle to keep the Hausa in control of the trade. Ethnicity is thus basically a political and not a cultural phenomenon, and it operates within contemporary political contexts and is not an archaic survival arrangement carried over into the present by conservative people.

The development and functioning of Sabo, as an autonomous polity is far from being a unique case of 'retribalization' in contemporary African society. The same processes have operated in the formation of other Hausa communities in other Yoruba towns. This is confirmed both by records and by partial observations which I made of a number of such communities. Similar processes have also been evident in the formation of other communities of this type in southern Ghana where I made some limited enquiries, and elsewhere in Ghana as indicated in the literature. Each one of these Hausa communities is unique in the sense that it has developed under a particular combination of historical, geographical, demographic, economic, cultural, and political circumstances. But the general pattern and the sociological interconnections between the major variables, and particularly between the economic and the political ones, are similar.

Nor is the phenomenon of the Hausa diaspora in West Africa unique in this respect, for there are other ethnic diasporas in other parts of the sub-continent.[18] If one goes further afield, one will meet similar situations in the organization of Lebanese and Syrian communities in West Africa,[19] and in the development of a network of Indian migrant communities in East and Southern Africa.[20] If one leaves the African continent, one will find similar examples in the organization of Chinese migrant communities in different parts of the Far East and of South-East Asia,[21] in the network of Arab Moslem trading communities in non-Arab lands during the Middle Ages, of Jewish trading communities around the Mediterranean, and so on.

But the processes of political 're-tribalization' are not confined to the formation of ethnic diasporas in pre-industrial societies. Everywhere in the world today there are ethnic groupings which are engaged in a struggle for power and privilege with other ethnic groupings, within the frameworks of formal political settings. Recent studies by sociologists and anthropologists of various communities in the U.S.A. reveal the dynamic nature of ethnic groupings in contemporary society. In a study of such groupings in New York city, Glazer and Moynihan find that: 'New York organizational life today is in large measure lived within ethnic bounds'.[22] These ethnic groups are not a survival from the age of mass immigration, but new social forms. In many cases members who are third or more generation immigrants, have lost their original language and many of their indigenous customs. But they have continuously re-created their distinctiveness in different ways, not because of conservatism, but because these ethnic groups are in fact interest groupings whose members share some common economic and political interests and who, therefore, stand together in the continuous competition for power with other groups.[23]

Political ethnicity has been particularly striking in the newly emerging states of the Third World because under colonial rule some ethnic groups succeeded in gaining a great deal of power while others became under-privileged.

With independence, the underprivileged closed their ranks to redress the balance whilst the privileged had to close their ranks to retain their privileges. In the course of the ensuing struggle, many of these ethnic groups exploited some of their traditional values, myths and ceremonial in order to establish an elaborate political organization. And because within the formal structure of the new state there is no place for the formal organization of these ethnic groups, this organization has been informally developed by being articulated in terms of some of these traditional symbolic forms.

This process is dramatically manifested in post-independent British West Africa, but it is also present, though only at certain levels of political organization even in those parts of Africa which have been characterized by a great deal of political de-tribalization. This can be seen in the now classic example of the industrial centres in Central Africa. Here, as Epstein shows in his study of the industrial town Luanshya,[24] the tribally heterogeneous African labour force, confronting the monolithic, bureaucratic industrial organization which had been set up by white employers, aligned their forces together in a struggle for higher wages and better working conditions. But, within the unions themselves, competition over positions of power was conducted on ethnic lines. What this means is that on this level of organization, ethnicity must have been political and each ethnic group must have organized itself for political action. A leader of such an ethnic group will do his best to emphasize ethnic distinctiveness and to mobilize power relations within the group to support him. Studies on this level of political organization have not yet been made in Central Africa. Mitchell has recently drawn attention to this gap in our knowledge:

'. . . the interaction of African townsmen in industrial and commercial environments has been little studied. Industrial sociologists have shown that in Europe and America informal relationships among workmen modify and augment the formal pattern of relationships among them. We would expect this to be true also of African workers. From a theoretical point of view it would be interesting to know whether such factors as tribalism and kinship play a more important role in informal relationships in the work situation in Africa than they do in Europe and America . . .'[25]

This means that even in the industrial towns of the Copper-belt tribalism *is* a live political and economic issue and is not just a method of categorization to help the African migrant to deal with the bewildering complexity of urban society or to regulate for him such 'domestic' matters as marriage, friend-ship, burial and mutual help. It has for long now been recog-nized by social anthropologists that political organization in a society does not exclusively consist in formal political institu-tions, but includes many institutions that are not formally political, like marriage, friendship, and security for old age.

Epstein must have been aware of all this because soon after indicating that tribalism *was* a live political issue within the unions he introduced into the picture of the African camp a new variable, that of social stratification, to indicate that this was a countervailing force against political tribalism.[26] But, here, too, our information is scanty and a great deal depends on whether the new lines of stratification cut across, or overlap with, tribal cleavages.

If status cleavages will cut across ethnic divisions, then the manifestations of ethnic identity and exclusiveness will tend to be inhibited by the emerging countervailing alignments of power. The less privileged from one ethnic group will co-operate with the less privileged from other ethnic groups against the privileged from the same ethnic groups. The privileged groups will, for their part, also close their ranks to protect their interests. If the situation continues to develop in this way, tribal differences will be weakened and will eventually disappear and the people will become politically detribalized. In time, class division will be so deep that a new sub-culture, with different styles of life, different norms, values and ideologies, will emerge and a situation may develop which is similar to that of 'the two nations' of Victorian Britain.

However, the situation will be entirely different if the new class cleavages will overlap with tribal groupings, so that within the new system the privileged will tend to be identified with one ethnic group and the under-privileged with another ethnic group. In this situation cultural differences between the two groups will become entrenched, consolidated, and strengthened in order to express the struggle between the two interest groups across the new class lines. Old customs will tend to persist, but within the newly emerging social system they will assume new values and new social significance. A great deal of social change will take place, but it will tend to be effected through the rearrangement of traditional cultural items, rather than through the development of new cultural items, or, more significantly, rather than the borrowing of cultural items from the other tribal groups. Thus to the casual observer it will look as if there is here stagnation, conservatism, or a return to the past, when in fact we are confronted with a new social system in which men articulate their *new roles* in terms of traditional ethnic idioms. This is why a concentration on the study of culture as such will shed little light on the nature of this kind of situation, and it is for this reason that Gluckman and others insisted that ethnicity should be studied within the social context of the town.[27]

The Political Dimension of Ethnic Groupings

In the heterogeneous African towns today we find various situations which reveal different degrees of political ethnicity. The situations can be heuristically arranged in a continuum between the two extremes. At the one end we have situations in which cultural differences between people in the town are being rapidly eroded by various cleavages which cut across ethnic differences and give rise to close co-operation and alignments between men from different ethnic groups. At the other end of the continuum we have situations where men emphasize their ethnic identity and separateness and adjust, within the contemporary setting, in terms of their endoculture.

In the first extreme type of situation, where political ethnicity is weakening, 'tribesmen' may still form some 'tribal' associations to help newcomers from the 'tribal' homeland, or to assist members in such respects as birth, marriage and burial, or to engage in some ceremonial activities. The significance of many of these ethnic associations, which abound in West African towns particularly, has been greatly exaggerated by some writers. Most of the associations are highly segmental, involving only one or a few roles of the individual members. They are voluntary and at any one time they include within their membership only a small fraction of the men from the same ethnic group in town. Many of them meet irregularly and in many cases large proportions of the members default in the payment of their fees.[28] Nearly all of these associations have elaborately written constitutions but these are often the composition of public letter-writers who charge a small fee for such service.

But even so, i.e., even when ethnicity at this end of the continuum is only a method of categorization, it will still play some political role, as a basis for a pressure group. The observance by such a group of a body of customs means that their members are interacting under some values, beliefs, and norms which create among them moral obligations that are governed by categorical imperatives. Such imperatives can be politically significant in various contexts. Groupings of this type may not form solid corporate blocks, but may nevertheless informally affect the performance of monolithic organizations of power.

The processes involved in this type of situation are well known from the general history of urban development in Europe and America. It is the processes involved in the other extreme type of situation that I have concentrated in this study. These processes have not yet been adequately studied. While in the first type we have a process of political 'detribalization', in the second we have a process of 'tribalization'. In the first, the longer a tribesman stays in town the more politically detribalized he becomes. In the second, the longer a tribesman stays in town the more politically tribalized he becomes.

I am referring here to types of situations, not to types of towns, since we can find both types of situation within one and the same town. The classification of towns into types may be convenient for some purposes but it is not sociologically significant and is rather misleading. The assumption by Durkheim and Radcliffe-Brown that it is possible to compare societies as wholes and to establish a typology of societies has long been discarded in the study of simple, small-scale societies. And if this is the case in the study of simple societies, it should be more so in the case of towns, where the variables involved are far more numerous and their combinations and interaction more complex. It may be legitimate to compare towns on the basis of a single criterion, such as demographic structure, economic organization, administrative system or so forth, but it will be futile to attempt to take all these, combined, as a basis for the classification.

But even if we compare towns in respect of a single political variable like that which I have called political ethnicity, it may not be possible to establish a typology of towns. In New York City, the Scandinavians and the Germans have been assimilated into the main body of white Anglo-Saxon Protestants. But the Negroes, Puerto Ricans, Jews, Italians and Irish, remain distinct because they are associated with distinct status groupings.[29] Similarly, in the city of Ibadan, we have a tribal group like the Western Ibos, who have gone a long way in integrating themselves economically and politically within the city, and we have on the other hand the Hausa who are now more tribally distinct than ever before. One may also expect to find the same kind of variation in situations of political ethnicity in the industrial urban centres of Africa, and there is certainly a growing body of evidence that this is so.[30]

In most types of situations which lie between the two extremes of the continuum of ethnic political grouping we have at one and the same time processes of political tribalization and detribalization operating simultaneously. The same tribal group may be going through a process of detribalization on one political level and through a process of tribalization on another level. Thus many tribal groupings in central African towns might have 'detribalized' in their collective struggle with white employers, but 're-tribalized' in the struggle for power within their own camp. What concerns anthropologists and sociologists here is to study the involvement of custom in this kind of situation. Indeed this is an ideal situation for the study of the dynamics of social and cultural change.

But despite its universal character, the process of political ethnicity has received little attention in sociology. This is only partly due to the unpopularity of the word 'tribalism' among Africans, especially the African élite, who have developed vested interests in controlling the strategic central institutions of political power, and among professional anthropologists and other scholars, who want to avoid being branded as reactionaries. But the main reason is something deeper and more theoretical. This is that many sociologists and social anthropologists are still influenced by the evolutionary formulations of the great sociologists of the turn of this century who have seen all social change leading in one direction: from status to contract (Maine), from community to association (MacIver) from *gemeinshaft* to *gesellschaft* (Tonnies) from mechanical solidarity to organic solidarity (Durkheim).[31]

It was only in recent years that the significance of informal, face to face, primary interaction and groupings in contemporary industrial societies, has been 're-discovered', principally by American sociology.[32] The process here is from single-interest relations to multiple relations, and from relations governed by hypothetical imperatives to relations governed by categorical imperatives. Homans explains this in terms of a 'social surplus' theory. This is that whenever men come together within the framework of a formal single-interest association, they interact as whole personalities and soon create informal social relations which are not a necessary part of the formal association.[33]

Greer expresses this with great clarity by conceiving a social group in terms of two dimensions: the *secondary*, which refers to the 'social product', and the *primary* which refers to the 'social process'. The social product represents the formal aim of the group while the social process refers to the informal relations that are created between people who are interacting in the course of achieving that aim. Few social groups are either wholly secondary or wholly primary, with most concrete groups ranging on the continuum between the two extremes.[34]

As LaPiere points out, the great sociologists over-simplified the nature of pre-industrial society by emphasizing its primary, communal character, as individuals are submerged in the world of multiplex relations.[35] On the other hand, they also over-simplified the nature of industrial, mainly urban, society by emphasizing its 'impersonal' character, as a man's personality is broken down to its constituent roles which are submerged within separate, different, single-interest associations.

Today many sociologists hold that in both the industrial and simple societies people spend their lives within a two-dimensional social world, where formal and informal relations are interconnected, interdependent and continually interacting. The structural significance of the system of moral values which govern these informal relations has been recently discussed, for the first time in a systematic way in social anthropology, by Fürer-Haimendorf, on the basis of his extensive field studies in several societies.[36]

Wolfe has pointed out the possibility that

'complex societies in the modern world differ less in the formal organization of their economic or legal or political systems than in the character of their supplementary interpersonal sets . . . [which] make possible the functioning of the great institutions.[37]

It is thus clear that within a multi-ethnic milieu, the members of an ethnic group are likely not only to retain primary inter-personal formations, but also to generate new ones more intensively and more readily than with members of other ethnic groups, because they speak the same language and have the advantage of having a common system of values and of customs under which these formations can be developed. These formations will, in their turn, be used by the ethnic group, for new purposes within their new surroundings. Some of these purposes are political and, under some circumstances, an ethnic polity will develop in connection with them.

The Informal Nature of Political Ethnicity

In the light of the foregoing discussion, a number of points can be made which can help in isolating the phenomena and processes of ethnicity.

Firstly, contemporary ethnicity is the result of intensive interaction between ethnic groupings and not the result of complete separatism. This is contrary to what one may call 'the glue theory of tribalism' which has been suggested by some writers. This theory states that during the colonial period, the colonial powers had acted as 'glue' in sticking together within the framework of new, artificially established, centralized states, some diverse 'tribal' groups, and that once the glue was removed when the colonial powers withdrew, each package state began to disintegrate and to fall into its original parts. It is of course true that many of the new states of Africa were originally created by the colonial powers. But during the colonial period a great deal of integration between the constituent tribal groups had taken place and this had given rise to increasing interaction between these groups. In British West Africa, this interaction was limited because of the policy of Indirect Rule and also because the strategic positions of centralized power were held by the foreign rulers. But the protective umbrella of Indirect Rule made it possible for some tribal groups to develop vital interests of their own while other tribal groups became relatively underprivileged. When the British withdrew an intense struggle for power ensued. The privileged became exposed to the danger of losing power and had to mobilize their forces in defence while the underprivileged aligned themselves to gain power.

Further and more bitter struggles broke out over new strategic positions of power: places of employment, taxation, funds for development, education, political positions, and so on. In many places the possibilities of capturing these new sources of power were different for different tribal groups, so that very often the resulting cleavages were on tribal lines. As a result of this intensified struggle, many tribal groups mobilized their forces and searched for ways in which they could organize themselves politically so as to conduct their struggle more effectively. In the process of this mobilization a new emphasis was placed on parts of their traditional culture, and this gave the impression that here there was a return to tribal tradition and to tribal separatism when in fact tribalism in the contemporary situation was one type of political grouping within the framework of the new state.

Secondly, tribalism involves a dynamic rearrangement of relations and of customs, and is not the outcome of cultural conservatism or continuity. The continuities of customs and of social formations are certainly there, but their functions have changed. As Gluckman pointed out a long time ago, 'where in a changing system the dominant cleavage is into two culture-groups, each of these groups will tend to set increasingly greater value on its own endo-culture, since this expresses the dominant cleavage'.[38]

Thirdly, ethnicity is essentially a political phenomenon, as traditional customs are used only as idioms, and as mechanisms for political alignment. People do not kill one another because their customs are different. Men may make jokes at the strange customs of men from other tribes but this by itself will not lead to serious disputes. If men do actually quarrel seriously on the grounds of cultural differences it is only because these cultural differences are associated with serious political cleavages. On the other hand men stick together under the contemporary situation only because of mutual interests. The Hausa of Sabo are united viz-à-viz the Yoruba because their unity is essential for their livelihood and for safeguarding their assets in the land and the buildings of the Quarter. Another tribal group may unite in order to mobilize votes in elections, to gain new benefits in development funds, or even to prevent the relatively scarce supply of women of the ethnic group from being taken by outsiders.

Finally, ethnic grouping is essentially informal. It does not form part of the official framework of economic and political power within the state. Otherwise, i.e. if an ethnic grouping is formally recognized, either as a state or as a region within a federal framework, then we are no longer dealing with ethnicity but with national or international politics. Thus according to this usage interaction between the regions of Nigeria should not be called ethnicity. Similarly the relations between various 'native authorities' during the colonial period cannot be called ethnicity since ethnic groupings under native authorities were officially recognized and a great part of their political organization was formally institutionalized. It is only when, within the formal framework of a national state or of any formal organization, an ethnic group informally organizes itself for political action, that we can say that we are dealing with ethnicity. Informally organized political groupings of this type have been called by different names. Bailey, borrowing a term from Easton, has called them 'parapolitical structures', and described them as those political structures

'which are partly regulated by, and partly independent of, larger encapsulating political structures; and which, so to speak, fight battles with these larger structures in a war which for them, seldom, if ever, ends in victory, rarely in dramatic defeat, but usually in a long drawn stalemate and defeat by attrition'.[39]

Wolfe refers to the same kind of groupings when he states that

'the formal framework of economic and political power exists alongside or intermingled with various other kinds of informal structures which are interstitial, supplementary, parallel to it'.[40]

SOCIAL AND CULTURAL STRATEGIES IN POLITICAL ETHNICITY: A COMPARATIVE SCHEME

Our main theoretical interest here is how ethnic groups whose political corporateness is not formally institutionalized within the contemporary situation seek to organize their political functions informally, in terms of other principles of social organization. More specifically, we are concerned with the processes whereby groups of this type have sought to find solutions to a number of basic problems in political organization which have been isolated by comparative analysis: (1) the problem of distinctiveness, (2) the problem of communication, (3) the problem of decision-making, (4) the problem of authority, (5) the problem of ideology, and (6) the problem of discipline. Ultimately, our interest is in the dynamics of cultural and structural changes in response to new political circumstances: what customs are retained, borrowed, or developed, and for what structural purposes.

(1) The Problem of Distinctiveness

To operate effectively, a tribal group must define its membership and its sphere of operation, by defining its identity and its exclusiveness, within the context of the contemporaneous political setting. A privileged status group will try to prevent men, from underprivileged status groups, from infiltrating into its ranks. An underprivileged status group, on the other hand will have to define its membership because it is only by organizing itself tightly that it can struggle effectively with the other status groups. The definition of the group depends on the size and power of the other groups with which it is in competition. Under some circumstances, two or more ethnic groups will have to stand together against a larger tribal group and will therefore have to define their alliance in terms of a super-ethnic entity.[41] On the other hand a status group, within an ethnic category, will sometimes have to define its distinctiveness in such a way as to exclude other members and groups from within the same tribal category. In a changing system a group will have to redefine its distinctiveness in order to adjust to the changing realities of the distribution and redistribution of power and to changes in the dominant political ideology of the encapsulating system.

Distinctiveness is achieved by a group in a number of ways:

(a) Myths of Origin and Claims to Superiority. Nearly all tribal groups combine special myths of origin with claims to superiority over other tribal groups. With the collapse of Indirect Rule in Ibadan the Hausa developed the claim that they were purer and more superior Moslems, to distinguish themselves from the masses of Yoruba Moslems in the city. On the other hand, they sought under some circumstances to distinguish themselves from other Hausa who were threatening their monopoly in trade by developing the myth that those other Hausa were 'undesirable'.

(b) Descent and Endogamy. Definition of membership of a group is always combined with the development of principles of descent and of endogamy. The observance of a strong descent principle, such as patriliny, or matriliny, may enable a group to retain its distinctiveness despite inter-marriage with other groups. But because we are dealing principally with migrants in towns, we are in effect dealing with people who, because they have left their tribal life in the rural hinterland, tend to be bilateral in their kinship organization. Descent will therefore have to be combined with group endogamy, and membership will thus be defined both paternally and maternally. Thus the Hausa in Northern Nigeria, whose kinship is patrilineally biased can and do marry non-Hausa wives, without running the risk of losing their children to the tribal groups of their wives or without running the risk of themselves losing their Hausa identity. But the Hausa of Sabo, being removed from their kinship groupings in the North, observe strict endogamy and prohibit marriage with the Yoruba, because in the Ibadan situation the Hausa family is nucleated and is thus more bilateral.

(c) Moral Exclusiveness. In-group endogamy is of crucial importance in maintaining and developing the distinctiveness of the group in yet another respect. Marriage is nearly everywhere a means of establishing friendships and alliances between groups and individuals. On the other hand, as Wagley and Harris point out,[42] endogamy is 'an almost certain sign of hostility and conflict between groups'. Marriage creates channels for the development of primary relations and thus leads to the formation of loyalties and of moral obligations. Emphasis on in-group endogamy, therefore, means the intensification of informal interaction between people within the group, and the inhibition of such interaction with members of the other groups.

But in the towns, marriage is of course not the only sphere of informal interaction, and an ethnic group which is seeking to sharpen its distinctiveness, will discourage all or much informal social interaction outside the group in order to intensify such interaction within the group. I discussed earlier in this book how the localization, intensification, and collectivization of rituals brought about by the entry of the Tijaniyya order into Sabo developed this moral exclusiveness for the Hausa in Ibadan. Essien-Udom also shows how in their efforts to create 'the Nation of Islam', the Black Moslems in the United States seek to insulate their members from much interaction with the Whites and with non-Moslem Blacks, while at the same time they put pressure on members to intensify interaction among themselves in order to deepen the distinctiveness of the emerging 'Nation'.[43] Studies of other ethnic groupings in U.S.A. and elsewhere show the employment of similar techniques by those groupings.

(d) Endo-Culture. Channelling informal interaction within a group deepens the distinctiveness of the group further by keeping alive and developing the endo-culture of the group.[44] Informal interaction creates primary relations that are governed by specific values, norms, and beliefs. Interaction within the group will therefore lead to the maintenance or revival of group customs. Interaction out of the group, on the other hand, will lead to either the adoption of foreign customs or to the creation of new, neutral, customs. Sometimes, as in the case of many ethnic groups in U.S.A. today, a group might have lost its original language and much of its original traditional culture, but moral relations between its members will still be guided by endo-cultural symbols.

(e) Spatial Proximity. The members of a status, ethnic, group will nearly always try to live in spatial proximity in order to facilitate co-operation and to intensify interaction among its members. This is particularly the case in large cities, like Ibadan. In the city of Oyo, the Hausa remained living in the town with the Yoruba until the early 1940's when, since the city had expanded, the Hausa demanded, and eventually succeeded, in having a separate quarter of their own. Spatial proximity by itself, however, is not a sufficient factor in the development of an ethnic grouping, unless—as was the case with the Makaah Indians' reservation,[45] and partly was the case of Sabo—the land and the buildings become a vital economic interest in their own right. There are many cases of tribal groups who were forced to live within special quarters but who eventually broke out of those quarters and dispersed. There are, on the other hand, cases of tribal groups who were deprived of having a special residential area but who later did their utmost to concentrate within special quarters. In nearly all big U.S.A. cities there are distinct residential areas which are associated with distinct ethnic or ethno-religious groupings. Spatial proximity can become a strong auxiliary factor in the development of effective ethnic grouping, as in the case of French Canadians.[46]

(f) Homogenization. An ethnic grouping which is engaged in a struggle with another ethnic grouping will, in the course of the struggle, go through a process of social and cultural homogenization among its members. Homogeneity increases the viability of the group in many ways. The Hausa of Sabo have originated from different Hausa areas and different Hausa sub-cultures. But because of the cleavage with the Yoruba, there is a continuous pressure on people to drop these differences. The different groups of Hausa in Sabo inter-marry without any restrictions and the operation of such common institutions as the Tijaniyya and the chieftaincy bring about further homogenization in a variety of respects. Homogenization is essential for increasing internal co-operation and interaction, and is indispensable in the development of communication within the polity. √

(2) *The Problem of Communication*

Distinctiveness alone will not make a tribal category into a tribal political grouping. A tribal polity can develop only to the extent, and within the limits, of the development of a system of communication between its constituent parts. Without communication, political and economic co-operation and interdependence will not be possible. A tribal group will seldom be subjected to pressure collectively and conspicuously. In a large tribally heterogenous African town the members of a tribal group may be dispersed in terms of residence and in terms of place of work. Each member may be involved in a struggle for power on his own and it is only when the members of the group exchange messages, pool their separate experiences, discuss their problems, and identify the common denominators of these problems, that it is possible for them to develop a common policy and a common political organization to put such policy into action.

As I indicated earlier, the malams in Sabo serve as an institutionalized channel through which communication is effected. Laymen express their current anxieties in divination sessions with the malams. In their regular interaction among themselves, the malams discuss the current problems that are afflicting people. The big malams discuss these problems with the landlords in the course of consultation and divinatory sessions. In frequent consultations with the Chief of the Quarter, information about the basic problems that are affecting the whole community is pooled. In this way one part of the community knows about the other parts.

Within the Black Moslem organization in the U.S.A. communication is effected through the theocratic politico-ritual hierarchy running from the Head of the movement, the Messenger, down to his Ministers, who are in charge of the local Temples, then down the hierarchy to the captains, secretary, treasurers, and investigators.[47]

In some cases, communication within a tribal grouping is effected through a hierarchy of associations. Thus, according to Parkin, the Luo and Luhya in Kampala, each have three levels of association: that of the maximal lineage or clan, that of the sub-tribe, and that of the whole tribe.[48]

Less formal and less systematic, but more pervasive channels for communication within a tribal group, are the chains of dyadic and other small groupings, whose boundaries cut across one another, within which people interact intensively and in the course of this interaction exchange views and discuss current problems.

(3) The Problem of Decision-Making

Communication alone is not sufficient for a distinct group to function politically. Some kind of an institutionalized agency must collect the political messages, discuss them, and take decisions. All political action is the result of decision making. Political scientists distinguish between three stages in the process of decision-making.[49] The first stage is that at which problems are formulated in the light of the information that is supplied through the channels of communication. In Sabo when the malams exchange information about the current afflictions of people they may discover a pattern in these problems and in the course of discussions among themselves and between themselves and the landlords and the Chief, a generalization from the particular problems may be established.

The formulation of general problems is followed by a stage of deliberation when the leaders try to find solutions. In Sabo this deliberation takes place in the course of theological discussions among the malams and in the course of divining sessions between the leading malams and the landlords. In addition there is the more direct formal discussion between the Chief and the *Hajjis*, i.e., the leading landlords and the leading malams.

In the analysis of every political system, it is thus important to find out who formulate the general problems, who deliberate about these problems, and who make the decisions. No matter how lacking it is in centralized authority, a political group must have some functionaries who take decisions. Failure to recognize the crucial importance of this point has for long vitiated the analysis of the so-called segmentary political systems, i.e. political systems that are by definition without centralized leaders.

(4) The Problem of Authority

In dealing with the problem of decision making we are dealing, partly, also with the problem of authority, though the two problems should be analytically separated. Decisions will be implemented only if they are backed by authority, which involves the legitimate use of power.

Among the Hausa of Sabo, a decision to boycott the Yoruba kola producers in a certain area, or the butchers from a specific slaughter house in the city, may be in the short run detrimental to the interests of one or more Hausa men from the Quarter who may therefore feel tempted not to abide by the decision. These men may realize that the decision was taken in the interest of the whole community and, indirectly in their own interest, but because they are immersed in their immediate problems they may not feel strongly enough to forego an immediate advantage or to avoid some possible loss. It is therefore of crucial importance that some kind of authority which is backed by sufficient power should apply pressure on such individuals to make them conform.

All political organizations need authority. Authority is needed also for administrative purposes, for the resolution of internal disputes, for the co-ordination of political action, and for symbolizing the political corporateness of the group against other groups.

Authority is always composite, in that the power on which it is based is derived from different kinds of social relationships. Power is nearly always inherent in social relationships and different kinds of social relationships are thus mobilized to support authority. Power mobilized in this way is routinized and institutionalized. Informally organized political groupings make more use of moral, ritual, and economic power than political groupings that are formally backed by physical power.

In the study of authority it is always important to distinguish between formal power, that is power which is associated with an office, and the personal network of power of the man occupying that office. In informally organized political systems like those of tribal groupings in African towns, more extensive use is made of the personal power of the incumbent of a position of authority than in a formal political system. This is one of the reasons why many tribal groupings in African towns today choose for positions of authority old settlers from the same tribe who have built for themselves an effective network of social relationships in their own right. In this way these old settlers bring with them into the position within the tribal polity all the power which they personally derive from their economic, moral, and other relations within the context of the town.

(5) The Problem of Ideology

It is evident from the discussion so far that the organization of a tribal polity requires the mobilization of different kinds of social relationships, the creation and strengthening and utilization of different kinds of myths, beliefs, norms, values, and motives, and the employment of different types of pressure and of sanctions. These different elements which are employed in the development of a political system become so interdependent that they tend to be seen in terms of an integrated ideological scheme which is related to the basic problems of man, his place in society and in the universe. This is achieved by the development or by the adoption of a political ideology by the community. Ultimately, it is the political ideology which gives legitimacy to power and thus converts power to authority.

A political ideology is not just a reflection of the various elements of the political system, but is itself a significant variable in its own right, contributing to the development and the functioning of the political system. Once developed, it becomes an autonomous factor which can motivate people to action. In every political system there is a continuous dialectical interaction between its ideology and its other constituent parts.

A political group may either develop its own political ideology or may adopt a ready-made one. But even when a ready-made ideology is adopted as a 'blueprint' for the development of its political organization, it will be given substance in terms of the particular circumstances of the group. Ideologies are seldom rigid. They are made of myths and symbols which can be variously interpreted and reinterpreted.

Political ideologies can take different *forms*. In simple societies two major forms of ideologies can be found. The first may be labelled as a predominantly 'kinship ideology', and the second as a predominantly 'ritual ideology'. These two forms are not mutually exclusive. Many kinship ideologies contain some ritual elements, such as the beliefs and practices that are associated with the ancestors of a group. Similarly, many ritual ideologies mobilize some of the primary relations within the elementary family by ritualizing them through rites of passage.

In the so-called segmentary political systems generally, the political ideology tends to take the form of a predominantly kinship ideology, while in centralized societies the ideology tends to take the form of a predominantly ritual ideology. Kinship ideologies exploit the strong sentiments and emotions that are associated with primary relationships between members of the elementary family in support of the political system. Religious ideologies, on the other hand, exploit the emotional anxieties of men in facing the perennial problems of existence, of life and death, health and illness, happiness and misery.

There is some partial evidence that some migrant ethnic groupings, like those of Luo and the Luhya in Kampala, seem to articulate their political organization in terms of a kinship ideology.[50] But cases of this type must be few because as a result of migration even those migrants who come from tribal societies which have traditions of extensive kinship organization tend to become bilateral as they settle in town.

Many ethnic political groupings in the towns seem therefore to organize themselves in terms of a ritual ideology, in the form of a separatist church, of an exclusive mystical order, or of some other type of cult.

This can be seen in dramatic way in the organization of ethnic groups in the U.S.A. today. When an immigrant is naturalized as a U.S. citizen he is asked to swear absolute allegiance to the American flag and to hold no loyalties towards any foreign country. Apart from this legalistic principle, there is a very strong ideology about American society being a 'melting pot' within which migrants from different ethnic groups shed their cultural differences. All this makes it very difficult for an ethnic group which is identified with a specific status grouping, to organize itself formally on ethnic lines. Instead, the group will make use of a religious ideology and organization in order to articulate its political organization. Thus, Glazer and Moynihan state that 'religious institutions are generally closely linked to distinct ethnic groups' and that in New York ethnic groupings have religious names. Indeed this may explain the nature of the so-called 'religious paradox' in the U.S.A. today. Recent studies of religious behaviour and religious organization in America have revealed that there is on the one hand increasing secularization and on the other increasing affiliation within religious organizations.[51] As Herberg puts it: 'Americans think, feel, and act in terms quite obviously secularist at the very time that they exhibit every sign of a widespread religious revival'.[52] Lenski, on the basis of intensive studies of religion in Detroit, detects 'a trend toward increased religious group communalism' and states that 'the successor to the ethnic subcommunity is the socio-religious sub-community, a group united by ties of race and religion'.[53]

Religion provides an ideal 'blueprint' for the development of an informal political organization. It mobilizes many of the most powerful emotions which are associated with the basic problems of human existence and gives legitimacy and stability to political arrangements by representing these as parts of the system of the universe. It makes it possible to mobilize the power of symbols and the power inherent in the ritual relationships between various ritual positions within the organization of the cult. It makes it possible to use the arrangements for financing and administering places of worship and associated places for welfare, education, and social activities of various sorts, to use these in developing the organization and administration of political functions. Religion also provides frequent and regular meetings in congregations, where in the course of ritual activities, a great deal of informal interaction takes place, information is communicated, and general problems are formulated and discussed. The system of myths and symbols which religion provides is capable of being continuously interpreted and re-interpreted in order to accommodate it to changing economic, political and other social circumstances.

I have shown earlier in this book how these various strategic advantages of a religious ideology have been exploited by the Hausa of Sabo, when the doctrine, practice and organization of the Tijaniyya order were made to organize them as a community.

(6) *The Problem of Discipline*

An ideology will function only if it is maintained and kept alive by continuous indoctrination, conditioning of moods and attitudes, and affirmation of belief. This can be achieved mainly through ceremonials. The symbols have to be continuously charged with meanings which deal with the current problems of the community. Men are usually immersed in their day-to-day private problems and immediate utilitarian interests and they have therefore to be regularly shaken out of their egocentric affairs and made to reaffirm their belief and support of the basic principles of their political organization. The more elements of the political organization that the ideology articulates the greater the need for frequent ceremonials.

This is the case in all political systems but it is particularly so when a polity is informally organized, as in cases of ethnicity, when, because of the absence of the use of organized physical coercion, increasing use is made of ritual and moral mechanisms. These mechanisms impose a heavy burden on the 'conscience' and will of men and require the continuous sharpening of their normative sensibilities.[54] I believe that this is one of the main reasons why members of some minority groups are said to be 'tense' for they are always under pressure to discipline themselves to think of their heavy obligations to their groups.

The different cultural variables which are mobilized to provide solutions to these problems in political organization assume in the new situation new values. The result is a cultural, as well as a social, reorganization.[55] The old 'compulsory institutions' and the new economic and political institutions interact with, and adjust to, one another and integrate within a new sociocultural system.[56] The new integration will develop within the biographies of the members of the community as these members assume new sets of roles.

The Challenge to Social Anthropology Today

It is evident from the foregoing discussion that political ethnicity is a complex social and cultural phenomenon in which different variables are involved. These variables can be isolated, and their interdependence analysed, by comparative research. It will be necessary to compare different structural situations which give rise to ethnic political groupings.[57] Comparison can then be made between the various cultural strategies which have been adopted by various ethnic groups in solving their basic problems in political organization, taking each one of these problems as a basis for comparison at a time.

As different cultural traditions provide different solutions to these problems, it will be possible to examine the question whether some cultural traditions are more effective than others in the organization of political functions within the same structural situation. For example, whether the culture of ethnic groups from traditionally segmentary 'tribes' is more, or less, effective in political articularation in the modern situation than the culture of ethnic groups from traditionally centralized 'tribes'.[58] Further comparison can be made on these lines to find out the relative importance of cultural, as against structural, factors in producing the phenomenon of political ethnicity. The question may be posed, for example, as to what extent can the continuity of Jewish ethnic groupings, over many centuries and in many parts of the world, be attributed to the strength of Judaic cultural tradition, as against the continuity of the structural conditions under which these groupings have developed. In this way, different cultural traditions can be compared within similar structural situations, and similar cultural traditions within different structural situations.

In considering such questions we are in fact dealing with the basic problems of the study of sociocultural interdependence and their analysis will thus shed substantial light on the major theoretical problems of social anthropology. Their investigation can no longer be adequately developed in the course of studying the static, isolated, 'tribal', society. 'Tribal' studies have provided a fundamental starting point in the analysis of sociocultural phenomena. Because of their simple technology, the homogenity of their culture, and of their relative isolation, the 'tribes' offered the anthropologist situations for dealing with a limited number of variables in the analysis of what would otherwise have been a hopelessly complex set of phenomena. And it is indeed only thanks to the insights gained in these 'tribal' studies that it is now possible to make sense of the more complex phenomena which one encounters in the contemporary complex society. But a new stage in the development of social anthropology has now been reached, not only because the static, small-scale, 'tribal' society has been rapidly disappearing, but also because little theoretical and methodologidal progress can be made by the multiplication of monographic studies on the old lines.[59]

The challenge to social anthropology today is the study of sociocultural change, of the involvement of custom in the change of social relations. Social change is essentially a change in the forms, distribution, and exercise of power and the struggle for it, and social anthropology is concerned mainly with the role of custom in this change. Social anthropology is thus essentially a branch of political science and is chiefly concerned with unfolding the political implications of custom under various structural conditions. In other words, it is mainly concerned with the political functions of what are formally non-political institutions, like marriage, kinship, friendship and religion. The social relationships which are governed by these formally non-political institutions have their own forms of power which are variously combined and utilized in political organization. As Russell puts it:

'Power, like energy [in physics] must be regarded as continually passing from any one of its forms into any other, and it should be the business of social science to seek the laws of such transformation.'[60]

This does not mean that we must search for 'laws of change'. As Fortes states:

'Social laws refer to ideally isolated features of social life and can be stated only in terms of probabilities. The combinations of factors that make up a particular occasion in the life of any society are not predictable and never will be, though each factor by itself may work in ways that can be foreseen within known limits of error.'[61]

What we look for are probabilities of this type. We seek to answer the broad question: Under what structural conditions, what customs, will perform what political functions, within which political unit? To study this question, we need to consider different combinations of social and cultural variables under different circumstances. It is in this respect that urban studies can be of crucial importance for social anthropology today. Varieties of social situations which are in the 'tribal' field dispersed over wide areas, among different peoples and under different traditions, are conveniently displayed within the small space of the town. Similarly, processes of sociocultural change which in the 'tribal' time perspective extend over many generations, are in the town telescoped within the span of a few years.

The towns thus afford ideal 'laboratory' conditions for the study of the dynamics of custom in political change. It is in this *technical* respect and not in the *theoretical* study of the so-called 'urbanism' or 'urbanization process', that the town is significant for anthropological research.[62] I believe that the search for *special principles* governing urban life is a blind alley for sociological research. A great deal of what is called 'urban sociology' is not sociology but is mainly a description of human ecology. When, on the other hand, an urban study *is* sociological, then it is no longer necessarily urban, but is just sociological. As Mitchell points out, the town should be treated as *a social field*, not as a single social system.[63]

Numerical Abstracts

INTRODUCTORY NOTE

In the course of the intensive part of my field work which was carried out within the Hausa Quarter in Ibadan, I sought to supplement the usual ethnographic material with numerical data. I did this in three ways. Firstly, I collected in a methodical and systematic way information on the biography and present social network of nearly 90 men, covering their business, kinship, friendship, political, marital and other family links. Secondly, I conducted with the help of one local assistant, 23 different surveys on different categories of men and women, with each survey covering several variables. Some of the surveys were exhaustive of all the people in the category, while the others dealt with samples, either systematic or random. Thirdly, I sought to gather, as a general quantitative background for the study, a general census for the whole population of the Quarter. It would not have been possible for me to carry out this census without the substantial and extensive work by two capable, paid, local assistants and by my wife. As it turned out, the bulk of the work was accomplished by them. Even so, the census would not have been possible if we did not have reference to an older census and to various kinds of lists of names of heads of households. A list was drawn up of the names of the people who were living in every house during 1963. I then constructed and printed a form for the house-to-house census in which several variables were covered, including age, place of birth, occupation and number of years spent in the Quarter.

When I returned to Britain the entire general census, together with two of the surveys, were coded and duly processed by I.B.M. The results were organized in scores of detailed and exhaustive tables in which correlations between the different variables are shown. As I believe in the motto that 'statistics can be a good servant but a very bad master', I have intentionally avoided indulging in any sophisticated statistical computations and used the data as a help in simple counting. In a varied, mobile, and differentiated population like the one with which this study is concerned, the importance of these numerical data cannot be overemphasized both in testing generalizations and in isolating variables.

The following tables have been abstracted from the original and more extensive ones, and they include only information which is directly relevant to the analysis in the text.

TABLE I

Occupational Distribution of Hausa Men
(aged 15 years and over) in 1963

Serial No.	Occupational Category	No. of Men
1	Cattle	112
2	Kola	340
3	Porters	175
4	Transporters	24
5	Malams	119
6	Services within Quarter	324
7	Labourers within Quarter	58
8	Labourer outside Quarter	47
9	Petty Traders within Quarter	117
10	Petty Traders out of Quarter	356
11	Beggars (formal)	82
12	Farmers	24
13	Others	206
	Total	1984

TABLE II

The Hausa Population of Sabo in the end of 1916
(based on data which was assembled by the D.O. in that year)

(a) Division by Age Group

Category	Male	Female	Total
Adult	261	120	381
Child	11	2	13
Total	272	122	394

(b) Destiny as in 1963 by Sex

Destiny	Male	Female	Total
Alive in Sabo	13	7	20
Died in Sabo	174	65	239
Left Sabo	29	14	43
Unknown	56	36	92
Total	272	122	394

[*This Table is continued on next page*]

[continuation of Table II]

(c) Adults by Sex and Occupation

Occupation	Male	Female	Total
Petty Trader	60	114[1]	174
Farmer	36	—	36
Trader	4	—	4
Tailor[2]	51	—	51
Cattle Trader[3]	56	—	56
Butcher	21	—	21
Barber	6	—	6
Woodseller	4	—	4
Arabic Scribe	3	—	3
Beggar-Musician	3	—	3
Blacksmith	2	—	2
Others	15	6	21
Total	261	120	381

[1] Most of these women were prostitutes. See the text pp. 61–2.

[2] Many of these were only part-time tailors who made Hausa gowns (riga) to sell to local Yoruba Moslems and to some Hausa strangers and to the Hausa settlers.

[3] The census collector obviously lumped together within this category both landlords and their clients in the cattle trade.

TABLE III

The Hausa Population of Sabo by Sex, Length of Settlement in Ibadan, and Segment of Quarter in 1963

Years in Ibadan	Original Quarter			Annexe			Total Sabo		
	M.	F.	Total	M.	F.	Total	M.	F.	Total
0 – 2	35	27	62	28	31	59	63	58	121
3 – 4	200	99	299	61	39	100	261	138	399
5 – 6	196	100	296	94	41	135	290	141	431
7 – 8	175	74	249	54	21	75	229	95	324
9 – 10	187	77	264	73	20	93	260	97	357
11 – 15	242	137	379	37	15	52	279	152	431
16 – 20	149	78	227	33	11	44	182	89	271
21 – 25	33	14	47	5	2	7	38	16	54
26 – 30	50	21	71	7	7	14	57	28	85
31 – 35	25	13	38	7	—	7	32	13	45
36 – 40	24	14	38	2	5	7	26	19	45
41 – 45	11	2	13	1	—	1	12	2	14
46 – 50	17	7	24	—	1	1	17	8	25
51 and over	6	6	12	—	—	—	6	6	12
{ Born in { Ibadan	610	793	1403	69	98	167	679	891	1570
Total	1960	1462	3422	471	291	762	2431	1753	4184

TABLE IV

Hausa Population of Sabo by Age and Sex in 1963

Age	Male	Female	Total
1 – 9	331	419	750
10 – 19	161	219	380
20 – 29	708	659	1367
30 – 39	683	272	955
40 – 49	303	94	397
50 – 59	155	55	210
60 and over	65	23	88
Total	2406	1741	4147

TABLE V

The Hausa Population in Sabo by Sex and No. of Years in the Quarter as in 1963

Years in Sabo	Males	Females	Total
1 – 2	63	58	121
3 – 4	261	138	399
5 – 6	290	141	431
7 – 8	229	95	324
9 – 10	260	97	357
11 – 15	279	152	431
16 – 20	182	89	271
21 – 25	38	16	54
26 – 30	57	28	85
31 – 35	32	13	45
36 – 40	26	19	45
41 – 45	12	2	14
46 – 50	17	8	25
51 and over	6	6	12
Born in Sabo	679	891	1570
Total	2431	1753	4184

TABLE VI

Hausa Population in Sabo by Sex and Birthplace (1963 Census)

Birthplace	Male	Female	Total
Kano Province	955	473	1428
Katsina Province	175	70	245
Sokoto Province	201	94	295
Zaria Province	114	76	190
Other North	300	146	446
Sabo	678	889	1567
Other W.R.	8	5	13
Total	2431	1753	4184

TABLE VII

Hausa Born in Sabo by Age and Sex as in 1963

Age	Male	Female	Total
1 – 9	318	397	715
10 – 19	123	170	293
20 – 29	153	241	394
30 – 39	64	70	134
40 – 49	12	8	20
50 – 59	7	4	11
60 and over	1	1	2
Total	678	891	1569

TABLE VIII

Hausa Population of Sabo by Age, Sex and Place of Birth, as in 1963

Age	Males			Females			Total		
	Mi-grant	Sabo Born	Total	Mi-grant	Sabo Born	Total	Mi-grant	Sabo Born	Total
1 – 9	13	318	331	22	397	419	35	715	750
10 – 19	38	123	161	49	170	219	87	293	380
20 – 29	555	153	708	418	241	659	973	394	1367
30 – 39	619	64	683	202	70	272	821	134	955
40 – 49	291	12	303	86	8	94	377	20	397
50 – 59	148	7	155	51	4	55	199	11	210
60 and over	64	1	65	22	1	23	86	2	88
Total	1728	678	2406	850	891	1741	2578	1569	4147

TABLE IX

Foster Parent and Foster Child by Sex:
A random sample, taken in 1963, of 120 cases of fostering

Foster Parent	Foster Child		
	Male	Female	Total
Male	15	15	30
Female	31	59	90
Total	46	74	120

Notes

INTRODUCTION

(1) See Mercier 1965, p. 486.

(2) For this typology of towns, see Southal 1961.

(3) See Eisenstadt 1966.

(4) On 'interest groups', see Eckstein 1960, Smelser 1962, and Castles 1967.

(5) For a detailed survey and analysis of various governmental arrangements, in the new states of Asia and Africa, for 'integrating' such
groups, see Geertz 1963.

(6) See Van Den Berghe 1965, pp. 1-11, and Mercier 1965, pp. 483-501.

(7) See Smith 1960.

(8) Van Den Berghe 1965, pp. 77-88.

(9) Gluckman 1958 (originally published in 1940-42), p. 63.

(10) See Bauer 1963, pp. 379-92, Cohen 1965 & 1966, Dorjahn and
Fyfe, 1962, Forde 1947, Skinner 1963 & 1964, Smith 1962, Oliver
and Fage 1962, Fage 1955, and Jones 1954.

(11) See Hill 1962, 1966a, and 1966b.

(12) See Skinner 1964.

(13) See Forde, 1947, p. 22.

(14) Indeed, it has been argued on psychological grounds that the Hausa
have poorer 'achievement motivations' than the Yoruba and the Ibo.
See LeVine 1966. This argument is discussed critically below, pp.
229-232.

(15) In Hausa, meaning 'New Town'.

(16) See Cohen, 1965b.

(17) *ibid.*

(18) See Table I, p. 216.

(19) As in many other parts of Africa, anything related to Islam is described as 'Arabic' by the Hausa.

(20) Ar. *Mukaddam*, in the singular. Plural, *mukaddamin*.

(21) Ar. *Salat el-Jumu'a*.

(22) Hausa: '*Lokacin da siyasa ta zo*'.

(23) There are about 750,000 people in Ibadan. But the city is often
described as 'the largest village on earth', because a very large
proportion of its population is engaged in farming. Oluwansanmi 1967.

(24) See the Map. Mokola was originally established as a quarter for the
Nupe, but in the course of a few years most of the Nupe sold their
plots of land and the majority now live as tenants in Yoruba-owned
houses. A large proportion of non-Nupe have joined the quarter and
the Nupe are now in effect a minority in Mokola. Ekotedo was
allotted for the residence of strangers from other parts of southern

Nigeria, mainly from the Eastern Region. But here too the tribal character of the area has been blurred.

(25) See Rouch, 1956.
(26) ibid.
(27) See Bauer 1963, Church 1957, Forde 1947, Pedlar 1955.
(28) *Trypanosomiasis.*
(29) Except for occasional experimental herds and a small local breed which is of no economic significance.
(30) See Table I, p. 216.
(31) From categories 8 and 9, Table I, p. 216.
(32) See Table I.
(33) See Cohen 1965b.
(34) See Cohen 1966.
(35) See also Bauer 1963.
(36) See Cohen 1967.
(37) See Fortes and Evans-Pritchard 1940, pp. 16-22. For further elaboration of this point, see Gluckman 1955, pp. 27-53 and Gluckman 1965, pp. 244-5.
(38) See pp. 129-40.
(39) See Mair 1958.
(40) This methodological problem is discussed in great depth by Bailey, Devons and Gluckman 1964.
(41) See Bailey 1964. On network analysis see Barnes 1968.
(42) This of course is a decision on lines of orientation rather than on strict methodological procedure. Indeed this is what is implied in Devons and Gluckman's (1964) advice: close the system but keep your mind open to the intrusion of other factors.
(43) For detailed discussion of these two kinds of process, see Gluckman 1958, and Mitchell 1966.
(44) See Cohen 1965b, for a similar procedure.
(45) This is not a theoretical, but a practical, necessity. See Evans-Pritchard 1961.
(46) See Evans-Pritchard 1961, for a detailed discussion of this point.
(47) See Turner 1957 and Gluckman 1961.

CHAPTER ONE

(1) See Table II, pp. 216-17.
(2) See Table III, p. 217.
(3) See Map (Frontispiece).
(4) The belief is that a true Hausa must have originated from one of the seven Hausa states: Biram, Katsina, Zaria, Kano, Gobir, Daura, and Sokotol.
(5) See Table V, p. 218.
(6) See Table II, p. 216-17.
(7) See Table V, p. 218.
(8) See Table V, p. 218.
(9) In Hausa: *Dan Kasa.*
(10) In Hausa: *Baki.*

(11) For the North, see Smith 1955 and 1964.

(12) See Table IV, p. 218.

(13) For migrants in Central Africa, see Gluckman 1960.

(14) In Islam alms are distinct from charity.

(15) See Government of the Gold Coast 1955. See also Clarkson 1963.

(16) Taxis provide the main means of public transport in Ibadan. They carry passengers for short standard journeys and charge about 6d. (in 1963) per passenger.

(17) See Government of the Gold Coast 1955.

(18) See Smith 1961.

(19) See Table VI, p. 218.

CHAPTER TWO

(1) See Rouch 1956.

(2) *ibid.*

(3) Prothero 1957 and 1959.

(4) See Table IV, p. 218.

(5) See Table VII, p. 219.

(6) See Table IV, p. 218.

(7) See Smith, M. G. 1959.

(8) See Cohen 1965b.

(9) I have been informed that in some emirates in Northern Nigeria, the local rulers are in the habit of ordering a mass expulsion of prostitutes from their cities when times are bad, such as during a drought.

(10) See Smith 1964, p. 26.

(11) See Greenberg 1946.

(12) See Levy 1957.

(13) See Cohen 1965b.

(14) In Arabic: *maddanha.*

(15) In Arabic: *sufur fallahi*

(16) In Arabic: *sufur madani.*

(17) See Smith 1955.

(18) See Cohen 1965b.

(19) See Table II, p. 216–17.

(20) See Table VII, p. 219.

(21) One petition was presented by a northern political party who pointed out that although they did not approve of prostitution, they could not accept that Hausa prostitutes should be singled out for persecution.

(22) See Table IX, p. 219.

(23) See Smith 1955.

(24) The situation may differ in the North.

(25) See Nadel 1957.

(26) See Smith 1959.

(27) See Table VII, p. 219.

CHAPTER THREE

(1) *Maigida*, singular; plural: *masu gida*. The literal meaning of the word is 'houseowner'. The Hausa refer to the house of a business man in

the same way as one refers to 'the house of Rothschild'.

(2) There is a great deal of ambiguity in these terms because of their connotations in English. As I explain further on, all these categories of men are 'clients' to the landlord, work only for him, and depend for their business and remuneration on the landlord exclusively.

(3) There is a great deal of ambiguity in the use of this term. A detailed discussion on the subject is given below, pp. 119–29.

(4) For details see below, pp. 119–29.

(5) By the term 'dealer' I am referring to a man who acts as a trader in his own right. This is different from the usage advocated by Hill 1966d.

(6) Throughout the Western Region of Nigeria the cattle markets are locally known by the Hausa word *Zango*, literally meaning a camping place or caravan, while the local Hausa quarter is known as Sabo. In Ghana, on the other hand, the word *Zango*, which is pronounced as *Zongo*, is used for the quarters where strangers from Northern territories, who are predominantly Hausa, live.

(7) This occurred during the 1962-3 'emergency situation' in the Western Region of Nigeria which was attended by a serious economic crisis.

(8) Apart from a few such free-lance commission agents there were a few Hausa men operating in the market as small scale speculators, known as *baranda*, who used to buy a few heads of cattle and sell them in some Yoruba villages around Ibadan.

(9) See Cohen 1965a.

(10) Throughout this book I use the term 'informal relations' in the sense of primary, personal, face-to-face relations. LaPiere refers to groups based on these relations as status groups. See LaPiere, 1954. See also Wolfe 1966 for a similar usage.

(11) See Sampson 1962, chapter 23-25.

(12) See Roberts 1966 and Gulliver 1963, pp. 287–8 and 293–6.

(13) See Wilson and Lupton 1959.

(14) See Table No. IX

(15) See, for a comparison, the close interconnection between marriage and status among the Arabs, Cohen 1965b

(16) The Hausa of Sabo differ in this respect from the Hausa of Northern Nigeria. See Smith 1959 and Yeld 1960.

(17) This, again, is the opposite of the practice among the Arabs. See Cohen 1965b.

(18) *Mahr*, or *sadaq*.

(19) In Hausa, *Zumunci*.

(20) See above pp. 53–4.

(21) It was not possible for me to ascertain the exact number of the houses which 'belonged' to the Chief. Many members of his family lived in houses which they declared as theirs when, according to informants, the houses were originally held by the Chief on behalf of the community. There were similar cases of some leading clients of the Chief who claimed the houses to be theirs.

CHAPTER FOUR

(1) See Epstein 1958, Gluckman 1961, and Mitchell, 1956.

(2) Epstein 1958 and 1961.

(3) See Cohen 1965a and 1966.

(4) See above, pp. 86–92.

(5) See Cohen 1965a.

(6) This is a procedure which I followed in a previous study (Cohen 1965b). It is essentially based on some leads and formulations in the use of case material, as a tool both of presentation and analysis by Turner 1957, and Gluckman 1961.

(7) Council Minutes of 13th October 1906 and of 30th October 1906. For a historical background of Ibadan see Awe 1967.

(8) Council Minutes of 23rd May 1907.

(9) Council Minutes of 22nd August 1907.

(10) See particularly Council Minutes of 3rd October 1910, and of 22nd July 1911.

(11) Akinyele 1946. (This is the late Sir Isaac B. Akinyele who became Olubadan from 1955 until his death in 1965).

(12) Council Minutes of 19th April 1913.

(13) See table II, pp. 216–17.

(14) Council Minutes of 23rd June 1916.

(15) Council Minutes of 18th December 1929. For details see below, pp. 120–1.

(16) See below, pp. 129–40.

(17) Native Authority Ordinance No. 43.

(18) See below, pp. 141–50.

(19) See Table II, p. 216. Administrative Department File, 20th December 1926, Mapo Hall.

(20) Administrative Department File, 20th December 1929, Mapo Hall.

(21) For detailed discussion of Indirect Rule, see Lugard 1922, Perham 1937, Flint 1960, Lloyd 1960, and Crowder 1964.

(22) Until this time, the group known in the Quarter as Kaka Gida still regarded themselves as Hausa and actively participated in the Quarter's public life.

(23) Native Administration Minutes of 29th January 1940.

(24) In 1914 Ibadan was incorporated within the Native Authority under the Alafin of Oyo. The Ibadans resented this subservience to a weak and less important town and after a great deal of agitation succeeded in 1936 in gaining independence. Since then the title 'Olubadan' has replaced that of 'Bale'. To avoid confusing the general reader I use the title 'Olubadan' throughout.

(25) See Map (frontispiece).

(26) These are 'Pastoral', not 'Town', Fulanis.

(27) Natives of Nigeria who travel in West Africa do not need a passport, but only a Travel Certificate.

(28) Sabo was in fact established within the wall of Ibadan.

(29) When the Quarter was founded, only simple cottages were built. Later, as the settlers became wealthier and as professional builders

came from the North, more solid and more expensive buildings were erected. Today, many expensively built houses in the Quarter can be found.

(30) Judicial Council Minutes of 18th December 1929. Also Ibadan Native Authority Minutes of 18th December 1929.

(31) Judicial Council Minutes of 3rd January 1930.

(32) Judicial Council Minutes of 18th January 1930.

(33) Judicial Council Minutes of 18th January 1930.

(34) Judicial Council Minutes of 7th February 1930.

(35) This point is discussed further in Cohen 1965a.

(36) Known in Hausa as *kankamba*.

(37) For detailed discussion of the cleavage into Hausa and Yoruba within the Market, see Cohen 1965a.

(38) Native Authority Council Minutes of 17th September 1942.

(39) This was 20th August 1942.

(40) For details see my paper, Cohen 1966.

(41) Yoruba Moslem theologians at the time argued that 'local community' meant an area within a radius of 20 miles.

(42) See Turner 1965.

(43) See Mitchell, 1956a, p. 56.

(44) In the forest areas in southern Nigeria, horses, like cattle, are prone to the diseases carried by the tse-tse fly. Special care is therefore needed to protect them.

CHAPTER FIVE

(1) Formerly known as the National Council of Nigeria and Cameroons.

(2) For detail on Nigerian political parties, see Coleman (1958), Sklar (1963), Post (1963), McIntosh (1966), and Bretton (1963). A detailed study of politics in Ibadan can be found in Jenkins (1964) and (1967) and in Jenkins and Post (forthcoming).

(3) I am referring here to the dispute between the Ibadans and the Ijebus about land.

(4) For details on the history and doctrine of the Order see Abun-Nasr (1965).

(5) See Crowder (1959).

(6) Parrinder mentions that 'some' Ibadan Moslems were Tijanis. See Parrinder (1953), p. 77.

(7) For details, see Tijani (no date).

(8) I attended one of these gatherings in 1963. Only a handful of Hausa were present. The Chief of the Quarter sent word that he was 'indisposed' and was represented by his son.

(9) See above, pp. 129–40.

(10) This was the second of the only two occasions in Sabo's history during 1916-1963 on which resort to collective physical violence was made. For factional disputes in terms of Friday mosque, see Fisher 1963.

(11) Or *Al-Ikhwan*.

(12) See Forde (1965).

(13) See Gluckman (1958), p. 53-77.

CHAPTER SIX

(1) Ar. *al-Ihram*.
(2) Ar. *Silsila*.
(3) See Greenberg 1941 and 1946, Smith, M. F. 1964, and Lewis 1966, pp. 64-5.
(4) In a Middle-Eastern Arab, Moslem village which I studied earlier, there were only two, part-time, religious functionaries in a population of about 2,300, though the village was reputed in the area as strongly orthodox.
(5) The average rent paid for a room in the Quarter in 1963 was nearly £3 a month.
(6) In Hausa: *Maroka*.
(7) In Hausa: *Maishela*.
(8) See above, pp. 129-40.
(9) See Turner 1957, 1965, 1966, 1968a and 1968b.
(10) Turner 1964.
(11) The reference here is to the scores of short prayers or invocations to Allah which Moslems pronounce on almost every current activity or event in daily life. For example, when one eats his meal one announces the *basmalah*; when one is angry and is afraid of losing one's temper or is afraid of temptation, one announces the *Isti'wadh*; when one finishes one's meal or when one belches, one pronounces the *Hamdalah*; and when one hears of a death or when one is witnessing an event that shows the powerlessness of man, one pronounces the *hawakala*.
(12) See Turner 1964.
(13) Known in Arabic as *tarikas*.
(14) Evans-Pritchard 1949.
(15) Known as *Jawaharat al-Kamal*.
(16) See Trimingham 1959, p. 98.
(17) For involvement of religious leaders in politics in a dffferent setting see Mayer, A. 1967.

CONCLUSIONS

(1) Some Yoruba became Tijanis, but because of the localization of ritual under local Mukaddams no interaction with Tijani Hausa could take place.
(2) It was initially established as University College associated with the University of London, and was meant to cater for the whole of British West Africa. It was converted into an independent university in 1963.
(3) Nearly half of the doctors of Nigeria were concentrated in Ibadan.
(4) Ibadan has been prolific in the formation of numerous types of voluntary associations, particularly since the Second World War.
(5) See B. Lloyd 1966, and P. Lloyd 1966.
(6) Except for the small group of men who learnt English privately. See above, pp. 148-9.
(7) See Okonjo, 1967.
(8) *ibid*.

(9) *ibid.*
(10) See Little 1957 and 1965, Parkin 1965, and Epstein 1958.
(11) Okonjo 1967.
(12) *ibid.*
(13) *ibid.*
(14) See LeVine 1966, p. 84.
(15) *ibid*, p. 93.
(16) See Schatz 1965, and Hunter 1962.
(17) See above pp. 82–3.
(18) See Hill 1966a, Goody 1954, Wilkes 1961, Fyfe 1962, Dorjahn 1962, Skinner 1964, Fallers 1962.
(19) See Winder 1962.
(20) See Morris 1968, Kuper 1958.
(21) See Crissman 1967. For a relevant study in Nepal see Caplan (in press).
(22) See Glazer and Moynihan 1965.
(23) *ibid.*
(24) Epstein 1958.
(25) Mitchell 1966, pp. 51-52.
(26) Epstein 1958.
(27) See Gluckman 1960.
(28) See Parkin 1965 and 1966.
(29) Glazer and Moynihan 1965.
(30) See Epstein 1967, also Mayer P. 1962, and McCulloch 1956.
(31) Maine 1861, MacIver 1917, Tonnies 1940, and Durkheim 1933.
(32) See Homans 1951, Shils 1951, Verba 1961, and LaPiere 1954.
(33) See Homans 1951, pp. 131-155.
(34) Greer 1955, pp. 33-39.
(35) LaPiere 1954.
(36) Fürer-Haimendorf 1967.
(37) Wolfe 1966.
(38) Gluckman 1958, p. 65.
(39) Bailey 1968.
(40) Wolfe 1966.
(41) See Rouch 1956 and Wallerstein 1964.
(42) Wagley and Harris 1964, p. 260.
(43) Essien-Udom 1966.
(44) Endo-culture is a term which has been coined by Gluckman to 'describe the culture of a social personality or group as perceived by that personality or by the members of that group respectively'. . . . See Gluckman 1958, p. 57.
(45) See Colson 1953.
(46) See Wagley and Harris.
(47) See Essien-Udom 1966, pp. 133-162.
(48) See Parkin 1966.
(49) See Macridis 1955, pp. 50-55.
(50) See Parkin 1966.
(51) See Lenski 1963, Herberg 1960, and Glazer and Moynihan 1965.
(52) Herberg 1960, p. 3.
(53) Lenski 1963, pp. 319-366.

(54) In a most penetrating study of the European community in Dakar, Mercier points out that before the Second World War, separation between European and African went without saying, as everyone knew 'his place'. But with independence such separation is to-day no longer legal and the Europeans have therefore been exerting *effort* to achieve exclusiveness informally, in order to separate themselves from the new African elites who are competing with them over economic power. See Mercier 1965.

(55) For discussion of the dialectical relations between social and cultural change, see Gluckman 1958 (originally published in 1942).

(56) See Smith 1960.

(57) See Fallers 1962, for a brief discussion of some structural conditions which favour the development of networks of ethnically exclusive trading communities in different parts of the world. See also Skinner 1963.

(58) It is here that the observations by Rouch (1956) and Banton (1957) about the relations between cultural tradition and the manner and effectiveness of grouping in the town, can be of great importance.

(59) I am of course assuming here that the main concern of social anthropology is the study of sociocultural interdependence in general and not the production of specific ethnographic studies.

(60) Russell 1965 (first published in 1938) p. 10.

(61) Fortes 1953, p. 36.

(62) For a brief survey of the attempt to search for special theories for explaining 'urban society' see Miner 1967, pp. 1-20.

(63) Mitchell 1966.

Bibliography

ABUN-NASR, J. M. 1965. *The Tijaniyya: A Sufi Order in the Modern World*. London: Oxford University Press.

AKINYELE, I. B. 1946. *The Outline of Ibadan History*. Lagos.

AWE, B. 1967. Ibadan, its Early Beginnings. In P. C. Lloyd, A. L. Mabogunje, B. Awe (eds.) *The City of Ibadan*. Cambridge: Cambridge University Press in association with the Institute of African Studies, University of Ibadan.

BAILEY, F. G. 1964. In E. Devons & M. Gluckman (eds.) *Closed Systems and Open Minds*. Edinburgh: Oliver & Boyd.

1968. Parapolitical Systems. In Marc Swartz (ed.) *Local Level Politics*. Chicago: Aldine Publishing Company.

BANTON, M. 1957. *West African City: A Study of Tribal Life in Freetown*. London: Oxford University Press for International African Institute.

BARNES, J. A. 1968. Networks and Political Process. In M. Swartz (ed.) *Local Level Politics*. Chicago: Aldine Publishing Company.

BAUER, P. T. 1963. *West African Trade*. Cambridge University Press.

BRETTON, H. L. 1963. *Power and Stability in Nigeria*. New York: Frederick A. Praeger.

CAPLAN, L. (Forthcoming). *Land & Social Change in East Nepal*.

CASTLES, F. G. 1967. *Pressure Groups and Political Culture*. London: Routledge & Kegan Paul.

CHURCH, R. J. H. 1957. *West Africa: A Study of the Environment and Man's Use of it*. Longmans.

CLARKSON, M. 1963. The Problem of Begging and Destitution in Urban Areas of the Gold Coast. In N.I.S.E.R. *Proceedings of the Fourth Annual Conference of the West African Institute of Social and Economic Research*. University of Ibadan (second edition) pp. 142–148.

COHEN, A. 1965a. The Social Organization of Credit in a West African Cattle Market. *Africa*. XXXV. 1.

1965b. *Arab Border-Villages in Israel: A study of Continuity and Change in Social Organization*. Manchester University Press.

1966. Politics of the Kola Trade. *Africa*. XXXVI, No. 1, pp. 18–36.

1967. Stranger Communities: The Hausa. In P. Lloyd, A.

Mabogunje & B. Awe (eds.) *The City of Ibadan*. pp. 117-127. Cambridge University Press.

COLEMAN, J. S. 1958. *Nigeria: Background to Nationalism*, University of California Press.

COLSON, E. 1953. *The Makah Indians: An Indian Tribe in Modern American Society*. Manchester University Press.

CRISSMAN, L. W. 1967. The Segmentary Structure of Urban Overseas Chinese. *Man*. 2:2 Pp. 185-204.

CROWDER, M. 1964. Indirect Rule—French and British Style. *Africa*. Vol. XXXIV, No. 3, pp. 197-205.

1959. *Pagans and Politicians*. Hutchinson.

DORJAHN, V. R. with FYFE, C. 1962. Landlord & Stranger. *Journal of African History*. III. 3.

DURKHEIM, E. 1933. *The Division of Labour in Society*. Glencoe, Illinois: Free Press.

ECKSTEIN, H. 1960. *Pressure Group Politics*. George Allen & Unwin.

EISENSTADT, S. N. 1966. *Modernisation: Protest and Change*, Prentice Hall.

EPSTEIN, A. L. 1958. *Politics in an Urban African Community*. Manchester University Press.

1961. The Network and Urban Social Organisation. *Rhodes-Livingstone Journal*. 29: pp. 29-62.

1967. Urbanization and Social Change in Africa, *Current Anthropology*, 8:4 pp. 275-296.

ESSIEN-UDOM, E. U. 1966. *Black Nationalism*. Penguin Books.

EVANS-PRITCHARD, E. E., with M. FORTES. 1940. Introduction. *African Political Systems*. Oxford University Press for International African Institute.

EVANS-PRITCHARD, E. E. 1949. *The Sanusi of Cyrenaica*. Oxford University Press.

1961. *Anthropology and History*. Manchester University Press.

FAGE, J. 1955. *An Introduction to the History of West Africa*. Cambridge University Press.

FAGE, J. with OLIVER, R. 1962. *A Short History of Africa*. Penguin Books.

FALLERS, L. A. 1962. Comment on 'Lebanese in West Africa'. *Comparative Studies in Society and History*. IV. pp. 334-336.

FISHER, H. J. 1963. *Ahmadiya: A Study in Contemporary Islam on the West African Coast*. London: Oxford University Press.

FLINT, J. E. 1960. *Sir George Goldie and the Making of Nigera*. London: Oxford University Press.

FORDE, D. 1947. The Native Economies. In M. Perham. *The Native Economies of Nigeria*. London: Faber & Faber. pp. 22-215.

1960. The Cultural Map of West Africa: Successive Adaptations to Tropical Forests and Grassland. In S. & P. Ottenberg (eds.) *Cultures and Societies of Africa*, Random House.

1965. Tropical African Studies. *Africa*. XXXV. No. 1.

FORTES, M. with EVANS-PRITCHARD, E. E. 1940. Introduction. *African Political Systems*. Oxford University Press.

FORTES, M. 1953. *Social Anthropology in Cambridge since 1900 (An Inaugural Lecture)*. Cambridge University Press.

FÜRER-HAIMENDORF, C. VON, 1967. *Morals and Merit: A Study of Values and Social Controls in South Asian Societies*. Weidenfeld & Nicolson.

FYFE, C. with V. R. DORJAHN. 1962. Landlord & Stranger. *Journal of African History*. III. 3.

GEERTZ, C. 1963. The Integrative Revolution. In his *Old Societies and New States*. Glencoe: The Free Press pp. 105-157.

GLAZER, N., with D. P. MOYNIHAN, 1965. *Beyond the Melting Pot*. The M.I.T. Press.

GLUCKMAN, M. 1955. *Custom and Conflict in Africa*. Oxford University Press.

1958. *Analysis of a Social Situation in Modern Zululand*. Rhodes Livingstone Institute. Manchester (Originally published in 1940-42).

1960. Tribalism in Modern British Central Africa. *Cahiers d'Études Africanines*. 6 Section: Sciences Économiques et Sociales: École Practique des Hautes Études, Sorbonne, pp. 55-70.

1961a. Anthropological Problems Arising from the African Industrial Revolution. In A. Southall (ed.) *Social Change in Modern Africa*, Oxford University Press. pp. 67-83.

1961b. Ethnographic Data in British Social Anthopology. *The Sociological Review*, N. S. Vol. 9, No. 1.

1964. Introduction and Conclusion. *Closed Systems and Open Minds: The Limits of Naivety in Social Anthropology*, Edinburgh: Oliver & Boyd.

1965. *Politics, Law & Ritual in Tribal Society*, Oxford: Basil Blackwell.

GOODY, J. 1954. *The Ethnography of N. Territories of the Gold Coast*. Colonial Office.

GREENBERG, J. H. 1946. *The Influence of Islam on a Sudanese Religion*. Augustin, American Ethnological Society, Monographs, No. 10.

1941. Some Aspects of Negro-Mohammedan Culture-Contact among the Hausa. *American Anthropologist*. 43. pp. 51-561.

1947. Islam and Cain Organization among the Hausa. *Southwestern Journal*. Vol. 3.

GREER, S. A. 1955. *Social Organization*. Doubleday & Company.

GOVERNMENT OF THE GOLD COAST. 1955. *Report on the Enquiry into Begging and Destitution in the Gold Coast 1954*. Published by the

Department of Social Welfare and Community Development.

GULLIVER, P. H. 1963. *Social Control in an African Society*. Routledge & Kegan Paul.

HARRIS, M. with WAGLEY, C. 1964. *Six Case Studies: Minorities in the New World* (third edition). Columbia University Press.

HERBERG, W. 1960. *Protestant, Catholic and Jew*. Doubleday & Co.

HILL, P. 1963a. Some Characteristics of Indigenous West African Enterprise. In Nigerian Institute of Social and Economic Research *Conference Proceedings March* 1962. Published by N.I.S.E.R.

1963b. Markets in Africa. *The Journal of Modern African Studies*. Vol. 1, No. 4, pp. 441-453.

1963c. *Migrant Cocoa-Farmers of Southern Ghana*. Cambridge University Press.

1966a. Landlord and Brokers. A West African Trading System. *Cahiers d'Études Africaines*. Vol. VI. pp. 351-66.

1966b. Notes on Traditional Market Authority and Market Periodicity in West Africa. *Journal of African History*. VII. 2. pp. 295-311.

1966c. A Plea for Indigenous Economics: The West African Example. *Economic Development and Cultural Change*. Vol. 15. No. 1. pp. 10-20.

1966d. Landlords and Brokers. In Centre for African Studies University of Edinburgh, *Markets and Marketing in West Africa*. pp. 1-14.

HOMANS, G. C. 1951. *The Human Group*. Routledge & Kegan Paul.

HUNTER, G. 1962. *The New Societies of Tropical Africa*. Oxford University Press.

JENKINS, G. 1964. *Politics in Ibadan*. Ph.D. Thesis, Northwestern University.

1967. Government and Politics in Ibadan. In *The City of Ibadan*. Lloyd, Maboginge, Awe (eds.) Cambridge University Press.

JENKINS, G. and POST, K. (Forthcoming). *The Price of Liberty*.

JONES, G. I., 1954. The Beef-cattle Trade in Nigeria. *Africa*. Vol. XVI.

KUPER, L. *et al*. 1958. *Durban: A Study in Racial Ecology*. Jonathan Cape.

LAPIERE, R. T. 1954. *A Theory of Social Control*. McGraw Hill.

LENSKI, G. 1963. *The Religious Factor: A Sociological Inquiry*. Doubleday.

LEVINE, R. A. 1966. *Dreams and Deeds*. The University of Chicago Press.

LEVY, R. 1957. *The Social Structure of Islam*. Cambridge University Press.

LEWIS, I. 1966. (ed.) Introduction. *Islam in Tropical Africa*. Oxford University Press. pp. 1-126.

LITTLE, K. 1957. The Role of Voluntary Associations in West African Urbanisation. *American Anthropologist*. 59: 579-96.

1965. *West African Urbanisation*. Cambridge University Press.

LLOYD, B. 1966. Education and Family Life in the Development of Class Identification Among the Yoruba. In P. Lloyd (ed.) *The New Elites of Tropical Africa*. Oxford University Press.

LLOYD, P. C. 1960. Lugard and Indirect Rule. *Ibadan*. No. 10.

1966. Introduction. *The New Elites of Tropical Africa*. Oxford University Press.

1967. With Awe and Mabogunje. (eds.) *The City of Ibadan*. Cambridge University Press.

LUGARD, F. D. 1922. *Dnal Mandate in British Tropical Africa*. Blackwood.

LUPTON, T. with WILSON, S. 1959. Background and Connections of Top Decision-Makers. *Manchester School*.

MACIVER, R. M. 1917. *Community*. Macmillan.

MACKINTOSH, J. P. 1966. *Nigerian Government and Politics*. George Allen & Unwin.

MACRIDIS, R. V. 1955. *The Study of Comparative Government*. New York: Random House.

MAINE, H. S. 1861. *Ancient Law*. London. Murray.

MAIR, L. P. 1958. African Chiefs To-day. *Africa*. XXVIII. No. 3. pp. 195-206.

MAYER, A. 1967. Pir and Murshid. *Middle Eastern Studies*. Vol. 3. No. 2. pp. 160-169.

MAYER, P. 1962. Migrancy and the Study of the African in Town. *American Anthropologist*. 64. 576-92.

MCCULLOCH, M. 1956. Survey of Recent and Current Field Studies on the Social Effects of Economic Development in Inter-Tropical Africa. In D. Forde (ed.) *The Social Implications of Industrialization and Urbanization in Africa South of the Sahara*. Tensions and Technology Series. Paris: U.N.E.S.C.O., pp. 53-229.

MERCIER, P. 1965. On the Meaning of 'Tribalism' in Black Africa. in P. L. Van Den Berghe (ed.) *Africa: Social Problems of Change and Conflict*. San Francisco: Chandler Publishing Co. pp. 483-501.

1965. The European Community of Dakar. *ibid*. pp. 283-300.

MINER, H. 1967. The City and Modernization: An Introduction. In H. Miner (ed.) *The City in Modern Africa*. London: Pall Mall Press. pp. 1-20.

MITCHELL, J. C. 1956a. *The Yao Village*. Manchester University Press.

1956b. *The Kalela Dance*. Manchester University Press.

1966. Theoretical Orientations in African Urbanization Studies. In M. Banton (ed.) *The Social Anthropology of Complex Societies*. ASA. Monograph No. 4. Tavistock Publications. pp. 37-68.

MORRIS, S. 1968. *Indians in Uganda: Caste and Sect in a Plural Society*. London: Weidenfeld Publishers Group.

MOYNIHAN, D. P. with GLAZER, N. 1965. *Beyond the Melting Pot*.

Cambridge (Massachusetts): The M.I.T. Press. Massachusetts Institute of Technology.

NADEL, S. F. 1954. *Nupe Religion*. Routledge & Kegan Paul.

1957. *The Theory of Social Structure*. London: Cohen & West.

OKONJO, C. The Western Ibo. In P. Lloyd, A. Mabogunje, and B. Awe (eds.) *The City of Ibadan*. Cambridge University Press.

OLIVER, R. with FAGE, J. 1962. *A Short History of Africa*. Penguin.

OLUWANSANMI, H. A. 1967. The Agricultural Environment. In P. C. Lloyd, A. L. Mabogunje, B. Awe (eds.) *The City of Ibadan*. Cambridge University Press.

OTTENBERG, S. 1959. Improvement Associations Among the Afikpo Ibo. *Africa*, Vol. XXXIX. pp. 1-29.

PARKIN, D. 1965. *The Social Structure of Two African Housing Estates in Kampala*. PhD. Thesis. London University (S.O.A.S.).

1966. Urban Voluntary Associations as Institutions of Adaptation. *Man*. Vol. 1. No. 1.

PARRINDER, G. 1953. *Religion in an African City*. Oxford University Press.

PEDLAR, F. J. 1955. *Economic Geography of West Africa*. Longmans.

PERHAM, M. F. 1937. *Native Administration in Nigeria*. Oxford University Press.

POST, K. W. J. 1963. *The Nigerian Federal Elections of* 1959. Oxford University Press. For N.I.S.E.R.

POST, K. W. J. with JENKINS, G. (forthcoming). *The Price of Liberty*.

PROTHERO, R. M. 1957. Migratory Labour from North Western Nigeria. *Africa*. Vol. XXVII. No. 3. pp. 251-61.

1959. *Migrant Labour from Sokoto Province Northern Nigeria*. Government Printer Northern Region. Kaduna.

ROBERTS, J. M. 1966. Oaths, Autonomic Ordeals and Power. In L. Nader (ed.) *American Anthropology*. Part 2. LXII. No. 6. 186-212.

ROUCH, J. 1956. Migration au Ghana. *Journal de la societe des africanistes*. *xxvi*.

RUSSELL, B. 1938. *Power: A New Social Analysis*. London: Arnold.

SAMPSON, A. 1962. *Anatomy of Britain*. Hodder & Stoughton.

SCHATZ, S. P. 1965. The Capital Shortage Illusion: Government Lending in Nigeria. *Oxford Economic Papers*. Vol. 17. 2. pp. 309-16.

SKINNER, E. P. 1963. Strangers in West African Societies. *Africa*. Vol. XXXIII. No. 4. pp. 307-320.

1964. West African Economic Systems. In M. Herskovitz (ed.) *Economic Transition in Africa*. Routledge.

SKLAR, R. L. 1963. *Nigerian Political Parties*. Princeton University Press.

SHILS, E. A. 1950. Primary Groups in the American Army. In Merton and Lazarsfeld (eds.) *Continuities in Social Research*. Glencoe, Illinois: Free Press.

1951. The Study of the Primary Group. In D. Lerner and H. D.

Lasswell (eds.) *The Policy Sciences.* Oxford University Press.

SMELSER, N. 1962. *The Theory of Collective Behaviour.* Routledge & Kegan Paul.

SMITH, M. F. 1964. *Baba of Karo.* Faber & Faber. (second ed.)

SMITH, M. G. 1955. *The Economy of Hausa Communities in Zaria.* H.M. Stationery Office. For the Colonial Office. Colonial Research Studies. No. 16.

1960. Social and Cultural Pluralism. *New York Academy of Sciences.*

1959. The Hausa System of Social Status. *Africa.* Vol. XXIX. No. 3. pp. 239-252.

1961. Kebbi and Hausa Stratification. *The British Journal of Sociology.* XII. No. 1. pp. 52-64.

1962. Exchange and Marketing Among the Hausa. In P. Bohannan & G. Dalton (eds.) *Markets in Africa.* Northwestern University Press. pp. 299-334.

1964. Introduction. M. F. Smith, *Baba of Karo.* Faber & Faber. pp. 11-34.

SOUTHAL, A. 1961. Introduction: *Social Change in Modern Africa,* Oxford University Press for International African Institute. pp. 1-46.

TIJANI, AHMAD. *Ahzab wa Awrad.* Edited by Muhammad el-Ghameawi. Cairo (in Arabic).

TONNIES, F. 1940. *Fundamental Concepts of Sociology: Gemeinschaft und Geselleschaft.* American Book. N.Y.

TRIMINGHAM, J. S. 1959. *Islam in West Africa.* Oxford University Press.

1964. *Islam in East Africa.* Oxford University Press.

TURNER, V. W. 1957. *Schism and Continuity in an African Society.* Manchester University Press.

1965. Symbols in Ndembu Ritual. In M. Gluckman (ed.) *Closed Systems and Open Minds.* Edinburgh: Oliver & Boyd.

1966. Colour Classification in Ndembu Ritual. In M. Banton (ed.) *Anthropological Approaches to the Study of Religion.* ASA. Monograph No. 3 Tavistock Publications.

1968a. Mukanda. In M. Swartz (ed.) *Local Level Politics.* Chicago: Aldine Publishing Company. pp. 135-50.

1968b. *The Drums of Affliction.* Oxford University Press for International African Institute.

VAN DEN BERGHE, P. L. 1965. *Africa: Social Problems and Conflict.* San Francisco: Chandler Publishing Company.

VERBA, S. 1961. *Small Groups and Political Behaviour: A Study of Leadership.* Princeton University Press.

WAGLEY, C. and HARRIS, M. 1964. *Six Case Studies: Minorities in the New World.* (third edition). Columbia University Press.

WALLERSTEIN, I. 1964. Voluntary Associations. In J. S. Coleman and C. G. Rosberg (eds.) *Political Parties and National Integration in Tropical Africa.*

WILKES, I. 1961. *The Northern Factor in Ashanti History.* The Institute of African Studies. University of Ghana.

WILSON, S. with LUPTON, T. 1959. Background and Connections of Top Decision-Makers. *Manchester School.*

WINDER, R. BAYLY. 1962. The Lebanese in West Africa. *Comparative Studies in Sociology and History.* IV. pp. 296-333.

WOLFE, E. R. 1966. Kinship, Friendship, and Patron-Client Relationships. In M. Banton (ed.) *The Social Anthropology of Complex Societies.* Tavistock Publications.

YELD, E. R. 1960. Islam and Social stratification in Northern Nigeria. *British Journal of Sociology*, Vol. XI, No. 2, pp. 112-28.

Index